Reading and Writing Short Essays

Reading and Writing Short Essays

Third Edition

MORTON A. MILLER

Random House
New York

For Shirley,
my wife

Third Edition

9 8 7 6 5 4 3 2 1

Library of Congress Cataloging-in-Publication Data

Reading and writing short essays.

Includes index.
1. College readers. 2. English language—Rhetoric.
I. Miller, Morton A., 1914–
PE1417.R37 1986 808'.0427 86-6459
ISBN 0-394-34394-8

Manufactured in the United States of America

Cover art:
TRADITIONAL JAPANESE STENCIL DESIGNS
Edited by Clarence Hornung
Dover Publications, Inc.

Cover design by Katharine Von Urban

Preface

THE third edition of *Reading and Writing Short Essays,* like its predecessors, attempts to help college students become more perceptive readers and more craft-conscious writers. It retains those components that teachers using the first edition found successful in their classes: a broad range of material rhetorically organized; extensive introductions; short nonfiction prose models chosen for ease of reading and comprehension; and exercises containing questions on reading and writing that encourage students to ascertain precisely what writers say as well as how they put their ideas into words. But the book has been changed to incorporate as many as practicable of the welcome recommendations of its users and to make it more effective as a teaching tool:

1. The mix of authors has again been changed to further increase the ratio of contemporary to classic essayists. Twenty-one of the book's sixty-six selections are new to this edition.
2. The subject matter of the essays has been updated by incorporating an even greater proportion of present-day authors writing on current topics.
3. This edition places greater stress than heretofore on writing as process.

Teachers report that they rearrange the book's contents in various ways. Since its six parts and eighteen sections are self-contained units and there are ample selections in each, *Reading and Writing*

Short Essays remains adaptable to the tastes and preferences of the teachers who use it and to the needs of their students.

I am grateful to the many persons whose useful suggestions helped shape this new edition, among them Arnie Davidson, Pima Community College; Joyce Dempsey, Arkansas Polytechnic; John Dick, University of Texas, El Paso; Marvin Garrett, University of Cincinnati; George Richards, Jacksonville State University; Stephen Weidenborner, Kingsborough Community College.

I acknowledge also the guidance of Richard L. Larson. For his continuing enthusiasm for *Reading and Writing Short Essays* I thank Steve Pensinger, English editor of Random House's College Department. For help with this edition I am obligated to him, to his assistant Cynthia Ward, and to project editor Fred Burns.

MORTON A. MILLER

Contents

Thematic Table of Contents

The Animal Kingdom

Childhood

The Environment

Growing Up

Nature and the Sciences

People

Society

Sports and Leisure

Values

Work

Writing

Miscellaneous

Writing is a deeply personal process, full of mystery and surprise. No two people go about it in exactly the same way. We all have little devices to get us started, or to keep us going, or to remind us of what we think we want to say, and what works for one person may not work for anyone else. The main thing is to get something written—to get the words out of our heads. There is no "right" method. Any method that will do the job is right for you.

—William Zinsser

I always write about a thing first and think about it afterwards, which is not a bad procedure because the easiest way to have consecutive thoughts is to start putting them down.

—E. B. White

My thoughts were a great excitement, but when I tried to do anything with them, it was like trying to pack a balloon in a shed in a high wind.

—William Butler Yeats

1

The Essay: Thesis

Unity is the anchor of good writing. It not only keeps the reader from straggling off in all directions; it satisfies his subconscious need for order and assures him that all is well at the helm.
—William Zinsser

AN essay is a short composition in prose that discusses a subject limited in scope. The degree of limitation will depend on the length of the essay. In an essay of from five hundred to one thousand words – such as you are likely to be called upon to write in your course in composition – you would not be able to treat adequately a broad subject such as weather, sailing, or architecture. But you could, in a short essay, do justice to limited or specific parts of those subjects:

The Cause of Hail; or, What Is a Thunderstorm?

The Difference Between a Catboat and a Sloop; or, How to Sail Against the Wind

The Purpose of the Flying Buttress; or, Why the Leaning Tower of Pisa Leans

To a subject sufficiently restricted for you to be able to explain it to your reader in a short essay, we will apply the term "topic."

When it is up to you to choose a topic, first choose a subject that appeals to you – for example, the energy crisis. Then, since the subject is vast, too large to be covered adequately in a short composition, limit it progressively, as follows:

Energy

Sources of Energy

Wind as a Source of Energy

How a Windmill Works

The Windmill on My Grandfather's Farm

This list of possible topics ranges from the most general to the most specific. Unless you have done so at the outset, your aim will be to pick a topic that is sufficiently limited for you to be able to discuss it in a short essay to the extent necessary to explain it to your reader. A diagram of the process of limiting a subject would resemble a triangle balancing on one of its points.

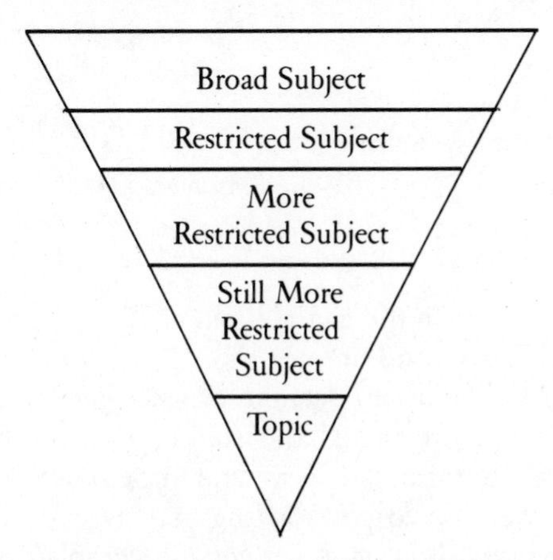

Preferable, among the subjects you might select, are ones that you already know something about. In your personal experiences and observations as well as in your reading, you will find ample material for intelligible short essays on a variety of topics. (I will discuss these and other sources of the writer's materials in Part Three.) If your broad subject is education, you might already know enough to write a short essay on topics such as

The Advantages of a Small College

The Importance of Learning a Foreign Language

A Proposal for Greater Freedom in Choosing Courses in College

Why I Chose to Attend a Two- Instead of a Four-Year College

Professor Jones, the Best Teacher I Ever Had

If necessary, you can supplement your knowledge of your topic with, for example, research in a library.

Here are other examples of broad and restricted subjects:

Broad Subject	***Restricted Subject***
Vacations	My Trip to Aruba and Back on an Oil Tanker
College Sports	Coaching an Intramural Softball Team
Television	The Humor of *The Cosby Show*
Hobbies	My Stamp Collection
Cooking	Baking a Pie

Whereas the subjects in the first column are too general for a short essay, those in the second are not. You could write about any of them briefly but in sufficient detail to explain them to your readers.

After you have restricted the subject of your composition, gather information, formulate ideas, and make notes about the relevant material available to you—before you start to write the first draft of your essay. Your notes might be complete sentences or merely phrases or single words. On the topic "My Trip to Aruba and Back on an Oil Tanker," you might jot down

> Harbor pilot. Navigational aids. Steering a big ship. Changes in the weather between New York and Aruba. A storm at sea. Thoughts on sighting land (Hispaniola) after five days at sea. Dolphins. Flying fish. The first mate lets me take the wheel of the ship in Mona Passage (between Hispaniola and Puerto Rico). Arrival in Aruba. Water ballast pumped out. Oil pumped in. Vessel turned around and on way back north (to Boston) with full tanks. Hull low in

the sea; decks barely above water. The ship's crew: friendly; make me feel at home.

When you have finished your jottings, you might find that you have more than enough material for a short essay. Your next steps would be to mull over and evaluate your ideas and then to restrict your subject still more by deciding on what part of your jottings you will focus. Let's assume that the essay about the trip to Aruba will flesh out the idea in the last note: "The ship's crew: friendly; make me feel at home." You would then jot down specific details relating to this idea, for example:

All-Italian crew. Only the captain and second mate speak English. We communicate with the help of an Italian-English dictionary. Also hand signs. Body communication? I'm invited to eat in the officers' mess. Entire crew considerate of me, the only woman on board. Played checkers with Aldo Barzolo, a Florentine, chief engineer; chess with Luigi Covici, steward, who is from Lerici on the Gulf of La Spezia. He tells me Shelley's last home still stands there. On its façade is a plaque with his words (in Italian): "Oh, bless the beaches where love, liberty, and dreams have not chains." Romanticism. Shades of Lit. 134. Exchanged addresses with crew members. Will we ever write to one another? Meet again? I have the run of the wheelhouse. First mate Enzo Finardi shows me how radar works; how to use loran to locate our position; how to read charts. Helmsman Alfredo Bettolucci lets me take a turn at the wheel.

These specific details may need to be winnowed until you discover a manageable central idea they seem to represent.

The preparation we have been considering is often referred to as *prewriting:* the thinking, reflecting, planning, outlining, substituting, note taking—even scribbling—that precede writing a first draft. For beginning writers especially, the more prewriting the better. It is at that stage of the writing process that they are first likely to discover the idea a proposed essay will focus on.

In prewriting, some writers find particularly useful an informal outline, which is simply the ordering of one's ideas by grouping them under appropriate headings in some logical sequence. An informal outline of the material above on the writer's experience with the crew of the oil tanker might be:

> The varied backgrounds of the crew.
>
> How their background and rank affected their treatment of me.
>
> How we communicated.
>
> Lessons on the working of the ship.
>
> Lasting benefits of my shipboard experience.

Sometimes the main idea that you ultimately focus on will not be evident at the outset, but will become clear to you as you rewrite the first draft of your essay. Generally, but not always, you will be able to express that idea explicitly in a single sentence. Such a statement is called a *thesis.* Often, but not always, it sums up an essay's content. A thesis for an essay about the trip to Aruba might be: "The best part of my trip to Aruba on an oil tanker was making friends with the ship's crew."

Sometimes you will find when you read your first draft that parts of what you have written do not relate to your thesis or that what appeared to be the expression of your main idea is not so. You could correct these defects in a second draft by cutting out the irrelevant material or by writing a new thesis statement that does express what you discover the main idea of your essay to be.

Jottings about the other topics just suggested might yield thesis statements such as these:

> Coaching an intramural softball team last term taught me that teamwork is more important to winning than is individual athletic ability.
>
> Much of the humor in *The Cosby Show* stems from commonplace familial predicaments.
>
> Buying commemorative issues is an easy way to start a stamp collection.
>
> The key element of a pie is the pie crust.

A thesis may be stated anywhere in an essay: its beginning, middle, or end. A writer may want to delay stating it because its meaning might be clearer to the reader after other material has been presented. Or a writer may choose to place the thesis in the middle or, to give it greater emphasis, at the end. But, more often than not, you will find that the best place to state a thesis is in the first paragraph:

> *If the ghosts of Franklin Roosevelt and George Marshall were to return today, they would—it is certain—find the role of the United States in the world a good deal changed since their time.* They would find American power and influence remarkably diminished, in spite of the growth of a vast strategic military arsenal. They would also find that the country had abandoned many of the policies and principles that in their view contributed to its greatness: the search for peace in a just world order, for a stable international economic system, and for an end to poverty, ignorance, and disease. In addition, they would find that the temper of the nation's leaders had changed considerably: instead of a jaunty self-confidence or a benign paternalism, they would encounter a defensive churlishness combined with adolescent self-promotion—a tendency to brag and strut [Frances FitzGerald, "The American Millennium." © 1985 by Frances FitzGerald. Originally in *The New Yorker*].

The reason for placing a thesis in the first paragraph of an essay or as soon after it as possible is that the sooner you state it, the more likely you are to remain aware of your main idea and the less likely you are to wander from that idea as you write.

Sometimes the main idea of an essay is not stated. Instead of making the thesis *explicit,* expressed in so many words—as in the paragraph just quoted—a writer may leave it *implied,* that is, suggested by the essay's contents. Whether explicit or implied, the thesis will help you to keep in mind your restriction of the broad subject, to avoid digressive information and ideas, and to focus on relevant material to explain and develop your essay's main idea.

There are three requirements for a good thesis:

1. *The thesis must be restricted.* It must limit the range of a subject to what the writer can discuss in adequate detail in an essay of a given length. Thus "restricted" is a relative term.

For a short essay to be written in your composition course, this thesis would not be sufficiently restricted:

Learning how to write well is essential for success.

But this thesis would be:

Learning how to write clearly is essential for achieving high grades in college courses in the humanities.

2. *The thesis must be unified.* It must state a single main idea:

Learning how to write well, to think clearly, and to study efficiently are essential for success in college.

This statement, although in three parts, enumerates the ingredients for "success in college," the one main idea of a proposed essay. Thus it is a unified thesis. Nonetheless, a student writing a short essay would do well to consider limiting it to a discussion of just one of the three ingredients because an essay of about five hundred words, for example, might not permit adequate explanation of all three.

The difference between unity and restriction is this: *unity* limits the number of main ideas—in a short essay, to one; *restriction* limits the scope of that single idea.

3. *The thesis must be precise.* The thesis

Learning how to write well is a wonderful idea for success in college.

is not precise, because "wonderful idea," being vague, can have more than one meaning. (For a discussion of vague words, see "Ambiguous and Vague Words," page 85.)

Now let's apply these criteria to this thesis:

Ronald Reagan's choice of cabinet members, his legislative programs, and his handling of foreign affairs show that he is a terrific president.

This statement is unified because it has a single main idea, Mr. Reagan's achievements. Nevertheless, it does not sufficiently restrict the subject of his accomplishments as president to a topic that could be discussed in adequate detail in a short essay. It commits the writer to discuss many, perhaps all, of Mr. Reagan's cabinet appointees; to write about some, if not many, of his legislative proposals; and to evaluate his dealings with two or more nations or groups of nations. Moreover, since "terrific" is vague, the thesis is not precise.

Compare it with this thesis:

> Ronald Reagan's choice of George Bush as his vice-president is sound.

This statement fulfills the requirements of a good thesis for a short essay: It is unified; it is restricted; and it is precise, because there are criteria for evaluating Mr. Reagan's choice of vice-president. The thesis could be improved, however, by adding "because" and the reason for the writer's judgment of Mr. Bush:

> Ronald Reagan's choice of George Bush as his vice-president is sound because Mr. Bush is well trained in government.

This statement, in addition to being a good thesis, clearly establishes the single direction its essay must take: a discussion of Mr. Bush's training in government.

A good thesis is to the writer what a compass is to a navigator: It establishes and helps maintain direction. In addition, by stating the limits of a topic it helps the writer to keep in mind the essay's main idea.

If, in an essay on highway safety, you were to include material on rural roads, jaywalking in cities, and riding a bicycle with no hands, you would end up with an essay lacking unity. To include this material would be to stray from your essay's main idea: *highway* safety. A good thesis, by pointing to the direction your essay should take—and maintain—will help you to avoid this defect.

TEENAGER'S PRIVACY

Haim Ginott

Haim G. Ginott (1922–1973) wrote the definitive *Group Psychotherapy for Children* (1961) and popular books such as *Between Parent and Teenager* (1969), which is based on his extensive experience in child psychotherapy and parental guidance. It is the source of this passage.

---

1 Teenagers need privacy; it allows them to have a life of their own. By providing privacy, we demonstrate respect. We help them disengage themselves from us and grow up. Some parents pry too much. They read their teenagers' mail and listen in on their telephone calls. Such violations may cause permanent resentment. Teenagers feel cheated and enraged. In their eyes, invasion of privacy is a dishonorable offense. As one girl said: "I am going to sue my mother for malpractice of parenthood. She unlocked my desk and read my diary."

2 One sixteen-year-old boy complained: "My mother has no respect for me. She invades my privacy and violates my civil rights. She comes into my room and rearranges my drawers. She can't stand disorder, she says. I wish she'd tidy up her own room and leave mine alone. I deliberately mess up my desk as soon as she cleans it up. But mother never learns."

3 Some teenagers complain that their parents participate too eagerly in their social life.

4 Bernice, age seventeen, speaks with bitterness: "My mother dresses up before my date arrives. She gossips with him while I'm getting ready. She even walks down with us to the car. When I return, I find her waiting for me, bursting with curiosity. She wants to know everything. What did he say? What did I answer? How did

From "Don't Violate His Privacy," in *Between Parent and Teenager* by Haim G. Ginott (New York: Macmillan, 1969), pp. 39–41. Reprinted by permission of Dr. Alice Ginott.

I feel? How much money did he spend? What are my future plans? My life is an open book; every page is a public announcement. My mother tries to be a pal. I don't want to hurt her feelings but I don't need a forty-year-old pal. I'd rather have some privacy."

5 Respect for privacy requires distance, which parents find hard to maintain. They want closeness and fraternization. For all their good will, they intrude and invade. Such familiarity does not breed mutual esteem. For respect to flourish, parents and teenagers must keep some distance. They can "Stand together yet not too near together." Respect encompasses an awareness of our teenager as a distinct and unique individual, a person apart from us. In the last analysis, neither parent nor teenager "belongs" to the other. Each belongs to himself.

Questions About "The Essay: Thesis"

1. Where does Ginott express the main idea of this essay?
2. Explain whether in his thesis he states precisely one restricted idea.
3. How does his thesis determine the content of the essay?
4. Does Ginott at any time digress from his subject? Explain.

Questions on Diction and Writing Techniques

1. How does your dictionary define "disengage" and "malpractice" (par. 1); "fraternization" (par. 5)? Use each of these words in a sentence.
2. Reporting in the third person instead of using dialogue, rewrite the last sentence of paragraph 1. Which version of the sentence do you prefer? Why? What is the writer's purpose in quoting the teenagers directly?
3. Ginott introduces the first quotation with "said" (par. 1). What is his purpose in introducing the second with "complained" (par. 2) and the third with "speaks with bitterness" (par. 4)?

4. Explain whether he cites sufficient evidence of "invasion of privacy" to convince you that "Some parents pry too much" (par. 1).
5. Whom did Ginott have in mind as his readers when he wrote this essay—child psychologists or the general public? What clues do you find in the essay to help you arrive at your conclusion? What changes might Ginott have made had he written for a different audience?

For Discussion, Reading, and Writing

1. Which of these statements, according to Ginott, is true (T), and which false (F)?

   A. ______ By providing privacy for teenagers, parents demonstrate their own maturity.

   B. ______ Teenagers should have an equal right to open parents' mail and to listen in on telephone calls.

   C. ______ One sixteen-year-old boy complained that his mother rewrote his homework.

   D. ______ For all their goodwill, parents intrude and invade.

   E. ______ Neither parent nor teenager belongs to the other.

2. The media have reported instances of children suing parents for malpractice. Should the courts permit such lawsuits? Why or why not?
3. Prewrite a short essay about teenagers, considering as much material as possible from your own experience and that of friends. In limiting the subject, you may find it useful to focus on and perhaps to further restrict one of the points in this passage from John E. Horrocks' *The Psychology of Adolescence* (2nd ed.):

   > In Western culture there are five points of reference from which to view adolescent growth and development:
   >
   > 1. It is a time of physical development and growth.
   > 2. It is a time when group relations become of major importance.
   > 3. Adolescence is a time of seeking status as an individual.

4. It is a time of intellectual expansion, development, and academic experience.
5. It is a time of development and evaluation of values.

Write the essay.

BUILDING SATISFACTION

Andy Rooney

The author of this essay writes a column that appears in more than 350 newspapers nationwide. He has won many honors for his TV essays, including "A Few Minutes with Andy Rooney" on *60 Minutes*.

---

1 For most of the last month I've been putting up a small building. I am not experienced in putting up buildings. My new structure is just behind the building we call the garage at our summer place. I don't know why we call that the garage, though, because it used to be an icehouse and has been full of tools for several years.

2 If Americans have a little bit of land near their house, they're possessed to put buildings on it. Most American farms, where there's plenty of land, are a cluster of haphazardly erected little buildings adjacent to the house and the barn. Most of the buildings were put up by someone who had an idea for their use at the time but that time has passed and they are now mostly used for what could only be called miscellaneous.

3 When I started my building I was going to use it for storing garden tools and a small tractor/lawnmower but now I think I may use it as a place in which to write. I'm getting to like it too much to just keep garden tools in.

4 My building is five-sided, eight feet tall at the sides and twelve

feet tall at the crown of the roof in the middle. It's about twelve feet across although in a pentagon no side is directly opposite any other side so it's hard to measure that dimension. The base is on heavy, flat stones and the timbers are treated five-by-fives. The uprights and the roof members are two-by-fours. The sides are three-quarter-inch plywood, which I covered with tarpaper and then red cedar shingles. The floor is rough oak I bought from a farmer who has a little sawmill, and now I think if I'm going to use it as an office, I'll insulate and panel the interior.

5 Don't ask me why I decided on a five-sided building and don't get thinking I'm any expert. I've bungled so many things putting it up that I'd be embarrassed to have a real carpenter see it. But it's up and it's mine and I built it and I had a wonderful time doing it.

6 It was very hard work. Every morning I'd get up at 6:15 and go to the garage/icehouse and write until about 8:30 and then go into the house and have breakfast. After breakfast I'd start on my building. Every evening at about 6:30 my wife would yell out the back door for me to quit. I'd work a little while longer, trying to anticipate how long I could stretch it out before she got really mad at me, then I'd go to the house, dripping wet with perspiration. I'd take a shower, have a drink, eat dinner and by 10:30 drop into bed.

7 It isn't often that I mix that much manual labor with writing and it got me thinking about which of the two is more satisfying. Writing is a great satisfaction to me but it's a wonderful feeling to go to bed dog-tired and twitching in every muscle after a long day's physical work in which you accomplished something. It always strikes me as surprising that it's so pleasurable to be physically tired from having used your muscles excessively. It makes me wish writing involved some kind of manual labor more strenuous than typing. If I got stiff writing, it might be even more satisfying.

8 Standing back and looking at my odd-shaped building, I've been impressed with how much like my writing it is. It's a little crude and not very well finished but it's direct and original.

9 My satisfaction in making it springs from the same well, too. For a man or a woman to take any raw material like lumber or words and shape these formless materials into a pattern that bears the stamp of his or her brain or hand, is the most satisfying thing to do in the whole world. It's what's wrong with cake mixes.

10 When, out of a scrambled mess of raw materials, some order

starts to emerge and it is an order you have imposed on those materials, it's a good feeling. It was nothing and now it's something.

11 For me, writing in the early morning and working on my building the rest of the day was the ultimate vacation and I never worked harder in my life.

12 Now I'm back at work and I can relax a little.

Questions About "The Essay: Thesis"

1. What meaningful conclusion(s) does Rooney draw from putting up his new structure?
2. What do paragraphs 8–12 contribute to the effectiveness of the essay? Explain whether the essay would be as appealing to you as it now is if Rooney had ended it with paragraph 7.

Questions on Diction and Writing Techniques

1. How does your dictionary define "possessed," "haphazardly," "miscellaneous" (par. 2), and "pentagon" (par. 4)? Use each of these words in a sentence.
2. Rooney might quite effectively have organized his material as a process (see pages 331–346): "How to Put Up a Small Building." Instead, he wrote about his experience, with little emphasis on building. How did his purpose in writing affect his choice of details?
3. Is the essay unified? Explain.

For Discussion, Reading, and Writing

1. Prepare to discuss in class the distinction between toil and leisure and whether hard work in the one can be as satisfying as hard work in the other. Be sure to have specific examples to support your judgment.
2. Write a paragraph based on personal experience that gives ample support to an assertion such as that in paragraph 9: "It was very hard work."

3. Make notes as you recall any kind of manual labor that gave you the satisfaction of imposing order on raw materials; for example, woodworking, gardening, sewing, painting, cooking, repairing a car, assembling a knocked-down bicycle. After ample prewriting, organize the material in a short essay that makes convincing to an audience (such as your classmates) why work such as you performed is satisfying.
4. Using the same material (but adding to it or subtracting from it as may seem to you appropriate), write a letter to a potential employer in which you cite your experience in woodworking or gardening, etc., as a qualification for a part-time or summer job. You might find it useful to respond to an ad in the classifieds section of your local or regional newspaper.

THE STUDENT ATHLETE

Red Smith

Walter W. (Red) Smith (1905–1982) was an American sports writer who regularly contributed articles on sports to *The New York Times*. He won a Pulitzer Prize for journalism in 1976.

---

1 Some edifying words about student athletes were heard on the air over the weekend. Whenever a college football game is on radio or television, it is accompanied by edifying words about student athletes, about the importance of intercollegiate athletics in a rounded educational program and about the vital role played by the National Collegiate Athletic Association. The edifying words are composed by writers for the N.C.A.A.

2 Student athlete is a term susceptible to various definitions. It can mean a biochemistry major who participates in sports, or a

Heisman Trophy candidate who is not necessarily a candidate for a bachelor's degree. Some student athletes are more studious than athletic, and vice versa.

3 There is at hand a piece written by a student athlete in his senior year at a major university that has been polishing young intellects for more than a century. He is an attractive young man, short months away from graduation, the best wide receiver in the school. One of his professors, who happens to be a football buff, asked him why his teammate, John Doe, never played first string although he was a better passer than Richard Spelvin, the starting quarterback. The young man said he would write the answer "like it was a quiz."

4 What follows is an exact copy of the young man's answer. That is, it is exact except for the names. The quarterbacks are not really named John Doe and Richard Spelvin and the university's athletic teams are not known as the Yankees.

5 "People (Some) feel that Doe did not have the ability to run the type of offense that the yankys ran. He also made some mistakes with the ball like fumbling.

6 "As a wide receiver it didnt make me any different who quarterback. But I feel he has the best arm I ever saw or play with on a team. Only why I feel the I do about the quarterback position is because I am a receiver who came from J.C. out of state I caught a lot of pass over 80 and I did not care a damn thing but about 24 in one year.

7 "Spelvin is my best friend and quarterback at my J.C. school. Spelvin has an arm but when you don't thrown lot of half the time I dont care who you are you will not perform as best you can. Spelvin can run, run the team and most of all he makes little mistakes.

8 "So since they didn't pass Spelvin was our quarterback. But if we did pass I feel Spelvin still should of start but Doe should have play a lot. Tell you the truth the yanky's in the pass two years had the best combination of receivers in a season that they will ever have. More—ask to talk about politics alum Doe problems just before the season coaches hate?"

9 The last appears to be a suggestion that alumni politics may have played a part in the coaches' decision on which quarterback would play first string. However, the professor who forwarded this material did so without comment or explanation.

10 The importance of disguising the names of these student athletes

and the identity of the university is obvious. It would be unforgivable to hold a kid up to public ridicule because his grip on a flying football was surer than his grasp of the mother tongue. He is only a victim. The culprit is the college, and the system.

11 The young man's prose makes it achingly clear how some institutions of learning use some athletes. Recruiters besiege a high school senior with bulging muscles and sloping neck who can run 40 yards in 4.3 seconds. The fact that he cannot read without facial contortions may be regrettable, but if his presence would help make a team a winner, then they want his body and are not deeply concerned about his mind.

12 Some colleges recruit scholar athletes in the hope that the scholar can spare enough time from the classroom to help the team. Others recruit athletes and permit them to attend class if they can spare the time from the playing field. If the boy was unprepared for college when he arrived, he will be unqualified for a degree four years later, but some culture foundries give him a degree as final payment for his services.

13 One widely accepted definition of the role of a college is "to prepare the student for life after he leaves the campus." If the young man quoted above gets a job as a wide receiver for the Green Bay Packers, then perhaps the university will have fulfilled its purpose. However, only a fraction of college players can make a living in the National Football League. Opportunities are even more limited for college basketball players, for pro basketball employs fewer players.

14 Where outside of pro football can our wide receiver go? He can pump gas. He can drive a truck. He has seen his name in headlines, has heard crowds cheering him, has enjoyed the friendship and admiration of his peers and he has a diploma from a famous university. It is unconscionable.

Questions About "The Essay: Thesis"

1. What is the general subject of this essay?
2. Reread the essay and mark the place where Smith first gave you an inkling of its thesis.

3. What is Smith's thesis? Is it expressed or implied? If expressed, underline it. If implied, express it in a sentence of not over twenty-five words.
4. Is the thesis sufficiently restricted for a short essay? Explain.
5. Explain whether Smith digresses anywhere in the essay from its main idea.

Questions on Diction and Writing Techniques

1. Mark in your text all words in this essay that, though new to you, you understood from their context. Define them in your own words. Compare your definitions with those in your dictionary. Look up in your dictionary all other words that are new to you. Use the words in both groups in sentences.
2. How many times, in paragraph 1, does Smith use "edifying"? What is his purpose in repeating the word?
3. What word(s) might Smith have used instead of "polishing" (par. 3)? Why did he choose the verb he did? Find, in paragraph 12, a phrase or phrases that Smith chose for the same reason.
4. What is Smith's purpose in writing, and the effect on you of reading, the student athlete's answer to the professor's question?
5. What is Smith's purpose in asking the question in the last paragraph?

For Discussion, Reading, and Writing

1. This essay is mainly about (circle one):
   A. College athletes who play football well but who write poorly.
   B. Colleges that fail to properly prepare student athletes for a degree.
   C. The graduation from college of student athletes who are unqualified for a degree.
   D. The victimization of students by their colleges.
   E. "Where outside of pro football can the wide receiver go?"

2. Who does Smith blame for the state of affairs he writes about? Do you agree with him? Why or why not?
3. Write a short essay in which you explain why preference in college admissions should or should not be given to applicants who excel in sports in high school. If your thesis is stated explicitly, underline it. If it is implied, state it in a sentence of not over twenty-five words.

THE KIND OF WORK DADDY DOES

Russell Baker

Russell Baker's keen, wide-ranging, humorous commentary on humankind and its institutions, regular features in his "Observer" column in *The New York Times*, have earned him the George Polk and Pulitzer prizes.

---

1 It is not surprising that modern children tend to look blank and dispirited when informed that they will someday have to "go to work and make a living." The problem is that they cannot visualize what work is in corporate America.

2 Not so long ago, when a parent said he was off to work, the child knew very well what was about to happen. His parent was going to make something or fix something. The parent could take his offspring to his place of business and let him watch while he repaired a buggy or built a table.

3 When a child asked, "What kind of work do you do, Daddy?" his father could answer in terms that a child could come to grips with. "I fix steam engines." "I make horse collars."

4 Well, a few fathers still fix engines and build things, but most

do not. Nowadays, most fathers sit in glass buildings performing tasks that are absolutely incomprehensible to children. The answers they give when asked, "What kind of work do you do, Daddy?" are likely to be utterly mystifying to a child.

5 "I sell space." "I do market research." "I am a data processor." "I am in public relations." "I am a systems analyst." Such explanations must seem nonsense to a child. How can he possibly envision anyone analyzing a system or researching a market?

6 Even grown men who do market research have trouble visualizing what a public relations man does with his day, and it is a safe bet that the average systems analyst is as baffled about what a space salesman does at the shop as the average space salesman is about the tools needed to analyze a system.

7 In the common everyday job, nothing is made any more. Things are now made by machines. Very little is repaired. The machines that make things make them in such a fashion that they will quickly fall apart in such a way that repairs will be prohibitively expensive. Thus the buyer is encouraged to throw the thing away and buy a new one. In effect, the machines are making junk.

8 The handful of people remotely associated with these machines can, of course, tell their inquisitive children "Daddy makes junk." Most of the work force, however, is too remote from junk production to sense any contribution to the industry. What do these people do?

9 Consider the typical twelve-story glass building in the typical American city. Nothing is being made in this building and nothing is being repaired, including the building itself. Constructed as a piece of junk, the building will be discarded when it wears out, and another piece of junk will be set in its place.

10 Still, the building is filled with people who think of themselves as working. At any given moment during the day perhaps one-third of them will be talking into telephones. Most of these conversations will be about paper for paper is what occupies nearly everyone in this building.

11 Some jobs in the building require men to fill paper with words. There are persons who type neatly on paper and persons who read paper and jot notes in the margins. Some persons make copies of paper and other persons deliver paper. There are persons who file paper and persons who unfile paper.

12 Some persons mail paper. Some persons telephone other persons and ask that paper be sent to them. Others telephone to ascertain the whereabouts of paper. Some persons confer about paper. In the grandest offices, men approve of some paper and disapprove of other paper.

13 The elevators are filled throughout the day with young men carrying paper from floor to floor and with vital men carrying paper to be discussed with other vital men.

14 What is a child to make of all this? His father may be so eminent that he lunches with other men about paper. Suppose he brings his son to work to give the boy some idea of what work is all about. What does the boy see happening?

15 His father calls for paper. He reads paper. Perhaps he scowls at paper. Perhaps he makes an angry red mark on paper. He telephones another man and says they had better lunch over paper.

16 At lunch they talk about paper. Back at the office, the father orders the paper retyped and reproduced in quintuplicate, and then sent to another man for comparison with paper that was reproduced in triplicate last year.

17 Imagine his poor son afterwards mulling over the mysteries of work with a friend, who asks him, "What's your father do?" What can the boy reply? "It beats me," perhaps, if he is not very observant. Or if he is, "Something that has to do with making junk, I think. Same as everybody else."

Questions About "The Essay: Thesis"

1. What is Baker's purpose in writing this essay? What, in a word, is the broad subject? What is the restricted subject? Is the subject sufficiently restricted for the length of the essay and for Baker's purpose in writing it? Explain.

2. State in a sentence of not over twenty-five words the thesis of the essay.

3. Mark in your text the paragraphs and underline the sentences and phrases that best explain the main idea of the essay. Making sure to indicate the sequence of Baker's ideas, write a summary (see page 39) of them in not over seventy-five words.

Questions on Diction and Writing Techniques

1. How does your dictionary define "dispirited" (par. 1), "mystifying" (par. 4), "systems" (par. 5), "inquisitive" (par. 8), and "quintuplicate" (par. 16)? Use each of these words in a sentence.
2. What is the tone of this essay? Where does Baker first reveal it to you? What other evidence do you find in his essay to support your answer?

For Discussion, Reading, and Writing

1. How does Baker support his statement: "In effect, the machines are making junk"? Do you agree with his conclusion? Support your answer with specific manufacturing processes and/or products that you are familiar with.
2. Write a short essay explaining what you know from observation of your father, mother, guardian, or anyone else you know well about what he or she experiences in going to work and making a living.
3. Much is being written nowadays about the workmanship and durability of American and Japanese products. Find in your school library two or three articles on the subject and, for the benefit of the students in your class, write a short essay about what you discovered in your reading.
4. If you know anyone who works or has worked in a factory, compare his or her views and Baker's about whether the production by machines of junk is inevitable nowadays. In preparation for a discussion in class of this subject, consider too the view of an American anthropologist:

> A man is not likely to fashion a spear for himself whose point will fall off in midflight; nor is a woman who weaves her own basket likely to make it out of rotted straw. Similarly, if one is sewing a parka for a husband who is about to go hunting for the family with the temperature at sixty below, all stitches will be perfect. And when the men who make boats are the uncles and fathers of those who sail them, they will be as seaworthy as the state of the art permits.

In contrast, it is very hard for people to care about strangers or about products to be used by strangers. In our era of industrial mass production and mass marketing, quality is a constant problem because the intimate sentimental and personal bonds which once made us responsible to each other and to our products have withered away and been replaced by money relationships [Marvin Harris, *America Now*].

2

Units of Composition

Paragraphs

There can be no general rule about the most suitable length for a paragraph; a succession of very short ones is as irritating as very long ones are wearisome. The paragraph is essentially a unit of thought, not of length: it must be homogeneous in subject-matter and sequential in treatment.

—H. W. Fowler

THE paragraph is the largest unit of composition that you will use to express your ideas when writing. It is a unit designed to divide longer writing into more readily readable and understood sections. Its length, structure, and density—the amount of information it contains—may be varied to suit the intended audience and the function the writer wants it to perform, especially as the beginning, part of the middle portion, or the end of an essay.

The basic paragraph is like an essay, and like an essay, it should be unified. Also, it should be complete and be developed in an orderly manner. And, just as in an essay there should be smooth transitions between paragraphs, so in a paragraph there should be smooth transitions between sentences.

Unity: The Topic Sentence

By unity in a paragraph, teachers of composition mean consistency of content. All the sentences in a paragraph must discuss one topic only—one restricted subject—and they must relate to one another, as they do in this example:

> Spain is the stronghold of the vultures. There are four listed species in Europe, two common and two rare; if they are anywhere, they are in Spain. The bearded vulture and the black survive there, the Egyptian flourishes, and the great griffon swarms. The further south you go the more numerous they become, until you reach the hot grazing plains of Andalusia. There, summer and winter through, they hang in hordes in the roofless sky, for Andalusia is the vulture country [John D. Stewart, "Vulture Country"].

The sentences must, without deviating from this objective, develop the main idea of the paragraph, the idea that the paragraph is all about, the one point that the paragraph makes.

The easiest way to assure the unity of a paragraph is to announce its main idea in a sentence, which, because it states the paragraph's topic, is called a *topic sentence.* In this example the topic sentence is in italics:

> *Each man had, to begin with, the great virtue of utter tenacity and fidelity.* Grant fought his way down the Mississippi Valley in spite of acute personal discouragement and profound military handicaps. Lee hung on in the trenches at Petersburg after hope itself had died. In each man there was an indomitable quality . . . the born fighter's refusal to give up as long as he can still remain on his feet and lift his two fists [Bruce Catton, "Grant and Lee: A Study in Contrasts"].

A topic sentence is to a paragraph what a thesis is to an essay. A topic sentence helps the writer to keep the main idea of the paragraph in mind while writing, to focus on it, to control it. It helps the writer to avoid sentences that would be extraneous—that would stray from the paragraph's main idea and thus destroy its unity.

A topic sentence is like a promise. In it the writer in effect says to the reader, "This is what I promise to explain to you in my paragraph." Readers have the right to expect that you will fulfill your promise. Having taken you at your word, they are sure to be disappointed if you don't. It is thus foolish to promise more than you can deliver. Accordingly, avoid making too broad a statement in a topic sentence if limited knowledge of the subject or the limitation of space will prevent you from giving your reader the information needed to prove it valid.

Like an arrow on the road sign that directs the traveler, a topic sentence points out to the writer the direction a paragraph should take. Thus, the sooner the topic sentence is presented, the sooner will the writer see what information is needed to develop it. This is not an unalterable rule, however. The topic sentence may be put anywhere in a paragraph: at its beginning, at the end, or in between.

Often it is more effective not to make the topic sentence the paragraph's first sentence. Preliminary information might clarify its meaning, or placement at or near the end of the paragraph may give it greater emphasis, as in this example (topic sentence in italics).

> If Man has benefited immeasurably by his association with the dog, what, you may ask, has the dog got out of it? His scroll has, of course, been heavily charged with punishments: he has known the muzzle, the leash, and the tether; he has suffered the indignities of the show bench, the tin can on the tail, the ribbon in the hair; his love life with the other sex of his species has been regulated by the frigid hand of authority, his digestion ruined by the macaroons and marshmallows of doting women. *The list of his woes could be continued indefinitely.* But he has also had his fun, for he has been privileged to live with and study at close range the only creature with reason, the most unreasonable of creatures [James Thurber, *Thurber's Dogs*].

Sometimes an author will not write a topic sentence at all. The main idea will not be expressed in so many words but will, nonetheless, be clear to the reader from the content of the paragraph. In this instance, we say that the paragraph's main idea is *implied,* as in this example:

> Riffling through the pages of the new magazines devoted to running, one could conclude from the advertisements that there are more kinds of running shoes on the market in America than there are feet. But this is not to speak of such auxiliary items as special arch supports, heel protectors, insoles; nor of fog-repellants for glasses, or skin lube to prevent chafing under the arms, or runner's mittens; nor of warm-up suits, singlets, socks, and shorts (one manufacturer sells shorts that he advertises as "almost like running in the nude"). Then there are metric conversion scales, chronographs and

> stopwatches, wallets that attach to running shoes, pouches to fit on the back of shorts. One of my favorite items is a "jogging stick," comparable to a military swagger stick, to be carried along while running and to be used, apparently, for beating off dogs, muggers, perhaps smokers [Joseph Epstein, "Running and Other Vices"].

Such a paragraph, though lacking the signpost I mentioned, is not barred from attaining the unity that a topic sentence is designed to ensure. In the paragraph just quoted, the main idea may be stated as follows:

> The ads in the new magazines devoted to the runner abound with special items for sale.

Often, when beginning a paragraph, a writer may not be aware of all that might be said in it and thus may not be able to state its main idea accurately at first. As the writing proceeds, the author may be expressing various unrelated ideas that come to mind. This is not unusual in a first draft. In the course of writing, the writer will realize what the main idea is to be and can then compose a suitable topic sentence and, by rewriting the paragraph, eliminate the extraneous material.

Finally, there are instances where a single topic sentence may serve more than one paragraph. This will be the case where two or more consecutive paragraphs form a unit with a single main idea.

Coherence: Smooth Sentence Flow

In addition to being unified, a paragraph should be coherent. "To cohere" means to stick together. To be coherent, a paragraph must have a smooth sentence flow. One sentence should lead easily to the next, requiring a minimum of effort from the reader. The function of coherence is to interrelate the ideas in a paragraph or essay; its effect is to make their meaning intelligible.

Here is an example of a coherent paragraph (italics added). A reading of this paragraph with and without the italicized words will demonstrate the function and effect of coherence.

> *When* the grave is finished, the wasp returns to the tarantula to complete her ghastly enterprise. *First* she feels it all over once more with her antennae. *Then* her behavior becomes more aggressive. She bends her abdomen, protruding her sting, and searches for the soft membrane at the point where the spider's leg joins its body—the only spot where she can penetrate the horny skeleton. *From time to time,* as the exasperated spider slowly shifts ground, the wasp turns on her back and slides along with the aid of her wings, trying to get under the tarantula for a shot at the vital spot. *During all this maneuvering,* which can last for several minutes, the tarantula makes no move to save itself. *Finally* the wasp corners it against some obstruction and grasps one of its legs in her powerful jaws. *Now at last* the harassed spider tries a desperate but vain defense. The two contestants roll over and over on the ground. It is a terrifying sight and the outcome is always the same. The wasp *finally* manages to thrust her sting into the soft spot and holds it there *for a few seconds* while she pumps in the poison. *Almost immediately* the tarantula falls paralyzed on its back. Its legs stop twitching; its heart stops beating. *Yet* it is not dead, as is shown by the fact that if taken from the wasp it can be restored to some sensitivity by being kept in a moist chamber for several months [Alexander Petrunkivitch, "The Spider and the Wasp"].

One way to attain smooth connections between sentences, as this paragraph demonstrates, is to make the order in a sequence of actions or events clear to the reader by using temporal words—words like "before," "now," "after," "when," and "at the same time" (see page 36).

This paragraph illustrates the distinction between unity and coherence. All its sentences deal with a single topic: the wasp's method of attacking the tarantula; thus the paragraph is unified. It would be unified even if the italicized words were omitted. But in that case the sentences would not flow smoothly, and the paragraph would not be coherent. With them, the paragraph is both unified and coherent.

Completeness

In addition to being unified and coherent, a paragraph must be complete. Your response to a person who makes a statement without supporting it is likely to be doubt or disbelief. You are likely to and would have the right to say, "I'm not convinced." Similarly, your reader will be skeptical – and disappointed – if you neglect to develop sufficiently the main idea of a paragraph you write.

How much development is needed depends in part on the topic and in part on your reader. In general, the more complicated the topic and the more specialized the knowledge required to understand it, the more extensive will the paragraph need to be. But even if the topic is simple, the writer must be sure to develop the topic sentence with sufficiently detailed information and ideas.

"Completeness" is a relative term. A paragraph is not necessarily complete because it is long. Nor is it necessarily incomplete because it is short. A paragraph is complete when it contains as much information as is needed to explain to its reader its main idea. The criterion of completeness is satisfied if the reader understands the paragraph's topic sentence or its implied central idea and accepts it as valid.

The paragraph just quoted, about the spider and the wasp, is relatively long and satisfies the criterion of completeness with its explanation of the wasp's "ghastly enterprise." From the same essay, here is a relatively short paragraph, which is also complete (topic sentence in italics):

> In all this the behavior of the wasp evidently is qualitatively different from that of the spider. *The wasp acts like an intelligent animal.* This is not to say that instinct plays no part or that she reasons as man does. But her actions are to the point; they are not automatic and can be modified to fit the situation. We do not know for certain how she identifies the tarantula – probably it is by some olfactory or chemo-tactile sense – but she does it purposefully and does not blindly tackle a wrong species.

Special Paragraphs: Transitional, Introductory, Concluding

The purpose of the paragraphs discussed so far in this introduction is expository; that is, they explain the essay's subject or some portion of it. There are other kinds of paragraphs with different purposes:

to *introduce*, to *conclude*, and to *serve as a transition between the parts of* an essay. We turn to the last of these first.

The *transitional paragraph* is a type that you will have occasion to use, especially in long essays. It is generally short, often only one sentence. A writer uses a transitional paragraph to inform readers that one section of an essay is completed and another is about to begin. Such a paragraph may summarize what has been written:

> In short, the defining characteristic of the valedictory address is its statement of the opposition between the university on one hand and the world on the other [Lionel Trilling, "A Valedictory"].

It may signal a change from general to more specific information:

> I am not talking pure theory. I will just give you two or three illustrations [Clarence Darrow, "Address to the Prisoners in the Cook Street Jail"].

It may hint at what is to come or announce the introduction of new material:

> Before the end of my trial period in the field I made two really exciting discoveries—discoveries that made the previous months of frustration well worth while [Jane van Lawick-Goodall, *In the Shadow of Man*].

> Looking back over my journal, I see that events of my first week in San Jose pretty much foreshadowed the shape of things to come [Jessica Mitford, "My Short and Happy Life as a Distinguished Professor"].

Or it may state explicitly what new material the writer is about to turn to:

> In what follows, the parallels are not always in physical events but rather in the effect on society, and sometimes in both [Barbara Tuchman, "History as Mirror"].

A transitional paragraph is a useful device for achieving coherence between paragraphs and groups of paragraphs:

> Certainly, there are additional liabilities, but those that I have indicated are a representative lot—perhaps the most serious ones. Let us turn now to the assets. What has technology done for the good life? [Stuart Chase, "Two Cheers for Technology"].

Note how, in this paragraph, the writer tries to connect—especially in sentence 2—his preceding paragraphs and the ones that are to follow.

You will be writing two other kinds of paragraph with special purposes: to introduce and to conclude an essay. You have seen an example of the former, by Frances FitzGerald, on page 7. The *introductory paragraph* has the distinctive purpose of engaging readers' attention.

The purposes of a *concluding paragraph* are to evaluate the rest of the essay, to summarize, or to draw a conclusion. Here are two examples of the third function:

> I have written at such length about this problem because any attempt to describe the America of today must take into account the issue of racial equality, around which much of our thinking and our present-day attitudes turn. We will not have overcome the trauma that slavery has left on our society, North and South, until we cannot remember whether the man we just spoke to in the street was Negro or white [John Steinbeck, *America and Americans*].

> It is not difficult to make a terrifying indictment of technology. It is not difficult to make a heartening list of benefits. The problem is so complex on one level, and yet, in essence, so simple. Granting the available resources of this planet, how many human beings and their fellow creatures can be supported at a level that makes life worth living? A dependable evaluation is very difficult. We can be sure, however, that nothing is to be gained by following the prophets of doom back to the Stone Age [Stuart Chase, "Two Cheers for Technology"].

Analysis of the Paragraphs of a Sample Essay

To further illustrate what I have been saying about paragraphs, I will analyze a sample five-paragraph, seven-hundred-word essay, "Menial Jobs Taught Me a Lot," which begins:

> 1 When I graduated from high school I decided that, having spent fourteen years without interruption in grammar and secondary schools, I would take a year or two, perhaps more, away from school before going on to college. Now, after three years of nondescript jobs, I am convinced that my decision to take a long break between high school and college was wise. *From the menial jobs I had I learned a valuable lesson.*

Here is an introductory paragraph—relatively short, as such a paragraph very often is—that attempts to engage the reader's attention. The writer, in addition to trying to induce his audience to read on, states the thesis of his essay (in italics).

Here is the second paragraph, the first of three paragraphs in the *body,* or middle section, of the essay:

> 2 I learned, first of all, that the jobs available to a teenager without special training do not pay well. Mowing lawns, my first job, paid $2.75 an hour. My second job, waiting on tables in a restaurant, paid, tips included, little more. Packaging groceries at the check-out counter of a supermarket paid somewhat less. Work on the production line of a hardware factory paid $3.00 an hour. My best-paying job, my last, was as a laborer on a construction project where my wages were $3.90 an hour.

Notice, first of all, that the second paragraph has a single main idea, expressed in a topic sentence: ". . . the jobs available to a teenager without special training do not pay well." Because the writer does not digress from this idea, the paragraph is unified. It contains ample evidence to convince us that indeed the jobs available to an unskilled worker do not pay well and is thus complete. It is developed in an orderly way, with the writer going from one job to another, beginning with his first and ending with his last. This development helps achieve coherence—smooth sentence flow—as does the repetition of the key word "paid." Finally, the use of "learned" in the first sentence helps to achieve coherence between the second paragraph and the opening paragraph, in whose last sentence the same word appears.

Here is the third paragraph:

> 3 More important, I found that my jobs, even if they weren't so at the outset, soon became boring. Take my last job, for example. The first thing each morning, I had to drive a truck to a supply depot to pick up odds and ends of building materials. Then, having driven back to the construction site, I had to unload them where they were needed. After that, I had to haul materials from one or another location on the site to others. That done, and for most of the rest of the day, I had to unload by hand from trailers and to stack in orderly piles tons and tons of bulky material such as rough lumber, roofing shingles, and kegs of nails. At the end of the day, I was obliged to clean up rubbish from the outside and inside of buildings under construction, load it on my truck and then unload it at a refuse dump on the site. As a laborer on a construction site, even though I found some variety in the day work, the routine of each day was like that of every other. However, in the factory where I worked pulling the levers on the same machine, every day and every hour of each day was like the next. Working there was like being on a treadmill; it was monotonous, unrelieved drudgery.

Here, too, since content is consistent, we have a unified paragraph. Its main idea is expressed at the outset in a topic sentence whose key word is "boring." The writer supports this idea with two examples of boring jobs, one on a construction project, the other in a factory. Since this information is sufficient to explain to the reader the paragraph's main idea, the paragraph is complete.

Notice how in this paragraph the writer establishes order and smooth sentence flow by arranging his sentences chronologically, with words indicating the passage of time: "the first thing each morning"; "then"; "after that"; "that done"; "and for most of the rest of the day"; "at the end of the day." The words "for example" and "however"—sometimes called *transition words*—also help achieve coherence within the paragraph. (A few more examples of transition words, not used here, are "thus," "for instance," "to illustrate," used to introduce an example; "in the second place," "moreover," "likewise," used to add a thought; "but," "on the contrary," "on the other hand," used to signal a qualification or contrast; and "consequently," "therefore," "to sum up," used to indicate a conclusion or result.) And "found," a synonym of "learned," helps achieve coherence between this paragraph and the other two, where "learned" is used.

Let's now take a look at the fourth paragraph:

> 4 Most important perhaps, I discovered that none of the jobs I had was fulfilling. The best that can be said for my lawn mowing is that it was good exercise and kept me outdoors during the summer months. Waiting on tables, after the newness of the job wore off, was uninteresting. Packaging groceries was unstimulating, to say the least. The same was true for my unchallenging work at a machine in the factory. Even my last job—which was the most satisfying because I was curious about how buildings were put together and because I had to make some decisions on my own even if they were as insignificant as directing a newly arrived trailer to stop here or there on the construction site so that its materials, when unloaded, would be conveniently placed for the skilled workers who would need them—failed to leave me, at the end of the day, with the feeling that I had fully realized my capabilities.

In the second paragraph of this essay, the writer begins with "I *learned,* first of all." In the third, he begins with "more important, I *found.*" In this paragraph, he starts with "Most important perhaps, I *discovered.*" Notice that "discovered," an alternative for "found" and "learned," refers, like "found," to the thesis in paragraph 1 and helps achieve coherence between paragraph 4 and the three preceding paragraphs. "Most important perhaps" has the same effect, since it reminds us of the points the writer made in the two preceding paragraphs. Saving the most important point for the end is also a commendable strategy.

In paragraph 4, as in paragraphs 2 and 3, the main idea is stated in the opening sentence. This idea is developed without digressions in the rest of the paragraph, and examples of the writer's jobs are given in the same order as in paragraph 2. The last part of the paragraph's last sentence, referring to the idea in its first part—a tactic that helps achieve coherence—is a rephrasing of that idea and a fitting summary of and conclusion to the paragraph.

Here is the essay's last paragraph:

> 5 Just what these were I hardly knew at the time; nor am I convinced now that I know just what they are. Nonetheless, I do know that without a skill, or a craft, or a profession, my options of ways to earn a living are limited to jobs that are poorly paying, boring, and unfulfilling. This much I did learn from my three years of work after graduation from high school.

Coherence between this paragraph and the preceding one is achieved by *pronoun reference:* the use of a pronoun or pronouns in one sentence to refer to a noun in a previous sentence. Here, "They" in the first sentence refers to "capabilities" in the previous paragraph. Coherence within the paragraph is helped by the transition word "nonetheless." Fittingly, for a concluding paragraph, the second sentence restates and amplifies the essay's thesis and includes the details of the lesson the writer learned and wrote about in the body (paragraphs 2, 3, and 4) of the essay:

> . . . I do know that without a skill, or a craft, or a profession, my options of ways to earn a living are limited to jobs that are poorly paying, boring, and unfulfilling.

The paragraph is comparable to the essay in that both should have unity, completeness, order, and coherence. Sometimes, an author will write a short essay in a single paragraph, as you will see in John Updike's "Beer Can" (pages 68–69). A good paragraph, whether it is a one-paragraph essay or part of a larger essay, is an integrated unit. Paragraphs have been called, rightly—by Richard M. Weaver in "The Function of the Paragraph"—"compositions in miniature."

Here is such a paragraph, annotated:

Rhetoric is the way the thoughts, feelings, and words of one person *interact* to influence another person. The *interaction* occurs quite spontaneously in speaking and writing. In fact, it is probably accurate to say that no one invented rhetoric. It sprang into being as soon as men saw the possibility of resolving their differences by speaking instead of fighting. Early rhetoric was concerned with the art of speaking in the law courts, the legislative assemblies, and councils of war. It was an art of persuading and exhorting. Ideally, it was designed to promote justice, to seek goodness, and to envision truth and beauty. As an art of persuasion, however, it was inevitable that rhetoric would be used by deceitful men for selfish purposes as well as by just men for virtuous causes. Thus, rhetoric has always had two implications. What we now call "mere rhetoric"–style without significance–need not obscure the fact that another kind of rhetoric can be made to serve good causes in honest ways [William F. Irmscher, *The Holt Guide to English,* 2d ed.].

topic sentence

key word

definition—what is rhetoric?

sentences develop writer's ideas—here and throughout ¶.

for emphasis

sentences help assure completeness

pronoun reference

transitional word—to introduce a restriction of previous idea.

transitional word—to indicate a consequence.

definition—to clarify; to help distinguish between two kinds of rhetoric.

conclusion leads to new judgment.

A special kind of paragraph you will have occasion to compose in college is the *summary*, a comprehensive but brief recapitulation of a piece of writing, which records only the writing's main ideas, as much as possible in one's own words. The summary is an effective means of preserving the essential points of what one reads for later use—in a term paper, for example, Since such a condensation requires the reader to uncover and digest the meaning of the original, it compels a close reading of the text. Effective summarizing makes for intelligent reading.

An example of such a summary, of a single paragraph, follows this original:

> In the Victorian home swarming with children sex was a secret. It was the skeleton in the parental chamber. No one mentioned it. Any untoward questions were answered with a white lie (it was the great age of the stork) or a shocked rebuke. From none of his elders—parent, teacher, or minister—did the Victorian child hear "so much as one word in explanation of the true nature and functions of the reproductive organs." This conspiracy of silence was partly a mistaken effort to protect the child, especially the boy, from temptation (initially from masturbation, which was condemned on grounds of health as well as morals), but at bottom it sprang from a personal feeling of revulsion. For the sexual act was associated by many wives only with a duty and by most husbands with a necessary if pleasurable yielding to one's baser nature: by few, therefore, with an innocent and joyful experience. The silence which first aroused in the child a vague sense of shame was in fact a reflection of parental shame, and one suspects that some women, at any rate, would have been happy if the stork had been a reality [Walter E. Houghton, *The Victorian Frame of Mind*].

> In the Victorian home, sex was a secret, the result of a mistaken effort to protect the child. The sexual act was regarded by many wives as a duty and by most men as a yielding to one's baser nature. The silence which first aroused in the child a vague sense of shame was in fact a reflection of parental shame.

WHAT I HAVE LIVED FOR

Bertrand Russell

Bertrand Russell (1872–1970), recipient of the Nobel Prize for Literature in 1950, was a British mathematician, philosopher, and social reformer. In this passage from his autobiography, he summarizes his personal philosophy.

---

1 Three passions, simple but overwhelmingly strong, have governed my life: the longing for love, the search for knowledge, and unbearable pity for the suffering of mankind. These passions, like great winds, have blown me hither and thither, in a wayward course, over a deep ocean of anguish, reaching to the very verge of despair.

2 I have sought love, first, because it brings ecstasy—ecstasy so great that I would often have sacrificed all the rest of my life for a few hours of this joy. I have sought it, next, because it relieves loneliness—that terrible loneliness in which one shivering consciousness looks over the rim of the world into the cold unfathomable lifeless abyss. I have sought it, finally, because in the union of love I have seen, in a mystic miniature, the prefiguring vision of the heaven that saints and poets have imagined. This is what I sought, and though it might seem too good for human life, this is what—at last—I have found.

3 With equal passion I have sought knowledge. I have wished to understand the hearts of men. I have wished to know why the stars shine. . . . A little of this, but not much, I have achieved.

4 Love and knowledge, so far as they were possible, led upward toward the heavens. But always pity brought me back to earth. Echoes of cries of pain reverberate in my heart. Children in famine, victims tortured by oppressors, helpless old people a hated burden to their sons, and the whole world of loneliness, poverty, and pain make a mockery of what human life should be. I long to alleviate the evil, but I cannot, and I too suffer.

5 This has been my life. I have found it worth living, and would gladly live it again if the chance were offered me.

Questions About "Paragraphs"

1. How does Russell achieve coherence in paragraph 1? In paragraph 2?
2. Considering the writer's purpose in paragraph 2, explain whether the paragraph is complete.
3. What is the topic sentence of paragraph 3? Of paragraph 4?
4. What does the phrase "with equal passion" (par. 3) contribute to the coherence of the essay?
5. What is the writer's purpose in writing "but" (par. 4)?
6. Explain whether paragraph 5 fulfills the requirement(s) of a concluding paragraph.

Questions on Diction and Writing Techniques

1. How does your dictionary define "passion"? What does the phrase "like great winds" (par. 1) contribute to your understanding of the word's meaning?
2. Define the following words and write sentences using each of them appropriately: "ecstasy" (par. 2), "unfathomable" (par. 2), "abyss" (par. 2), "mystic" (par. 2), "reverberate" (par. 4), "mockery" (par. 4).
3. What is the thesis of this piece?
4. How are the central ideas of paragraphs 2, 3, and 4 related to the main idea of the essay?
5. Comment on the essay's unity. Where, if at all, does the writer digress?

For Discussion, Reading, and Writing

1. One of the writing suggestions following "Building Satisfaction" (pages 13–15) is to write a paragraph with a topic sentence such

as "It was hard work." If you wrote such a paragraph, reread it and then rewrite it, keeping in mind the new information about paragraphs you now have. Rewrite any other paragraph you have written in this course so far.

2. What passions have governed your life? Write about one of them in a single paragraph that is unified, orderly, coherent, and complete.
3. Write a short essay on any subject—sports, hobbies, music, or anything else—imitating the organization of Russell's essay. Include (a) a statement in an introductory paragraph of three related ideas to be developed; (b) development of the ideas in separate paragraphs; and (c) a summary in a concluding paragraph.

DARKNESS AT NOON

Harold Krents

Harold Krents, a graduate of Harvard College and Harvard Law School, is a practicing attorney and an advocate of the employment of handicapped people.

---

1 Blind from birth, I have never had the opportunity to see myself and have been completely dependent on the image I create in the eye of the observer. To date it has not been narcissistic.

2 There are those who assume that since I can't see, I obviously also cannot hear. Very often people will converse with me at the top of their lungs, enunciating each word very carefully. Conversely, people will also often whisper, assuming that since my eyes don't work, my ears don't either.

3 For example, when I go to the airport and ask the ticket agent for assistance to the plane, he or she will invariably pick up the

phone, call a ground hostess and whisper: "Hi, Jane, we've got a 76 here." I have concluded that the word "blind" is not used for one of two reasons: Either they fear that if the dread word is spoken, the ticket agent's retina will immediately detach, or they are reluctant to inform me of my condition of which I may not have been previously aware.

4 On the other hand, others know that of course I can hear, but believe that I can't talk. Often, therefore, when my wife and I go out to dinner, a waiter or waitress will ask Kit if "*he* would like a drink" to which I respond that "indeed *he* would."

5 This point was graphically driven home to me while we were in England. I had been given a year's leave of absence from my Washington law firm to study for a diploma in law degree at Oxford University. During the year I became ill and was hospitalized. Immediately after admission, I was wheeled down to the X-ray room. Just at the door sat an elderly woman—elderly I would judge from the sound of her voice. "What is his name?" the woman asked the orderly who had been wheeling me.

6 "What's your name?" the orderly repeated to me.

7 "Harold Krents," I replied.

8 "Harold Krents," he repeated.

9 "When was he born?"

10 "When were you born?"

11 "Nov. 5, 1944," I responded.

12 "Nov. 5, 1944," the orderly intoned.

13 This procedure continued for approximately five minutes at which point even my saint-like disposition deserted me. "Look," I finally blurted out, "this is absolutely ridiculous. Okay, granted I can't see, but it's got to have become pretty clear to both of you that I don't need an interpreter."

14 "He says he doesn't need an interpreter," the orderly reported to the woman.

15 The toughest misconception of all is the view that because I can't see, I can't work. I was turned down by over forty law firms because of my blindness, even though my qualifications included a cum laude degree from Harvard College and a good ranking in my Harvard Law School class.

16 The attempt to find employment, the continuous frustration of being told that it was impossible for a blind person to practice

law, the rejection letters, not based on my lack of ability but rather on my disability, will always remain one of the most disillusioning experiences of my life.

17 Fortunately, this view of limitation and exclusion is beginning to change. On April 16, the Department of Labor issued regulations that mandate equal-employment opportunities for the handicapped. By and large, the business community's response to offering employment to the disabled has been enthusiastic.

18 I therefore look forward to the day, with the expectation that it is certain to come, when employers will view their handicapped workers as a little child did me years ago when my family still lived in Scarsdale.

19 I was playing basketball with my father in our backyard according to procedures we had developed. My father would stand beneath the hoop, shout, and I would shoot over his head at the basket attached to our garage. Our next-door neighbor, aged five, wandered over into our yard with a playmate. "He's blind," our neighbor whispered to her friend in a voice that could be heard distinctly by Dad and me. Dad shot and missed. I did the same. Dad hit the rim. I missed entirely. Dad shot and missed the garage entirely. "Which one is blind?" whispered back the little friend.

20 I would hope that in the near future when a plant manager is touring the factory with the foreman and comes upon a handicapped and nonhandicapped person working together, his comment after watching them work will be, "Which one is disabled?"

Questions About "Paragraphs"

1. Krents expresses two ideas in paragraph 2. What is the first of these? How does he support it? How does he signal to you that the paragraph contains a second idea? What is the idea?
2. What is Krents' purpose in writing paragraph 3? How does he signal that purpose to you?
3. If this were your essay, would you begin paragraph 3 with the last sentence of paragraph 2? Combine paragraphs 2 and 3? Leave the two paragraphs as they are? Why?

4. How does Krents achieve coherence between paragraphs 3 and 4? Between paragraphs 4 and 5?
5. Why, in paragraph 4, does Krents write "therefore"? Find, elsewhere in this essay, his use of that word for a similar purpose.
6. What is the topic sentence of paragraph 15? Of paragraph 17?
7. Is paragraph 20 an apt concluding paragraph? Why?
8. This essay was written for and edited by a daily newspaper. How does this fact help to explain its paragraphing?

Questions on Diction and Writing Techniques

1. Define, in your own way, any words in this essay that are new to you, but whose meaning you can surmise from their context. Then compare your definitions with those in your dictionary. Also, write in your text the dictionary definitions of all other words that are new to you. Use the words in both groups in sentences.
2. Is the thesis of this essay expressed or implied? If expressed, state where. If implied, state it in your own words.
3. What does the anecdote in paragraph 19 contribute to an explanation of the essay's main idea?
4. To better appreciate the organization of this essay and the progression of its ideas, summarize it in a coherent paragraph of not over one hundred words.

For Discussion, Reading, and Writing

1. What, according to Krents, was the toughest misconception of all?
2. Fill the blanks in this sentence to make it intelligible:

   I would hope that in the near future ______ a plant manager is touring the ______ with the foreman and comes upon a ______ and nonhandicapped person ______ together, his comment after ______

them work will be, "Which one of them is ______?"

Compare your choice of words with those in paragraph 20.

3. Think about the difference between lack of ability and disability, making notes as you do. Then, (a) write a one-paragraph letter on the subject to a friend; (b) write a one-paragraph letter to the president of a company in support of a real or imaginary disabled person's application for a job.

A FABLE FOR TOMORROW

Rachel Carson

Rachel Carson (1907–1964) was a marine biologist and author. She was the first scientist to document the dangers of insecticides, in *Silent Spring* (1962), in which this essay appeared.

---

1 There was once a town in the heart of America where all life seemed to live in harmony with its surroundings. The town lay in the midst of a checkerboard of prosperous farms, with fields of grain and hillsides of orchards where, in spring, white clouds of bloom drifted above the green fields. In autumn, oak and maple and birch set up a blaze of color that flamed and flickered across a backdrop of pines. Then foxes barked in the hills and deer silently crossed the fields, half hidden in the mists of the fall mornings.

2 Along the roads, laurel, viburnum and alder, great ferns and wildflowers delighted the traveler's eye through much of the year. Even in winter the roadsides were places of beauty, where countless birds came to feed on the berries and on the seed heads of the dried

weeds rising above the snow. The countryside was, in fact, famous for the abundance and variety of its bird life, and when the flood of migrants was pouring through in spring and fall people traveled from great distances to observe them. Others came to fish the streams, which flowed clear and cold out of the hills and contained shady pools where trout lay. So it had been from the days many years ago when the first settlers raised their houses, sank their wells, and built their barns.

3 Then a strange blight crept over the area and everything began to change. Some evil spell had settled on the community: mysterious maladies swept the flocks of chickens; the cattle and sheep sickened and died. Everywhere was a shadow of death. The farmers spoke of much illness among their families. In the town the doctors had become more and more puzzled by new kinds of sickness appearing among their patients. There had been several sudden and unexplained deaths, not only among adults but even among children, who would be stricken suddenly while at play and die within a few hours.

4 There was a strange stillness. The birds, for example—where had they gone? Many people spoke of them, puzzled and disturbed. The feeding stations in the backyards were deserted. The few birds seen anywhere were moribund; they trembled violently and could not fly. It was a spring without voices. On the mornings that had once throbbed with the dawn chorus of robins, catbirds, doves, jays, wrens, and scores of other bird voices there was now no sound; only silence lay over the fields and woods and marsh.

5 On the farms the hens brooded, but no chicks hatched. The farmers complained that they were unable to raise any pigs—the litters were small and the young survived only a few days. The apple trees were coming into bloom but no bees droned among the blossoms, so there was no pollination and there would be no fruit.

6 The roadsides, once so attractive, were now lined with browned and withered vegetation as though swept by fire. These, too, were silent, deserted by all living things. Even the streams were now lifeless. Anglers no longer visited them, for all the fish had died.

7 In the gutters under the eaves and between the shingles of the roofs, a white granular powder still showed a few patches; some weeks before it had fallen like snow upon the roofs and the lawns, the fields and streams.

8 No witchcraft, no enemy action had silenced the rebirth of new life in this stricken world. The people had done it themselves.

9 This town does not actually exist, but it might easily have a thousand counterparts in America or elsewhere in the world. I know of no community that has experienced all the misfortunes I describe. Yet every one of these disasters has actually happened somewhere, and many real communities have already suffered a substantial number of them. A grim specter has crept upon us almost unnoticed, and this imagined tragedy may easily become a stark reality we all shall know.

Questions About "Paragraphs"

1. Find examples of how Carson tells you of the validity of the main idea of paragraph 3.
2. What is the main idea of paragraph 4? Where is it expressed?
3. The topic sentence of paragraph 5 is implied. Write a suitable topic sentence for the paragraph.
4. What is the main idea of paragraph 6? How does Carson make the idea clear to you?
5. Find examples of Carson's use of transition words in paragraphs 4, 5, and 9.

Questions on Diction and Writing Techniques

1. Mark in your text all words in this essay that, though new to you, you understood from their context. Define them in your own words. Compare your definitions with those in your dictionary. Look up in your dictionary all other words that are new to you. Use the words in both groups in sentences.
2. What is Carson's purpose in writing "in fact" (par. 2)?
3. Why does she write "once so attractive" (par. 6)?
4. This essay may be divided into three parts: paragraphs 1–2, 3–8, and 9. Explain the function of each part.

For Discussion, Reading, and Writing

1. The first and last sentences of this passage are complete. Fill in the blanks in the other sentences.

   This town does not actually exist, but it might easily have a thousand counterparts in America or elsewhere in the world. I know of no ______ that has experienced all the ______ I describe. ______ every one of these ______ has actually happened somewhere, and many real ______ have already ______ a substantial number of ______.

   A grim specter has crept upon us almost unnoticed, and this imagined tragedy may easily become a stark reality we all shall know.

   Compare your choice of words with those in paragraph 9.

2. A fable is a short, uncomplicated story told to point a moral. What is Carson's message in this essay? State it in a sentence of not over twenty-five words.

3. Starting out with a clearly stated topic sentence, write a paragraph (one that you might want to see published) to the editor of your school's newspaper, explaining your views on environmental abuse of your college campus or of some place such as a park, wood, or lake.

4. In 1962, when *Silent Spring,* the source of this selection, was published, pesticides had been in use for about twenty years. Carson, criticized severely by some for being an alarmist, was then particularly worried about the "enormous biological potency" of synthetic insecticides. In your lifetime, new questionable chemicals have proliferated. What are some of them? What are their uses? What is their effect on you and me, on the rest of the animate world, on the environment? Should new dangerous chemicals, as Carson said of pesticides, be "of concern to us all"? In *Silent Spring* she wrote: "If we are going to live so intimately with these chemicals—eating and drinking them, taking them into the very marrow of our bones—we had better know something about their nature and power." Is this a subject that interests you? Might there be in it a topic for an essay to be

completed weeks from now, about midterm, say? If so, start gathering material for it. A good place to start might be *Silent Spring,* especially pages 15–37 ("Elixirs of Death").

DO DOCTORS REALLY LISTEN?

Lewis Thomas

Rarely does anyone achieve the distinction in two professions that Lewis Thomas has attained in medicine and in writing. Now chancellor of Memorial Sloan-Kettering Cancer Center in New York City, he is perhaps even better known as an essayist. A member of the National Academy of Sciences, he is also the recipient of the National Book Award for *The Lives of a Cell* (1974), his first book of essays.

---

1 Medicine was once the most respected of all the professions. Today, when it possesses an array of technologies for treating (or curing) diseases which were simply beyond comprehension a few years ago, medicine is under attack for all sorts of reasons. Doctors, the critics say, are applied scientists, concerned only with the disease at hand but never with the patient as an individual, whole person. They do not really listen. They are unwilling or incapable of explaining things to sick people or their families. They make mistakes in their risky technologies; hence the rapidly escalating cost of malpractice insurance. They are accessible only in their offices in huge, alarming clinics or within the walls of terrifying hospitals. The word "dehumanizing" is used as an epithet for the way they are trained, and for the way they practice. The old art of medicine has been lost, forgotten.

2 The American medical schools are under pressure from all

sides to bring back the family doctor—the sagacious, avuncular physician who used to make house calls, look after the illnesses of every member of the family, was even able to call the family dog by name. Whole new academic departments have been installed—some of them, in the state-run medical schools, actually legislated into existence—called, in the official catalogues, *Family Practice, Primary Health Care, Preventive Medicine, Primary Medicine.* The avowed intention is to turn out more general practitioners of the type that everyone remembers from childhood or from one's parents' or grandparents' childhood, or from books, movies, and television.

3 What is it that people have always expected from the doctor? How, indeed, has the profession of medicine survived for so much of human history? Doctors as a class have always been criticized for their deficiencies. Montaigne in his time, Molière in his, and Shaw had less regard for doctors and their medicine than today's critics. What on earth were the patients of physicians in the nineteenth century and the centuries before, all the way back to my professional ancestors, the shamans of prehistory, hoping for when they called for the doctor? In the years of the great plagues, when carts came through the town streets each night to pick up the dead and carry them off for burial, what was the function of the doctor? Bubonic plague, typhus, tuberculosis, and syphilis were representative examples of a great number of rapidly progressive and usually lethal infections, killing off most of the victims no matter what was done by the doctor. What did the man do, when called out at night to visit the sick for whom he had nothing to offer for palliation, much less cure?

4 Well, one thing he did, early on in history, was plainly magic. The shaman learned his profession the hardest way: he was compelled to go through something like a version of death itself, personally, and when he emerged he was considered qualified to deal with patients. He had epileptic fits, saw visions, and heard voices, lost himself in the wilderness for weeks on end, fell into long stretches of coma, and when he came back to life he was licensed to practice, dancing around the bedside, making smoke, chanting incomprehensibilities, and *touching* the patient everywhere. The touching was the real professional secret, never acknowledged as the central, essential skill, always obscured by the dancing and the chanting, but always busily there, the laying on of hands.

5 There, I think, is the oldest and most effective act of doctors, the touching. Some people don't like being handled by others, but not, or almost never, sick people. They *need* being touched, and part of the dismay in being very sick is the lack of close human contact. Ordinary people, even close friends, even family members, tend to stay away from the very sick, touching them as infrequently as possible for fear of interfering, or catching the illness, or just for fear of bad luck. The doctor's oldest skill in trade was to place his hands on the patient.

6 Over the centuries, the skill became more specialized and refined, the hands learned other things to do beyond mere contact. They probed to feel the pulse at the wrist, the tip of the spleen, or the edge of the liver, thumped to elicit resonant or dull sounds over the lungs, spread ointments over the skin, nicked veins for bleeding, but the same time touched, caressed, and at the end held on to the patient's fingers.

7 Most of the men who practiced this laying on of hands must have possessed, to begin with, the gift of affection. There are, certainly, some people who do not like other people much, and they would have been likely to stay away from an occupation requiring touching. If, by mistake, they found themselves apprenticed for medicine, they probably backed off or, if not, turned into unsuccessful doctors.

8 Touching with the naked ear was one of the great advances in the history of medicine. Once it was learned that the heart and lungs made sounds of their own, and that the sounds were sometimes useful for diagnosis, physicians placed an ear over the heart, and over areas on the front and back of the chest, and listened. It is hard to imagine a friendlier human gesture, a more intimate signal of personal concern and affection, than those close bowed heads affixed to the skin. The stethoscope was invented in the nineteenth century, vastly enhancing the acoustics of the thorax, but removing the physician a certain distance from his patient. It was the earliest device of many still to come, one new technology after another, designed to increase that distance.

9 Today, the doctor can perform a great many of his most essential tasks from his office in another building without ever seeing the patient. There are even computer programs for the taking of a history: a clerk can ask the questions and check the boxes on a printed

form, and the computer will instantly provide a printout of the diagnostic possibilities to be considered and the laboratory procedures to be undertaken. Instead of spending forty-five minutes listening to the chest and palpating the abdomen, the doctor can sign a slip which sends the patient off to the X-ray department for a CT scan, with the expectation of seeing within the hour, in exquisite detail, all the body's internal organs which he formerly had to make guesses about with his fingers and ears. The biochemistry laboratory eliminates the need for pondering and waiting for the appearance of new signs and symptoms. Computerized devices reveal electronic intimacies of the flawed heart or malfunctioning brain with a precision far beyond the touch or reach, or even the imagining, of the physician at the bedside a few generations back.

10 The doctor can set himself, if he likes, at a distance, remote from the patient and the family, never touching anyone beyond a perfunctory handshake as the first and only contact. Medicine is no longer the laying on of hands, it is more like the reading signals from machines.

11 The mechanization of scientific medicine is here to stay. The new medicine works. It is a vastly more complicated profession, with more things to be done on short notice on which issues of life or death depend. The physician has the same obligations that he carried, overworked and often despairingly, fifty years ago, but now with any number of technological maneuvers to be undertaken quickly and with precision. It looks to the patient like a different experience from what his parents told him about, with something important left out. The doctor seems less like the close friend and confidant, less interested in him as a person, wholly concerned with treating the disease. And there is no changing this, no going back; nor, when you think about it, is there really any reason for wanting to go back. If I develop the signs and symptoms of malignant hypertension, or cancer of the colon, or subacute bacterial endocarditis, I want as much comfort and friendship as I can find at hand, but mostly I want to be treated quickly and effectively so as to survive, if that is possible. If I am in bed in a modern hospital, worrying about the cost of that bed as well, I want to get out as fast as possible, whole if possible.

12 In my father's time, talking with the patient was the biggest part of medicine, for it was almost all there was to do. The doctor–patient relationship was, for better or worse, a long conversation in which the patient was at the epicenter of concern and knew it. When I was an

intern and scientific technology was in its earliest stage, the talk was still there, but hurried, often on the run.

13 Today, with the advances of medicine's various and complicated new technologies, the ward rounds now at the foot of the bed, the drawing of blood samples for automated assessment of every known (or suggested) biochemical abnormality, the rolling of wheelchairs and litters down through the corridors to the X-ray department, there is less time for talking. The longest and most personal conversations held with hospital patients when they come to the hospital are discussions of finances and insurance, engaged in by personnel trained in accountancy, whose scientific instruments are the computers. The hospitalized patient feels, for a time, like a working part of an immense, automated apparatus. He is admitted and discharged by batteries of computers, sometimes without even learning the doctors' names. The difference can be strange and vaguely dismaying for patients. But there is another difference, worth emphasis. Many patients go home speedily, in good health, cured of their diseases. In my father's day this happened much less often, and when it did, it was a matter of good luck or a strong constitution. When it happens today, it is more frequently due to technology.

14 There are costs to be faced. Not just money, the real and heavy dollar costs. The close-up, reassuring, warm touch of the physician, the comfort and concern, the long, leisurely discussions in which everything including the dog can be worked into the conversation, are disappearing from the practice of medicine, and this may turn out to be too great a loss for the doctor as well as for the patient. This uniquely subtle, personal relationship has roots that go back into the beginnings of medicine's history, and needs preserving. To do it right has never been easy; it takes the best of doctors, the best of friends. Once lost, even for as short a time as one generation, it may be too difficult a task to bring it back again.

15 If I were a medical student or an intern, just getting ready to begin, I would be more worried about this aspect of my future than anything else. I would be apprehensive that my real job, caring for sick people, might soon be taken away, leaving me with the quite different occupation of looking after machines. I would be trying to figure out ways to keep this from happening.

Questions About "Paragraphs"

1. Pronoun reference is one of the means of achieving coherence that Thomas utilizes in paragraph 1. Find in his essay another paragraph in which he uses a pronoun in the same way for a similar reason.
2. How are the ideas in paragraph 2 related to those in paragraph 1?
3. In what paragraph(s) does Thomas answer the question(s) raised in paragraph 3?
4. What is the main idea of paragraph 9? Explain whether Thomas' support of that idea in that paragraph convinces you of its validity. Is the paragraph complete? Explain.
5. How do the ideas in paragraph 10 relate to those in paragraph 9? Can you justify combining the two paragraphs? Explain.
6. Explain the relationship of the ideas in paragraph 8 with those in paragraph 9 and the relationship of the ideas in paragraphs 8 and 9 with those in paragraph 10. Can you justify regarding all three paragraphs as a unit? How? Of what larger group of paragraphs might paragraphs 8–10 be considered an integral part? Explain.
7. What is the main idea of the paragraph? Is the idea amply supported? Is the paragraph complete? Explain.
8. Underline, or mark in one way or another, or write next to each paragraph of this essay—in a word, a phrase, or a complete sentence—its gist. To better understand the relationship of the paragraphs and of their ideas and to better appreciate Thomas' organization of his essay, use your marks and jottings as a starting point in writing, in a coherent paragraph of not over one hundred words, a summary of the essay.

Questions on Diction and Writing Techniques

1. How does your dictionary define "technologies" and "escalating" (par. 1); "sagacious" and "avuncular" (par. 2); "lethal" and "shamans" (par. 3); "perfunctory" (par. 10)? Use each of these words in a sentence.
2. Where and why does Thomas take pains to explain the term "family doctor"?
3. Making specific reference to the text, justify your judgment of

whom Thomas took to be his audience when he sat down to write this essay.

4. List the important ideas that Thomas discusses. Considering their variety, explain whether it is fair to conclude that the essay has one main idea. If it does, state that idea in a sentence of not over twenty-five words.
5. What does the essay tell you about its author and about the kind of doctor he is? Support your answer with specific reference to the text.

For Discussion, Reading, and Writing

1. Why, according to Thomas, is medicine today under attack?
2. What, according to him, are the American medical schools under pressure to do?
3. For what have doctors as a class always been criticized?
4. What was the doctor's "oldest skill in trade"?
5. What, over the centuries, did that skill become?
6. What was "one of the great advances in the history of medicine"?
7. Why, according to Thomas, is the mechanization of medicine here to stay?
8. What, according to him, does the hospitalized patient feel like nowadays?
9. What, in the contemporary practice of medicine, are the costs to be faced?
10. What recommendation does Thomas make to "a medical student or an intern, just getting ready to begin"?
11. Recall as best you can, making notes of the experience as you do so, waiting in any doctor's outer office. Write a short essay on the subject.
12. If you have ever been hospitalized, comment, in a short essay, on "The hospitalized patient feels, for a time, like a working part of an immense, automated apparatus."
13. Explain in a short essay whether the practice of medicine or any related occupation—nursing, hospital administration, pharmacology, dentistry, paramedical care, etc.—appeals to you.

Sentences

Besides having its own semantic content, i.e., besides saying, asking, or commanding something, each sentence in any paragraph accomplishes—or should accomplish—an identifiable task, a piece of work, in cooperation with the sentences that surround it.

—Richard L. Larson

YOU have been using sentences all your life and probably know more about them than you realize. The purposes of this section are to make you conscious of what you already know, to describe techniques of sentence building that may be unfamiliar, and to increase your awareness of the variety of possibilities for constructing the units of composition called sentences.

The most common sentence—the *standard sentence*—consists of two parts: a subject and a predicate. The *predicate* is the part of a sentence that tells us something about the *subject.* "Bill Smith [subject] hit the ball [predicate]" is a standard sentence, but the amount of information it contains is small. This amount—the *density* of the sentence—can be increased by *modification, subordination* (a form of modification), and *coordination.*

Modification

"To modify" means to limit or describe a grammatical element. In the sentence,

Powerful Bill Smith hit the ball.

we modify "Bill Smith" with an adjective. In

> *After two bunting attempts, powerful* Bill Smith hit the ball *over the head of Jake Johnson.*

we expand the sentence more by modifying "hit" with "after two bunting attempts," a prepositional phrase (a preposition, its object, and any modifier of the object) and with another prepositional phrase, "over the head of Jake Johnson." We could continue to rewrite, using adjectives, adverbs, phrases, and clauses—building to an information-packed sentence:

> *After two bunting attempts and two foul tips, league-leading State U.'s slugging center fielder, powerful* Bill Smith, hit the ball *over the head of A. & M.'s Jake (alias "Flatfoot") Johnson, past the right-field fence of Kennedy Stadium to the top row of the stands where a proud State supporter speared the speeding sphere.*

By means of *modification,* we have expanded the original sentence, increasing the amount of information it contains by adding specific details.

To learn how writers utilize modification, consider these four sentences:

1. America needs a new kind of college.
2. I do not really live in that world.
3. I observed two large ants.
4. A saxophone player stands on the sidewalk.

These sentences are the cores and main clauses (constructions containing a subject and a predicate that can stand alone as a sentence) of enlarged sentences:

1. American needs a new kind of college, *in which the teachers are not drawn primarily from the academic profession, and the pedagogy does not rely primarily on classrooms* [Christopher Jencks, "An Anti-Academic Proposal"].

2. *And I do not really live in that world, so narrow and so trivial, so cruel and so unconscious; I was a mere visitor* [Katherine Anne Porter, "The Bullfight"].

3. *One day when I went out to my woodpile, or rather my pile of stumps,* I observed two large ants, *the one red, the other much larger, nearly half an inch long, and black, fiercely contending with one another* [Henry David Thoreau, *Walden*].

4. *Each afternoon in New York* a *rather seedy* saxophone player, *his cheeks blown out like a spinnaker,* stands on the sidewalk *playing Danny Boy in such a sad, sensitive way that he soon has half the neighborhood peeking out of windows tossing nickels, dimes and quarters at his feet* [Gay Talese, "New York"].

In each instance, the writer—by adding details—made the main clause more specific. Jencks stated the characteristics of "a new kind of college." Porter listed attributes of "that world" she referred to. Thoreau described the "two large ants." Talese particularized his subject. Each writer, by means of modification, increased the amount of information in the sentence and thereby made it of greater interest to readers.

Subordination

Adjectives, adverbs, phrases, and clauses that limit or describe other elements in a sentence are subordinate—of less importance, secondary—to them. Their placement in modifying roles is called *subordination.*

Often, writers use this technique to de-emphasize one idea while emphasizing another. Compare the first two examples with the third:

1. Bill Smith attempted two bunts. He hit a home run.

2. Bill Smith attempted two bunts, and then he hit a home run.

3. *After two attempts to bunt,* Bill Smith hit a home run.

Two sentences in the first example and two main clauses in the second example describe actions whose importance is not differentiated.

In the third example the writer de-emphasized one of the actions by making it subordinate, in a modifying prepositional phrase (in italics), to the action in the sentence's main clause, "Bill Smith hit a home run." The writer could change the relative importance of the two actions by reversing their roles in the sentence, placing the idea of bunting in the main clause and the idea of hitting a home run in a modifying phrase:

> *Before hitting a home run,* Bill Smith attempted to bunt twice.

Here are some other examples of the use of subordination to show which idea the writer wishes to emphasize (subordinate, de-emphasized elements in italics):

> *Even though Secretary of War Stimson opposed the move,* President Truman ordered the A-bombing of Japan.
>
> *When the Japanese surrendered,* most American troops in the Pacific were returned to the United States.
>
> *Except for those who chose to make soldiering their career,* returning American troops were discharged from the Army.
>
> Many veterans were able to go to college *because of the G.I. Bill.*
>
> *Older and more mature than most of the other college students,* many veterans distinguished themselves in college.
>
> *Although World War II is long since past,* the war's combat veterans still remember its horrors.

Useful in signaling a subordinate element in a sentence are words like "even though," "when," "except for," "because of," and "although."

Generally, a writer, when using subordination to increase the density of a sentence, has a choice of ways to construct the expanded sentence. Consider how this information might be merged in a sentence:

a. The mile race was run in Madison Square Garden.
b. Twenty thousand spectators were there.
c. Tom Jones trailed during most of the contest.
d. He reached the tape five yards ahead of his nearest rival.
e. He won the race in four minutes flat.

Among the possible combinations are:

1. After trailing during most of the contest held in Madison Square Garden before twenty thousand spectators, Tom Jones won the mile race in four minutes flat, reaching the tape five yards ahead of his nearest rival.

2. Tom Jones won the mile race in four minutes flat, reaching the tape five yards ahead of his nearest rival after trailing during most of the contest held in Madison Square Garden before twenty thousand spectators.

3. After trailing during most of the contest held in Madison Square Garden before twenty thousand spectators, Tom Jones reached the tape five yards ahead of his nearest rival to win the mile race in four minutes flat.

In these sentences, the writer indicates the importance of the information in sentences (a) through (e) by putting secondary information in modifying elements—prepositional phrases introduced by "after" and "before" and a participial phrase introduced by "reaching"—that are subordinated to the main clauses in the sentences.

This is not all the writer does. She also increases or decreases the emphasis of the information in sentences (a) through (e) by the place assigned to it in the expanded sentences.

The beginning and the end are a sentence's most emphatic positions—especially the end, for what we read last we remember best. In sentence 1, even though the beginning and end are subordinate to the main clause, the writer de-emphasizes the main clause by placing it in the less emphatic middle position. In sentence 2, she emphasizes the information in the main clause by putting it in the beginning, but the emphasis is diminished by the stress achieved by the information placed at the end. In sentence 3, the writer better emphasizes the idea in the main clause—that Jones won the mile race in four minutes flat—by putting it at the end.

For another example of the function and effect of subordination, consider how the author of "Menial Jobs Taught Me a Lot" (presented in its entirety in "Paragraphs," pages 34–37) might have written its first paragraph:

Original	*Alternate*
1. When I graduated from high school I decided that, having spent fourteen years without interruption in grammar school and secondary schools, I would take a year or two, perhaps more, away from school before going on to college.	1. I spent fourteen years without interruption in grammar and secondary schools. 2. Then I graduated from high school. 3. I decided I would take a year or two, perhaps more, away from school before going on to college.

The alternate sentences, all grammatically correct, contain the information that is in the first sentence of the original paragraph. But, regardless of the importance of the information they contain, the emphasis is the same in the three individual sentences. In the first sentence of the original paragraph, however, one idea is stressed and the others are deemphasized by means of subordination.

In sentence 1 of the original, the writer assigned less importance to the ideas in alternate sentences 1 and 2—"*when* I graduated from high school"; "*having* spent fourteen years without interruption in grammar and secondary schools"—than he did to the idea in alternate sentence 3, which he emphasized by putting its idea in the original sentence's main clause: "I decided that I would take a year or two, perhaps more, away from school before going on to college."

Original	*Alternate*
2. Now, after three years of nondescript jobs, I am convinced that my decision to take a long break between high school and college was wise.	4. I had nondescript jobs for three years. 5. I am convinced that my decision to take a long break between high school and college was wise.

The writer's construction of the original sentence 2 reveals the importance he assigns to the ideas expressed in the alternate paragraph's sentences 4 and 5: In sentence 2, a prepositional phrase—"after three years in nondescript jobs"—is subordinate to the sentence's main clause, "I am convinced. . . ."

Original	*Alternate*
3. From the menial jobs I had I learned a valuable lesson.	6. The jobs I had were menial. 7. But I learned a valuable lesson.

The writer makes clear the relative importance of the ideas in sentence 3 of the original by subordinating sentence 6 of the alternate in a prepositional phrase, "*from* the menial jobs I had," that modifies the idea in sentence 7, originally expressed—and emphasized—in a main clause: "I learned a valuable lesson."

A comparison of the two groups of sentences just discussed will reveal another benefit of subordination: the alleviation of monotony, which may result from a series of short, standard sentences with little modification. It must not be concluded, however, that a sentence is necessarily less desirable because it is uncomplicated or short. The sentences in paragraph 2 of "Menial Jobs Taught Me a Lot" are relatively simple and short, averaging eighteen words per sentence, six less than the average length of the sentences in the first paragraph of the essay. They are, nonetheless, sound sentences.

The criteria for judging whether a sentence is good are the exactness with which it expresses its writer's ideas and the clarity with which it communicates them to the reader. Thus the second sentence of paragraph 3, containing six words, and the last sentence of paragraph 4, containing eighty-nine words (seventy-two of them subordinated to its seventeen-word split main clause: "My last job . . . failed to leave me . . . with the feeling that I had fully realized my capabilities"), are equally good.

The short second sentence in paragraph 3 not only adds variety—an antidote to monotony—but also makes an impact because of the staccato effect of its brevity. It draws attention to itself and the idea it contains. The long last sentence in paragraph 4 has the virtue of emphasizing its main idea and of serving as the climax of the sentence (and of the paragraph as well). The writer achieved these effects by postponing the completion of the main idea until the end of the sentence, a construction that produces a *periodic sentence.*

The effect that a writer can achieve with a periodic sentence can be highlighted by comparing one with a *standard sentence,* also called a *loose sentence.* A loose sentence does not end with the completion of its main clause but continues with additional information; the writer attaches information that modifies and is subordinate to the sentence's main clause. In this example, the main clause is in italics (added):

> *January 11, 1965, was a bright warm day in Southern California,* the kind of day when California floats on the Pacific horizon and the air smells of orange blossoms and it is a long way from the bleak and difficult East, a long way from the cold, a long way from the past [Joan Didion, *Slouching Towards Bethlehem*].

The reader of a periodic sentence, in contrast, is held in suspense because grammatical construction and meaning are not complete until the end. Again, the main clauses are in italics (added):

> If neither men nor gadgets nor both combined can control the earth from the earth, *we fail to see how they will do so from the moon* [Eric Sevareid, "The Dark of the Moon"].

> In an era when huge television audiences watch surgical operations in the comfort of their living rooms, when, thanks to the animated cartoon, the geography of the digestive system has become familiar territory even to the nursery school set, in a land where the satisfaction of curiosity about almost all matters is a national pastime, *the secrecy surrounding embalming can, surely, hardly be attributed to the inherent gruesomeness of the subject* [Jessica Mitford, *The American Way of Death*].

Coordination

In addition to modification and subordination, the writer may use *coordination* to expand a sentence. Instead of writing

> Smith stepped into the batter's box. He faced the pitcher.

she might combine the two sentences by giving them a common subject and pairing the two predicates:

> Smith stepped into the batter's box and faced the pitcher.

Instead of writing

> Johnson checked first base. He turned to the batter. He raised his arm. He threw a screwball.

she might combine these sentences by giving them a common subject and linking their predicates:

> Johnson checked first base, turned to the batter, raised his arm, and threw a screwball.

Coordination is the joining of grammatical elements of identical construction in pairs or series. It is often signaled by the conjunctions "and," "but," "for," "nor," "or," and "yet":

> . . . among these are Life, Liberty *and* the Pursuit of Happiness.
> He studied hard *but* flunked the course.
> He ran all the way, *for* he was eager to get home in time for dinner.
> Neither snow, *nor* rain, *nor* heat, *nor* gloom of night stays these couriers from the swift completion of their appointed rounds.
> Give me liberty *or* give me death.
> She was outgoing *yet* had few friends.

There are examples of coordination in paragraph 3 of "Menial Jobs Taught Me a Lot."

> I had *to unload* by hand from trailers and *to stack* in orderly piles [pair of coordinate infinitives] . . . material such as rough *lumber*, roofing *shingles*, and *kegs* of nails [coordinate nouns in a series]. . . . I was obliged *to clean up rubbish* . . . *load it on my truck*, and then *unload it* [coordinate series of infinitive phrases]. . . .

Notice that the coordinate elements are of the same grammatical kind; "to unload" and "to stack," for example, are both infinitives. Unlike subordination, which makes one element less important than another, coordination combines in pairs or series elements—single words, phrases, or clauses—that are similar in kind and function and equal in importance.

The following sentences are diagrammed to point out examples of coordinate (1) verbs, (2) nouns, (3) prepositional phrases and nouns, (4) gerund phrases, and (5) predicates (all in italics):

1. *Having once got hold they never let go, but*
struggled and
wrestled and
rolled
on the chips incessantly.[1]

2. One hundred years later,
the life of the Negro is
still badly crippled by
the manacles of segregation and
the chains of discrimination.[2]

3. It is his privilege
to help man endure
by lifting his heart,
by reminding him of the
courage and
honor and
hope and
pride and
compassion and
pity and
sacrifice
which have been the glory of his past.[3]

4. We observe today not a
victory of a party but
a celebration of freedom—
symbolizing an end as well as a beginning—
signifying renewal as well as change.[4]

5. He has
plundered our seas,
ravaged our coasts,
burnt our towns, and
destroyed the lives of our people.[5]

[1] Henry David Thoreau, *Walden.*
[2] Martin Luther King, "I Have a Dream."
[3] William Faulkner, "Man Will Prevail."
[4] John F. Kennedy, "Inaugural Address."
[5] Thomas Jefferson, "Declaration of Independence."

Observe that each writer, by using similar elements, shows which ideas belong together and thereby conveys them succinctly and with clarity to the reader. Notice too that each sentence draws attention to itself and to its ideas by the repetition of similar elements.

Another effect that a writer can achieve with coordination is shown in example 5. The writer arranged the coordinate elements so that the sentence's most important idea comes at the end, where it makes the longest-lasting impression on the reader.

I have discussed modification, subordination, and coordination —three major methods of expanding a sentence—separately merely for convenience. Coordinate elements, as you have observed in the examples just presented, may modify and be made subordinate to other elements in a sentence just as other elements may modify and be made subordinate to them.

In this discussion of isolated sentences, one must not lose sight of their function within the paragraph where they interact with one another, each contributing meaning to the larger unit of composition as, for example, in this paragraph, diagrammed and annotated:

main point stated in topic sentence

(1) Patriotism is a very complex feeling, built up out of primitive instincts and highly intellectual convictions.

key idea—summary of much that follows

support for the topic sentence

(2) There is love of home and family and friends, making us peculiarly anxious to preserve our own country from invasion.

(3) There is the mild instinctive liking for compatriots against foreigners.

(4) There is pride, which is bound up with the success of the community to which we feel that we belong.

(5) There is a belief, suggested by pride, but reinforced by history, that one's

own nation represents a great tradition and stands for ideals that are important to the human race.

main point supported but also added to

(6) But besides all these, there is another element, at once nobler and more open to attack, an element of worship,

coordinate elements—support both for main point and for added idea

of willing sacrifice,
of joyful merging of the individual in the life of the nation.

idea in (6) expanded

(7) This religious element in patriotism is essential to the strength of the State, since it enlists the best that is in most men on the side of national sacrifice [Bertrand Russell, *Why Men Fight*].

BEER CAN

John Updike

John Updike (born 1932), American novelist and short-story writer, contributes to *The New Yorker* magazine, where you will find some of the most consistently meticulous contemporary prose. Here is one of his single-paragraph pieces that appeared there.

$_{1}$This seems to be an era of gratuitous inventions and negative improvements. $_{2}$Consider the beer can. $_{3}$It was beautiful—as beautiful as the clothespin, as inevitable as the wine bottle, as dignified and reassuring as the fire hydrant. $_{4}$A tranquil cylinder of delightfully resonant metal, it could be opened in an instant, requiring only the application of a handy gadget freely dispensed by every grocer. $_{5}$Who can forget the small, symmetrical thrill of those two triangular punctures, the dainty *pffff*, the little crest of suds that foamed eagerly in the exultation of release? $_{6}$Now we are given, instead, a top beetling with an ugly, shmoo-shaped "tab," which, after fiercely resisting the tugging, bleeding fingers of the thirsty man, threatens his lips with a dangerous and hideous hole. $_{7}$However, we have discovered a way to thwart Progress, usually so unthwartable. $_{8}$*Turn the beer can upside down and open the bottom.* $_{9}$The bottom is still the way the top used to be. $_{10}$True, this operation gives the beer an unsettling jolt, and the sight of a consistently inverted beer can might make people edgy, not to say queasy. $_{11}$But the latter difficulty could be eliminated if manufacturers would design cans that looked the same whichever end was up, like playing cards. $_{12}$What we need is Progress with an escape hatch.

Questions About "Sentences"

1. Updike's first sentence is an example of coordination: "of *gratuitous inventions* and *negative improvements*." Find in the paragraph two other sentences that combine similar grammatical elements into pairs or series.

2. What is the main idea of sentence 4? What ideas does Updike subordinate to it? He might have written the sentence: "It was a tranquil cylinder of delightfully resonant metal. It could be opened in an instant. It required only the application of a handy gadget freely dispensed by every grocer." What purpose is served by combining these sentences as he did? Which version do you prefer? Why?

3. Updike might have written sentence 11 like this: "But if manufacturers would design beer cans that looked the same whichever

end was up, like playing cards, the latter difficulty would be eliminated." Which version do you prefer? Why?

Questions on Diction and Writing Techniques

1. Define the following words and write sentences using each of them appropriately: gratuitous, symmetrical, exultation, thwart, queasy.
2. What do the italicized words contribute to your understanding of the idea in sentence 3: "It was beautiful—as beautiful *as the clothespin*, as inevitable *as the wine bottle*, as dignified and reassuring *as the fire hydrant*"?
3. What are the transitional words in Updike's paragraph? What is the function of each?
4. What does "like playing cards" contribute to your understanding of the idea in the sentence in which it appears?
5. "Most paragraphs have an internal unity, and they can be analyzed as compositions in miniature. . . . They will have a relative self-containment, or basic unity and coherence, and they will emphasize some point or idea" (Richard M. Weaver, *Composition*). Comment on Updike's one-paragraph essay as a composition "in miniature."

For Discussion, Reading, and Writing

1. Write a sentence that, except for "beer can," is like Updike's sentence 2 (for example, "Consider the Model T Ford"). Then write a sentence containing a series of coordinate elements and beginning with "It was beautiful—."
2. Imitating the structure of Updike's fourth sentence, write a standard sentence with a simple subject-predicate arrangement and then expand it by placing a modifying element before it and another after it.
3. Take any standard sentence and expand it in any way you can. For example, starting with "Bill loves to eat," you might end up with

My older stepbrother Bill, a jock at the College of the Holy Cross, in Worcester, Mass., where he plays football, lacrosse, and baseball, loves to eat, his favorite food being Italian: spaghetti, lasagna, ravioli—pasta of any kind—a taste he acquired a year ago when he spent a summer in Rome enrolled in Holy Cross' study-abroad program.

4. Can you think of other "gratuitous inventions and negative improvements" to which you might apply Updike's conclusion, "What we need is Progress with an escape hatch"? If so, imitating the organization of "Beer Can," write a one-paragraph essay about one of them.
5. The beer can would seem to be too lowly an object to be a fitting topic for an essay, yet Updike managed to write a successful piece about it. Select as another possible topic for a one-paragraph essay—among whose sentences are examples of modification, subordination, and coordination—a ballpoint pen, a paper clip, an alarm clock, a calendar, a wall poster, a wastebasket, or any object often taken for granted.

IN AND OUT OF SCHOOL

Margaret Mead

Margaret Mead (1901–1978), American anthropologist, did most of her fieldwork among the peoples of Oceania, reporting on them in *Coming of Age in Samoa* (1928) and in others of the twenty-five books she wrote on problems of child rearing, personality, and culture.

1 Some years we went to school. Other years we stayed at home and Grandma taught us. That is one way of describing my schooling. Another way is to explain that between the ages of five and

seventeen I spent two years in kindergarten, one year—but only half-days—in the fourth grade, and six years in high school. If I had not very much wanted to go to school or if I had been a sickly child, probably I would have spent even less time in school.

2 It is curious that a family of teachers—for Mother, too, had taught before I was born—should have had such paradoxical views about schools. As a family we took an active interest in schools wherever we lived, and many of our frequent moves to a new place for the winter months were made with the expectation of finding a particular kind of school. However, my family deeply disapproved of any school that kept children chained to their desks, indoors, for long hours every day.

3 Kindergarten—the one I attended was a private kindergarten in the home of well-to-do people with a large house—was an expression of the most modern ideas about education. The training of eye and hand, learning about color and form and pattern by sewing with bright wools, cutting and pasting, and stringing brightly colored beads made of different materials, and singing in time to rhythmic play—these were all activities that my grandmother and mother and father regarded as good for children. Father appreciated the precision, the command over my fingers, and the ability to make things I learned in kindergarten; Grandma and Mother were more interested in the freedom to move. In their minds these two things went together. They were complementary, not contradictory—as is so often the case when one examines what underlies the more recent belief that children can be, simultaneously, spontaneous and obedient.

4 Looking back, my memories of learning precise skills, memorizing long stretches of poetry, and manipulating paper are interwoven with memories of running—running in the wind, running through meadows, and running along country roads—picking flowers, hunting for nuts, and weaving together old stories and new events into myths about a tree or a rock. And there were long intervals, too, that were filled with reading, reading as many hours a day as I could manage between playing outdoors and doing formal lessons. Of course, reading was a good thing, but too much reading was believed to be bad for a child. And so it became, in part, a secret pleasure I indulged in at night when I was supposed to be asleep or in the daytime hours I spent curled up in a hollow at the roots of a tree while I was supposed to be off on some more active quest.

5 From the time I was six, the question was not when does school open, but what, if anything, is to be done about school. We lived in a different house in a different place each year—first in Lansdowne, then in Philadelphia on the edge of Fairmont Park, near the zoo, in an apartment house managed by a distant relative of my grandmother's, then for two years in Swarthmore—one year "on the hill" where the college people lived and one year at the edge of town. The owner of that second house lived nearby in a smaller house, and we used to steal corn from his corncrib and feed it to his chickens. Prank-stealing was a part of life that was pickled in songs and stories, and we had to act it out. In all that time I had only one period of formal schooling—and then I was allowed to go to school for only half a day. I was envied by the other children, but the teacher was annoyed—and I was, too, for I felt singled out and forced to be different. But that one year, the winter of my ninth birthday, gave me a clear idea of what school was like. Before that I had known only about kindergarten, a kind of school from which I had never wanted to come home. In the first month of that fourth-grade class I failed dismally in arithmetic. But by the third month I had worked my way up to 90 percent in arithmetic and had discovered that school was a system you had to learn about, just as you had to learn about each new house and garden and explore the possibilities of each new town.

6 Mother thought about every place we lived not only in terms of its schools, but also as a more or less promising source of "lessons." Whatever form such lessons took—drawing, painting, carving, modeling, or basketry—she thought of them as a supplement to formal education within the context of the most advanced educational theories. In Hammonton I had music lessons and also lessons in carving, because the only artist the town boasted was a skillful wood-carver. In Swarthmore we were taught by an all-round manual training teacher under whose tutelage I even built a small loom. In Bucks County I had painting lessons from a local artist and later from an artist in New Hope. And one year Mother had a local carpenter teach Dick and me woodworking. She was completely eclectic about what we were taught in these lessons, provided the person who was teaching us was highly skilled.

7 Looking back, it seems to me that this way of organizing teaching and learning around special skills provided me with a model for

the way I have always organized work, whether it has involved organizing a research team, a staff of assistants, or the available informants in a native village. In every case I try to find out what each person is good at doing and then I fit them together in a group that forms some kind of whole.

Questions About "Sentences"

1. Mead might have begun paragraph 1:

   One way of describing my schooling is to say that some years we went to school and that other years we stayed at home and Grandma taught us.

   Which version do you prefer? Why?

2. Instead of the first sentence of paragraph 2, she might have written:

   It is curious that a family of teachers should have had such paradoxical views about schools. For Mother, too, had taught before I was born.

   Which version, in the context of the paragraph, is preferable? Why?

3. The construction of sentence 2 of paragraph 3 marks it as what kind of sentence? Rewrite it as a standard or loose sentence.

4. By subordination, combine the following into one sentence:

   John is my best friend. He is twenty-one-years old. He has been tinkering with engines since he was a kid. He has been building his own stock racing cars for five years. During this time he rose to the top rank of racing-car drivers in the state. He earns a meager living. But he is content.

   Using the same material, write another sentence with a different idea in its main clause. Write a third sentence, using the same material, with still another idea expressed in its main clause. Underline the main clauses in each.

5. Revise any paragraph you have written so far this term in any

of your classes by combining its short sentences into one or more longer, denser sentences.

Questions on Diction and Writing Techniques

1. How does your dictionary define "paradoxical" (par. 2), "complementary" and "contradictory" (par. 3), "myths" (par. 4), "eclectic" (par. 6)? Use each of these words in a sentence.
2. Explain why, in paragraph 2, Mead writes "However."
3. Underline each instance of Mead's use of "but" in paragraph 5. Explain her purpose in writing the word within and between the sentences of the paragraph.
4. What is the main idea of paragraph 6? Where is it expressed? In which sentence(s) is it supported? What is the role of the last sentence of the paragraph?

For Discussion, Reading, and Writing

1. Looking back on your experience at home and at school, find evidence to support a judgment on whether children can be simultaneously spontaneous and obedient.
2. Write a paragraph of not over one hundred words beginning with "Looking back, my memories of . . ." or "Looking back, it seems to me. . . ."
3. Write a short essay comparing any period of your life with what Mead tells about a comparable period of hers.

THE FACE OF THE WATER

Mark Twain

Mark Twain is the pen name of Samuel L. Clemens (1835–1910). Among his numerous works is *Life on the Mississippi* (1883), based on his experience as a steamboat pilot on the Mississippi River.

1 The face of the water, in time, became a wonderful book—a book that was a dead language to the uneducated passenger, but which told its mind to me without reserve, delivering its most cherished secrets as clearly as if it uttered them with a voice. And it was not a book to be read once and thrown aside, for it had a new story to tell every day. Throughout the long twelve hundred miles there was never a page that was void of interest, never one that you could leave unread without loss, never one that you would want to skip, thinking you could find higher enjoyment in some other thing. There never was so wonderful a book written by man; never one whose interest was so absorbing, so unflagging, so sparklingly renewed with every reperusal. The passenger who could not read it was charmed with a peculiar sort of faint dimple on its surface (on the rare occasions when he did not overlook it altogether); but to the pilot that was an *italicized* passage; indeed, it was more than that, it was a legend of the largest capitals, with a string of shouting exclamation-points at the end of it, for it meant that a wreck or a rock was buried there that could tear the life out of the strongest vessel that ever floated. It is the faintest and simplest expression the water ever makes, and the most hideous to a pilot's eye. In truth, the passenger who could not read this book saw nothing but all manner of pretty pictures in it, painted by the sun and shaded by the clouds, whereas to the trained eye these were not pictures at all, but the grimmest and most dead-earnest of reading-matter.

2 Now when I had mastered the language of this water, and had come to know every trifling feature that bordered the great river as familiarly as I knew the letters of the alphabet, I had made a valuable acquisition. But I had lost something, too. I had lost something which could never be restored to me while I lived. All the grace, the beauty, the poetry, had gone out of the majestic river! I still kept in mind a certain wonderful sunset which I witnessed when steamboating was new to me. A broad expanse of the river was turned to blood; in the middle distance the red hue brightened into gold, through which a solitary log came floating, black and conspicuous; in one place a long, slanting mark lay sparkling upon the water; in another the surface was broken by boiling, tumbling rings, that were as many-tinted as an opal; where the ruddy flush was faintest, was a smooth spot that was covered with graceful circles

and radiating lines, ever so delicately traced; the shore on our left was densely wooded, and the somber shadow that fell from this forest was broken in one place by a long, ruffled trail that shone like silver; and high above the forest wall a clean-stemmed dead tree waved a single leafy bough that glowed like a flame in the unobstructed splendor that was flowing from the sun. There were graceful curves, reflected images, woody heights, soft distances; and over the whole scene, far and near, the dissolving lights drifted steadily, enriching it every passing moment with new marvels of coloring.

3 I stood like one bewitched. I drank it in, in a speechless rapture. The world was new to me, and I had never seen anything like this at home. But as I have said, a day came when I began to cease from noting the glories and the charms which the moon and the sun and the twilight wrought upon the river's face; another day came when I ceased altogether to note them. Then, if that sunset scene had been repeated, I should have looked upon it without rapture, and should have commented upon it, inwardly, after this fashion: "This sun means that we are going to have wind to-morrow; that floating log means that the river is rising, small thanks to it; that slanting mark on the water refers to a bluff reef which is going to kill somebody's steamboat one of these nights, if it keeps on stretching out like that; those tumbling 'boils' show a dissolving bar and a changing channel there; the lines and circles in the slick water over yonder are a warning that that troublesome place is shoaling up dangerously; that silver streak in the shadow of the forest is the 'break' from a new snag, and he has located himself in the very best place he could have found to fish for steamboats; that tall dead tree, with a single living branch, is not going to last long, and then how is a body ever going to get through this blind place at night without the friendly old landmark?"

4 No, the romance and beauty were all gone from the river. All the value any feature of it had for me now was the amount of usefulness it could furnish toward compassing the safe piloting of a steamboat. Since those days, I have pitied doctors from my heart. What does the lovely flush in a beauty's cheek mean to a doctor but a "break" that ripples above some deadly disease? Are not all her visible charms sown thick with what are to him the signs and

symbols of hidden decay? Does he ever see her beauty at all, or doesn't he simply view her professionally, and comment upon her unwholesome condition all to himself? And doesn't he sometimes wonder whether he has gained most or lost most by learning his trade?

Questions About "Sentences"

1. Instead of writing sentence 1 of paragraph 1 as he did, Mark Twain might have written "The face of the water, in time, became a wonderful book." Which version do you prefer? Why?
2. What is Mark Twain's purpose in the repetition of similar grammatical elements in the second half of sentence 3 of paragraph 1?
3. Rewrite the first sentence of paragraph 2, placing its main clause at the beginning. Which version gives greater emphasis to the sentence's main idea?
4. What are the purpose and the effect of the short second sentence in paragraph 2? Find, in paragraph 3, a short sentence used for a similar reason.

Questions on Diction and Writing Techniques

1. Mark in your text all words in this essay that, though new to you, you understood from their context. Define them in your own words. Compare your definitions with those in your dictionary. Look up in your dictionary any other words that are new to you. Use the words in both groups in sentences.
2. What does Twain achieve with his comparison of "the face of the water" with "a wonderful book"? Throughout paragraph 1 and in paragraph 2 he amplifies the comparison, using such phrases as "a book that was *a dead language* to the uneducated passenger" and "it had *a new story* to tell every day." Underline in your text three or more examples of Twain's use of this technique to make his meaning clear in those paragraphs.

For Discussion, Reading, and Writing

1. Why was the book of the river not to be read once and thrown aside?

2. What did Mark Twain say he lost from "mastering the language of this water"?

3. Why has he pitied doctors?

4. Which of these sentences better emphasizes its main idea?

   A. The doctor advised Jones to stop smoking immediately, after examining the x-rays of his lungs and checking his medical record.

   B. The doctor, after examining the x-rays of Jones' lungs and checking his medical record, advised him to stop smoking immediately.

5. Revise these sentences to emphasize the most important ideas in each:

   A. Patrick Henry, the patriot who became governor of Virginia during the Revolutionary War, said, "Give me liberty or give me death," a phrase familiar to all Americans.

   B. The clerk of the court said that the jury would not leave the room until it reached a verdict, except to return to the courtroom to ask the judge for further instructions or to go out for lunch.

   C. Frank Jones won an astounding election victory, beating the incumbent congressman, Walter Brown, by three thousand votes after trailing during most of the evening's counting of the ballots that was slowed down by a power failure in the lower part of the state.

THE SAN FRANCISCO EARTHQUAKE

Jack London

Jack London (1876–1916) was a popular writer of stories such as *The Call of the Wild* (1903), based on romantic adventures. His ability to report vividly his observations is evident in this account of the great San Francisco earthquake of 1906.

---

1 The earthquake shook down in San Francisco hundreds of thousands of dollars worth of walls and chimneys. But the conflagration that followed burned up hundreds of millions of dollars worth of property. There is no estimating within hundreds of millions the actual damage wrought.

2 Not in history has a modern imperial city been so completely destroyed. San Francisco is gone. Nothing remains of it but memories and a fringe of dwelling houses on its outskirts. Its industrial section is wiped out. Its social and residential section is wiped out. The factories and warehouses, the great stores and newspaper buildings, the hotels and palaces of the nabobs, all are gone. Remains only the fringe of dwelling houses on the outskirts of what was once San Francisco.

3 Within an hour after the earthquake shock, the smoke of San Francisco's burning was a lurid tower visible a hundred miles away. And for three days and nights this lurid tower swayed in the sky, reddening the sun, darkening the day, and filling the land with smoke.

4 On Wednesday morning at quarter past five came the earthquake. A minute later the flames were leaping upward. In a dozen different quarters south of Market Steet, in the working class ghetto and in the factories, fires started. There was no opposing the flames. There was no organization, no communication. All the cunning adjustments of a twentieth century city had been smashed by the earthquake. The streets were humped into ridges and depressions,

From *Collier's*, May 5, 1906, pp. 22–23.

and piled with the debris of fallen walls. The steel rails were twisted into perpendicular and horizontal angles. The telephone and telegraph systems were disrupted. And the great water mains had burst. All the shrewd contrivances and safeguards of man had been thrown out of gear by thirty seconds' twitching of the earth-crust.

5 By Wednesday afternoon, inside of twelve hours, half the heart of the city was gone. At that time I watched the vast conflagration from out on the bay. It was dead calm. Not a flicker of wind stirred. Yet from every side wind was pouring in upon the city. East, west, north, and south, strong winds were blowing upon the doomed city. The heated air rising made an enormous suck. Thus did the fire of itself build its own colossal chimney through the atmosphere. Day and night this dead calm continued, and yet, near to the flames, the wind was often half a gale, so mighty was the suck.

6 Wednesday night saw the destruction of the very heart of the city. Dynamite was lavishly used, and many of San Francisco's proudest structures were crumbled by man himself into ruins, but there was no withstanding the onrush of the flames. Time and again successful stands were made by the firefighters, and every time the flames flanked around on either side, or came up from the rear, and turned to defeat the hard won victory.

7 An enumeration of the buildings destroyed would be a directory of San Francisco. An enumeration of the buildings undestroyed would be a line and several addresses. An enumeration of the deeds of heroism would stock a library and bankrupt the Carnegie medal fund. An enumeration of the dead—will never be made. All vestiges of them were destroyed by the flames. The number of the victims of the earthquake will never be known.

Questions About "Sentences"

1. What is London's purpose in writing the short sentence "San Francisco is gone" (par. 2)? Find in paragraph 5 two examples of his use of sentences to achieve the same effect.
2. London might have written the next-to-last sentence of paragraph 2 like this: "Gone are all the factories and warehouses,

the great stores and newspaper buildings, the hotels and the nabobs." Which version better emphasizes the writer's main idea?

3. What effect does London achieve with coordination in sentence 3 of paragraph 4? Find in that paragraph two other sentences structured similarly to achieve the same effect.
4. Rewrite sentence 3 of paragraph 4 as a standard, or loose, sentence. Which version is more suspenseful? Why?
5. By what means does London achieve the effect of paragraph 7?

Questions on Diction and Writing Techniques

1. Define "nabobs" (par. 2) and write a sentence using it appropriately.
2. What is the effect of similarly constructed sentences 4 and 5 of paragraph 2?
3. What do "lurid tower" (par. 3) and "colossal chimney" (par. 5) contribute to your understanding of the ideas the writer is trying to communicate in the sentences in which they appear?
4. Does London give you enough information in paragraph 4 to convince you to accept as true the main idea of the paragraph? Explain.
5. By what means does London establish order among paragraphs 4, 5, and 6? Are the paragraphs coherent?

For Discussion, Reading, and Writing

1. Which of these statements, according to London, are true (T), which false (F)?

   A. ______ Insurance company adjustors came close to estimating the damage wrought by the earthquake.

   B. ______ If dynamite had been used, many of San Francisco's proudest structures might have been saved.

   C. ______ An enumeration of the buildings destroyed would be a directory of San Francisco.

D. ______ The number of the victims of the earthquake will never be known.

E. ______ Jack London suffered minor injuries.

2. Think back to any dramatic event to which you were an eyewitness. Prewrite and then write a first draft of a short essay about the event. Revise what you have written, paying particular attention to the density of your sentences, emphasis, and sentence variety.
3. Turn to profitable account your new knowledge of sentences by revising any paragraph or essay you have written so far for this course.

Words

Limited vocabulary, like short legs on a pole-vaulter, builds in a natural barrier to progress beyond a certain point.

—John Gardner

ONE of the benefits of reading is an increase in the supply of words that you can draw upon to express your ideas. You no doubt have met in this text words that were new to you. The meaning of some of them was reasonably clear from their contexts. The meaning of others you found in your dictionary. When you come across them another time, you likely will recognize them and know what they mean. To make new words a part of your active vocabulary it is a good idea to practice using them. List them and, when appropriate in your writing, try them out.

Words have primary or explicit meanings, *denotations,* which we find (along with information about pronunciation and derivation) in dictionaries. They have *connotations* as well—secondary, implied meanings based on associations. "Hearth," for example, is defined as the floor of a fireplace, but the word may *suggest* warmth and friendship. "Beach" means a stretch of sand or pebbles along a seashore, but the word may suggest expansiveness or freedom from restraint. When choosing a word, you must take into account both its explicit and its implicit meanings.

The choice of words is called *diction.* Good diction requires the writer to select words with care and take pains to arrange them in a way that will best convey meaning. You should not assume that your reader is a mind reader and must not lay on him or her the burden of trying to unravel the meaning of what you have written.

Your job is to sort out ideas and then, utilizing suitable words, to express them clearly to the reader.

No word is in itself bad. But any word you choose must be apt, meaningful, consistent with the rest of the words you use, and appropriate for your audience and the occasion of your writing.

Words may usefully be grouped as *ambiguous* or *vague, specific* or *general, abstract* or *concrete.*

Ambiguous and Vague Words

Ambiguous words are words that can be understood in more than one sense. An example is "un-American." The word is ambiguous because it may mean different things to different people. Using a word without making clear which of its meanings you intend can confuse your reader. (I will discuss the need for definition to avoid misunderstanding in "Definition," pages 291–311.)

Vague words are words that do not communicate an exact meaning. "Fantastic," as in "He's a *fantastic* person," is vague because it doesn't specifically modify "person." Among the more precise words that might be substituted for it are "charming," "outgoing," and "enthusiastic."

Among the many words that beginning writers often use inaccurately are "cool," "marvelous," "remarkable," "terrific," and "wonderful." These words, as your dictionary will reveal, have precise meanings, but in certain contexts they are inexact. Compare their use in these sentences with the possible alternative words in parentheses:

> Mr. Smith is a marvelous (knowledgeable, understanding, helpful) teacher.
>
> I had a remarkable (fulfilling, relaxing, instructive) weekend.
>
> The movie was terrific (entertaining, enlightening, terrifying).
>
> Sarah has a wonderful (loving, supportive, compassionate) father.

In each instance, the more definite alternative conveys more exact meaning.

Specific and General Words

In addition to differentiating between vague and precise words, we can classify words according to whether they are specific or general. Specific words—for example, "hamburger," "jeans," "house," "dog," "quarterback"—convey more particular meaning than do general words: "food," "clothing," "building," "animal," "athlete." "The cook served John a *hamburger*" creates a better defined image than does "The cook served John *food*."

"Specific" and "general" are relative terms, as you can see from this series:

substance, food, meat, beef, hamburger

"Food" is more specific than "substance" but more general than "meat," and "beef," is more specific than "meat" but more general than "hamburger." Here are more examples of the gradation of words from general to specific:

clothing, outerwear, trousers, jeans, Levis

structure, building, dwelling, house, dormitory

animal, mammal, dog, poodle, Fido

animal, man, athlete, football player, quarterback

You can make a specific word more specific by adding one or more modifiers. "*Broiled* hamburger" is more specific than "hamburger"; "*charcoal-broiled* hamburger" is still more specific; "*medium-rare charcoal-broiled* hamburger" is more specific yet.

Compare the image called forth by

The cook served John a hamburger

with the one evoked by

The cook served John a *medium-rare charcoal-broiled* hamburger.

To appreciate the function and effect of specific diction, compare the words in these different reports of the same event:

The men walked into the bank with guns drawn. One stayed near the door while the other went behind the counter and put currency into a bag.

The masked gunmen rushed into the Main Street branch of the United Bank and Trust Company, brandishing Colt .45s. One bandit stationed himself just inside the front door while the other desperado leaped over the teller's counter and stuffed bundles of brand-new 10-, 20-, and 50-dollar bills into a brown paper bag.

To emphasize more the importance of the writer's carefully choosing specific words to convey meaning vividly, here are the two sentences arranged schematically:

The men	The masked gunmen
walked	rushed
into the bank	into the Main Street branch of the United Bank and Trust Company
with guns drawn.	brandishing Colt .45s.
One	One bandit
stayed	stationed himself
near the door	just inside the front door
while the other	while the other desperado
went behind	leaped over
the counter	the teller's counter
and put	and stuffed
currency	bundles of brand-new 10-, 20-, and 50-dollar bills
into a bag.	into a brown paper bag.

The specific words in the right-hand column depict in detail what happened and give the reader a more precise picture than do the words in the left-hand column.

Abstract and Concrete Words

Words may be classified as abstract or concrete. The words in the first column denote abstractions–intangibles, ideas. The words in the second column are concrete–relating to the experience of our senses, to things that are actual or real.

friendship	handshake
love	embrace
femininity	woman
beauty	rainbow
calamity	earthquake
color	blue

Like "specific" and "general," "abstract" and "concrete" are relative terms. Consider, for example, this series:

> justice, the law, rules of the road, speeding limit, 55 m.p.h.

When writers deal with concepts they will of course have occasion to use abstract words: "We hold these *truths* to be sacred and undeniable. . . ." But to convey particulars they will use concrete words because, like specific words, concrete words are more vivid.

Imagery

Another way to enliven your writing is with imagery. "Imagery" refers to mental pictures representing an actual scene and to the nonliteral use of language in figures of speech such as *simile* and *metaphor.*

Here are examples of simile:

> . . . he was *as nervous as a race horse* fretting to be on the track [Willa Cather, "When I Knew Stephen Crane"].

> The visitor was lively and eager; her mind lay open and orderly, *like a notebook ready for impressions* [Mary McCarthy, "America the Beautiful"].

O, my luve is *like a red, red rose,*
That's newly sprung in June
[Robert Burns, "A Red, Red Rose"]

Notice that in each instance a comparison is expressed between dissimilar things (a man with a nervous race horse; a mind with a notebook; a beloved with a rose) and that, as in most similes, the comparisons are introduced by "as" or "like."

A metaphor is an implied comparison that identifies one thing with an unlike other thing. If Burns had written, "my luve *is* a rose," instead of "my luve is *like* a rose," he would have created a metaphor. Here are two examples of metaphor:

> . . . we drove my father through a *wilderness* of smashed plate glass [James Baldwin, *Notes of a Native Son*].

> In the middle of the *journey* of our life I came to myself within a dark wood where the straight way was lost [Dante Alighieri, *Inferno*].

Here the streets of Harlem covered with smashed plate glass after a riot are identified with a wilderness, and life with a journey. Like similes, metaphors animate writing by evoking visual images.

Formal and Informal Language

Another distinction between types of diction is formal and informal language. Formal language is likely to contain scholarly, multisyllabic, and abstract words; informal language tends to contain everyday, short, concrete words, as well as some slang.

Just as the attire you would choose for a church wedding or a funeral would differ from what you would wear to a tennis match or a picnic, the selection of formal or informal words will depend on the occasion. Would you use the same language in a letter to the admissions officer of a graduate school as you would in a letter to a fellow student? When writing to a friend, you probably would use everyday language and slang, language that is very informal. However informal your letter to the admissions officer, you most likely would not use slang.

Degrees of formality and informality, in descending order, may be observed in these passages:

This was the American Dream: a sanctuary on the earth for individual man: a condition in which he could be free not only of the old established closed-corporation hierarchies of arbitrary power which had oppressed him as a mass, but free of that mass into which the hierarchies of church and state had compressed and held him individually thralled and individually impotent [William Faulkner, "On Privacy"].

There are two ways in which one can own a book. The first is the property right you establish by paying for it, just as you pay for clothes and furniture. But this act of purchase is only the prelude to possession. Full ownership comes only when you have made it a part of yourself, and the best way to make yourself a part of it is by writing in it. An illustration may make the point clear. You buy a beefsteak and transfer it from the butcher's icebox to your own. But you do not own the beefsteak in the most important sense until you consume it and get it into your bloodstream. I am arguing that books, too, must be absorbed in your bloodstream to do you any good [Mortimer J. Adler, "How to Mark a Book"].

Richard Nixon's Vice-President, Spiro Agnew, writing about Attica under his byline in *The New York Times* newspaper the other day, said: "To compare the loss of life by those who violate society's law with the loss of life of those whose job it is to uphold it—represents not simply an assault on human sensibility but an insult to reason."

Beautiful. I think it was the greatest article I read in my whole life. . . . Because of it I finally was able to brush off the last shreds of the stupid ideas Sister Anna Gertrude outfitted us with in St. Benedict Joseph Labre School, Queens, New York City.

That silly Jesus Christ. The way that old nun made us learn it, Jesus spent the whole last morning of his Life standing in Part XXXII with a real bum named Barabbas. Instead of making a deal to sink Barabbas, Christ stood around rooting for Barabbas to get his case severed and dropped. One description of Barabbas was that he was a boss of thieves in Jerusalem. The first Jewish button man. I used to sit in class and picture Barabbas as Lepke [a notorious American gangster] with a beard [Jimmy Breslin, "The Greatest Article I Read in My Whole Life"].

Observe in the last passage the writer's use of ordinary, everyday words, among them the informal "bum" and "making a deal" and the slangy "button man." These words are not improper in themselves; no words ever are. The propriety of a word depends on the writer's purpose and the occasion of its use.

Inflated Language

Some people try to use language to impress their audience. In an article that appeared not too long ago in the newspaper of a university in southern New England, a young man wrote, "As a graduate student . . . I have come to realize the blatant dysfunctionality of this process we call education." Not satisfied with a simple word such as "fault," the writer—trying to score a verbal home run—stretched beyond the possible three-syllable "dysfunction" to the six-syllable "dysfunctionality," which is not a word at all, in an attempt to wow his audience.

In the same essay there is this sentence: "I arrived at school with open arms and an open mind." "With open arms" and "an open mind" are *clichés*—overused, colorless expressions like "fit as a fiddle," "water over the dam," "call a spade a spade," and "no flies on him"—which writers use to avoid the mental exertion needed to clarify their own thinking and to make their meaning clear to their readers. "What," a reader has the right to ask, "do you mean by 'with open arms and an open mind'? That you were eager to learn? That you were not prejudging the school?"

The young man also wrote in his article, "As an impressionable 17-year-old high school student, ideas of materiality pervaded my world. The pursuance of a college degree and the 'rewards' associated with it seemed to me an entirely pragmatic outlook." This is gobbledegook—pretentious, long-winded, unintelligible, and dull. What the writer probably meant to say is: "When I was 17 years old, possessions were important where I lived, and getting a college degree in order to make money seemed proper."

The same student finally managed to work into his article the currently popular and overused "viable." He wrote, "At this time I can't offer any viable alternatives," instead of saying simply that he has no alternatives.

Wordiness is of course not limited to students. "At this point in time" is widely used as a substitute for "now." Edwin Newman, the television commentator, in *Strictly Speaking,* reminds us that a former White House press secretary requested an extension of time so that the President's attorney could "evaluate and make a judgment in terms of a response." What he meant was that the attorney "wanted more time to think about it."

Careful writers use language economically. Knowing what they want to communicate, they put ideas into as few precise, apt words as possible. Not:

> I intend to express my own opinions, hoping with them to make clear to the reader of this paper the background and origins, the whys and wherefores of the deterioration and decline in the viability in the marketplace of our currency at this time.

But:

> My purpose is to explain the present decline in the purchasing power of the dollar.

The first of these sentences, containing forty-four words, is meandering, pretentious, and unintelligible. The second, of fifteen words, is compact and meaningful.

In lieu of a twenty-seven-word sentence with needless introductory phrases and useless repetition of words with similar meaning, such as

> In my opinion it seems necessary to point out that the plaintiff in this case is making statements that are lies, untrue, and not at all believable.

the effective writer creates a concise, forceful sentence of four words:

> The plaintiff is lying.

Wordiness

Wordiness is the use of more words than are necessary to make one's meaning clear. In your writing, make a special effort to eliminate needless words when you rewrite your first draft. Here is how you might revise wordy sentences.

Original:

> Concerning the question of whether or not the power of the legislative branch of the government should be allowed to proliferate, it seems to me that it depends basically on the crucial factor of how great you want the strength of the executive branch of the government to be. (49 words)

Revised:

> Whether congressional power should be increased depends on how strong you want the presidency to be. (16 words)

At least five common faults appear in the original sentence.

1. *Useless phrases*—that is, phrases that contribute nothing to the meaning of a sentence: "concerning the question of" and "it seems to me that."
2. *Redundancy*—unneeded repetition of words: "or not" ("whether" implies "or not").
3. *A useless word*—one that contributes nothing to the meaning of the sentence containing it: "basically."
4. *A vague word:* "factor."
5. *Pretentious diction*—words used to impress the reader: "crucial factor."

Containing only a third as many words as the original, the revised sentence conveys concisely and more clearly as much information as the original does.

Original:

> For the period of a year, there has been no observable improvement in the area of crime for the simple reason that there has not been a fundamental change for the better in crime prevention capability. (36 words)

Revised:

> For a year the rate of crime has been stable because the police force is still inadequate. (17 words)

The original sentence contains at least three common faults:

1. *Circumlocutions*–roundabout expressions: "for the period of a year" and "for the simple reason that."
2. *Needless words:* "in the area of," "observable," and "fundamental."
3. *Pretentious diction:* "crime prevention capability."

In the revised sentence, the writer has replaced the vague and uneconomical "there has not been a fundamental change for the better in crime prevention capability" with the precise, concise, and vigorous "the police force is still inadequate."

Original:

> With reference to your question, I came to discover at that point in time that I was definitely a religious person due to the fact that I was completely impressed concerning the matter of a belief in a life after death among the people in my family. (47 words)

Revised:

> I discovered that I was religious then because I was impressed with my family's belief in a life after death. (20 words)

This original sentence has at least four common faults:

1. *Useless beginning:* "with reference to your question."
2. *Useless words:* "came to" and "among the people."
3. *Circumlocutions:* "at that point in time" and "due to the fact that."
4. *Unnecessary qualifiers,* which fail to achieve the intended emphasis: "definitely" and "completely."

The revised sentence is simple and direct.

The best comment on wordiness that I know, and a model of brevity itself (sixty-three words), is E. B. White's quotation of his composition teacher at Cornell, William Strunk, Jr., in *The Elements of Style:*

> Vigorous writing is concise. A sentence should contain no unnecessary words, a paragraph no unnecessary sentences, for the same reason that a drawing should have no unnecessary lines and a machine no unnecessary parts. This requires not that the writer make all his sentences short, or that he avoid all detail and treat his subjects only in outline, but that every word tell.

Make "every word tell." See how much meaning Abraham Lincoln packed into the 173 words of the Gettysburg Address.

About every word you put on paper ask yourself, "What does it contribute to the meaning, clarity, and conciseness of my writing?"

THE DEATH OF BENNY PARET

Norman Mailer

Norman Mailer wrote the important World War II novel *The Naked and the Dead* (1948). His nonfiction works include the Pulitzer Prize–winning *Armies of the Night* (1968), written in the style of the so-called new journalism.

---

1 On the afternoon of the night Emile Griffith and Benny Paret were to fight a third time for the welterweight championship, there was murder in both camps. "I hate that kind of guy," Paret had said earlier to Pete Hamill about Griffith. "A fighter's got to look and talk and act like a man." One of the Broadway gossip columnists

had run an item about Griffith a few days before. His girl friend saw it and said to Griffith, "Emile, I didn't know about you being that way." So Griffith hit her. So he said. Now at the weigh-in that morning, Paret had insulted Griffith irrevocably, touching him on the buttocks, while making a few more remarks about his manhood. They almost had their fight on the scales.

2 The rage in Emile Griffith was extreme. I was at the fight that night, I had never seen a fight like it. It was scheduled for fifteen rounds, but they fought without stopping from the bell which began the round to the bell which ended it, and then they fought after the bell, sometimes for as much as fifteen seconds before the referee could force them apart.

3 Paret was a Cuban, a proud club fighter who had become welterweight champion because of his unusual ability to take a punch. His style of fighting was to take three punches to the head in order to give back two. At the end of ten rounds, he would still be bouncing, his opponent would have a headache. But in the last two years, over the fifteen-round fights, he had started to take some bad maulings.

4 This fight had its turns. Griffith won most of the early rounds, but Paret knocked Griffith down in the sixth. Griffith had trouble getting up, but made it, came alive and was dominating Paret again before the round was over. Then Paret began to wilt. In the middle of the eighth round, after a clubbing punch had turned his back to Griffith, Paret walked three disgusted steps away, showing his hindquarters. For a champion, he took much too long to turn back around. It was the first hint of weakness Paret had ever shown, and it must have inspired a particular shame, because he fought the rest of the fight as if he were seeking to demonstrate that he could take more punishment than any man alive. In the twelfth, Griffith caught him. Paret got trapped in a corner. Trying to duck away, his left arm and his head became tangled on the wrong side of the top rope. Griffith was in like a cat ready to rip the life out of a huge boxed rat. He hit him eighteen right hands in a row, an act which took perhaps three or four seconds, Griffith making a pent-up whimpering sound all the while he attacked, the right hand whipping like a piston rod which has broken through the crankcase, or like a baseball bat demolishing a pumpkin. I was sitting in the second row of that corner—they were not ten feet away from me, and like everybody else, I was hypnotized. I had never seen one man hit another

so hard and so many times. Over the referee's face came a look of woe as if some spasm had passed its way through him, and then he leaped on Griffith to pull him away. It was the act of a brave man. Griffith was uncontrollable. His trainer leaped into the ring, his manager, his cut man, there were four people holding Griffith, but he was off on an orgy, he had left the Garden, he was back on a hoodlum's street. If he had been able to break loose from his handlers and the referee, he would have jumped Paret to the floor and whaled on him there.

5 And Paret? Paret died on his feet. As he took those eighteen punches something happened to everyone who was in psychic range of the event. Some part of his death reached out to us. One felt it hover in the air. He was still standing in the ropes, trapped as he had been before, he gave some little half-smile of regret, as if he were saying, "I didn't know I was going to die just yet," and then, his head leaning back but still erect, his death came to breathe about him. He began to pass away. As he passed, so his limbs descended beneath him, and he sank slowly to the floor. He went down more slowly than any fighter had ever gone down, he went down like a large ship which turns on end and slides second by second into its grave. As he went down, the sound of Griffith's punches echoed in the mind like a heavy ax in the distance chopping into a wet log.

Questions About "Words"

1. Instead of "murder" (par. 1), Mailer might have written "bad feelings." Which do you prefer? Why?
2. Mailer might have written "reaction" instead of "rage" (par. 2). Why did he choose the word he did?
3. Why is the word "maulings" (par. 3), in the context of this essay, an apt choice?
4. In paragraph 4, Mailer wrote "wilt" and "clubbing punch." He might have written, instead, "to slow up" and "heavy blow." Which words express more meaning? Explain.

5. What is the effect on you of "like a cat ready to rip the life out of a huge boxed rat" (par. 4)? Find three more examples in this essay of Mailer's use of a similar figure of speech for the same purpose.

6. What is your feeling about the Griffith-Paret fight? Does Mailer, by his choice of words, try to affect your attitude toward it? Explain.

Questions on Diction and Writing Techniques

1. Mailer might have written sentence 1 of paragraph 3: "Paret, a proud club fighter who had become a welterweight champion because of his unusual ability to take a punch, was a Cuban." Which version better emphasizes the main idea of the sentence? Why?

2. "Griffith caught him in the twelfth." Does this version of a sentence in paragraph 4 better emphasize the main idea of the sentence? Why or why not?

3. Is there any point in this essay where your interest wanes? If so, explain why.

For Discussion, Reading, and Writing

1. What was the first hint of weakness Paret showed?

2. Why do you think boxing attracts such a large audience?

3. Does Mailer, in this essay, express or imply a comment about boxing? Explain.

4. Write a draft of a paragraph about any violent encounter you have observed. In a second draft, add one or more similes or metaphors.

5. Attend a sports event, or any other kind of event. Using as many apt, vivid words as possible, write a short essay about it.

A HILL OF FUR

John McPhee

A staff writer for *The New Yorker,* John McPhee also has numerous books to his credit, including *Coming into the Country* (1977), the source of this excerpt.

---

1 We passed first through stands of fireweed, and then over ground that was wine-red with the leaves of bearberries. There were curlewberries, too, which put a deep-purple stain on the hand. We kicked at some wolf scat, old as winter. It was woolly and white and filled with the hair of a snowshoe hare. Nearby was a rich inventory of caribou pellets and, in increasing quantity as we moved downhill, blueberries–an outspreading acreage of blueberries. Fedeler stopped walking. He touched my arm. He had in an instant become even more alert than he usually was, and obviously apprehensive. His gaze followed straight on down our intended course. What he saw there I saw now. It appeared to me to be a hill of fur. "Big boar grizzly," Fedeler said in a near-whisper. The bear was about a hundred steps away, in the blueberries, grazing. The head was down, the hump high. The immensity of muscle seemed to vibrate slowly–to expand and contract, with the grazing. Not berries alone but whole bushes were going into the bear. He was big for a barren-ground grizzly. The brown bears of Arctic Alaska (or grizzlies; they are no longer thought to be different) do not grow to the size they will reach on more ample diets elsewhere. The barren-ground grizzly will rarely grow larger than six hundred pounds.

2 "What if he got too close?" I said.

3 Fedeler said, "We'd be in real trouble."

4 "You can't outrun them," Hession said.

5 A grizzly, no slower than a racing horse, is about half again as

fast as the fastest human being. Watching the great mound of weight in the blueberries, with a fifty-five-inch waist and a neck more than thirty inches around, I had difficulty imagining that he could move with such speed, but I believed it, and was without impulse to test the proposition. Fortunately, a light southerly wind was coming up the Salmon valley. On its way to us, it passed the bear. The wind was relieving, coming into our faces, for had it been moving the other way the bear would not have been placidly grazing. There is an old adage that when a pine needle drops in the forest the eagle will see it fall; the deer will hear it when it hits the ground; the bear will smell it. If the boar grizzly were to catch our scent, he might stand on his hind legs, the better to try to see. Although he could hear well and had an extraordinary sense of smell, his eyesight was not much better than what was required to see a blueberry inches away. For this reason, a grizzly stands and squints, attempting to bring the middle distance into focus, and the gesture is often misunderstood as a sign of anger and forthcoming attack. If the bear were getting ready to attack, he would be on four feet, head low, ears cocked, the hair above his hump muscle standing on end. As if that message were not clear enough, he would also chop his jaws. His teeth would make a sound that would carry like the ringing of an axe.

6 One could predict, but not with certainty, what a grizzly would do. Odds were very great that one touch of man scent would cause him to stop his activity, pause in a moment of absorbed and alert curiosity, and then move, at a not undignified pace, in a direction other than the one from which the scent was coming. That is what would happen almost every time, but there was, to be sure, no guarantee. The forest Eskimos fear and revere the grizzly. They know that certain individual bears not only will fail to avoid a person who comes into their country but will approach and even stalk the trespasser. It is potentially inaccurate to extrapolate the behavior of any one bear from the behavior of most, since they are both intelligent and independent and will do what they choose to do according to mood, experience, whim. A grizzly that has ever been wounded by a bullet will not forget it, and will probably know that it was a human being who sent the bullet. At sight of a human, such a bear will be likely to charge. Grizzlies hide food sometimes—a caribou calf, say, under a pile of scraped-up moss—and a person

the bear might otherwise ignore might suddenly not be ignored if the person were inadvertently to step into the line between the food cache and the bear. A sow grizzly with cubs, of course, will charge anything that suggests danger to the cubs, even if the cubs are nearly as big as she is. They stay with their mother two and a half years.

7 None of us had a gun. (None of the six of us had brought a gun on the trip.) Among nonhunters who go into the terrain of the grizzly, there are several schools of thought about guns. The preferred one is: Never go without a sufficient weapon—a high-powered rifle or a shotgun and plenty of slug-loaded shells. The option is not without its own inherent peril. A professional hunter, some years ago, spotted a grizzly from the air and—with a client, who happened to be an Anchorage barber—landed on a lake about a mile from the bear. The stalking that followed was evidently conducted not only by the hunters but by the animal as well. The professional hunter was found dead from a broken neck, and had apparently died instantly, unaware of danger, for the cause of death was a single bite, delivered from behind. The barber, noted as clumsy with a rifle, had emptied his magazine, missing the bear with every shot but one, which struck the grizzly in the foot. The damage the bear did to the barber was enough to kill him several times. After the corpses were found, the bear was tracked and killed. To shoot and merely wound is worse than not to shoot at all. A bear that might have turned and gone away will possibly attack if wounded.

Questions About "Words"

1. McPhee might have written his first two sentences:

   We passed first through stands of fireweed, and then over ground that was covered with leaves. There were curlewberries, too, which put a stain on the hand.

   Which version do you prefer? Why?

2. McPhee chooses "hill of fur" (par. 1) and "great mound of weight" (par. 5) to convey the immensity of the bear. Mark in

your text two or more examples of specific diction that he chooses to add to this portrayal of the animal.

3. In the third sentence of paragraph 5, instead of "wind" or "southerly wind" McPhee wrote "light southerly wind." As an exercise in making a specific noun more specific by adding a modifier, do with the words that follow as McPhee does with "wind" to achieve greater specificity:

balloon	grass	sweater
cloud	pear	tomato
dog	strawberry	village
forest		

4. Find in paragraph 5 an example of simile.

Questions on Diction and Writing Techniques

1. How does your dictionary define "adage" (par. 5), "extrapolate" and "cache" (par. 6), "inherent" (par. 7)? Use each of these words in a sentence.

2. What effect does McPhee achieve with the short sentences (par. 1): "Fedeler stopped walking. He touched my arm."

For Discussion, Reading, and Writing

1. However familiar you may be with a pet or any other animal, observe the creature again at some length, making notes of its behavior and mannerisms as you do so. Then, in a paragraph or two, portray it colorfully and with as much specific diction as may be appropriate to the purpose of making it seem real to your classmates.

2. Visit a pet shop in your area to observe any animal or group of animals and the response to them of any person(s) in the store. Make notes of what you notice, particularly of vivid, revealing details of what you see and hear. Using words appropriate to your purpose in conveying the scene in the pet store to readers unfamiliar with such a place, write a short essay about your experience.

AMERICANS AND THE LAND

John Steinbeck

John Steinbeck (1902–1968) wrote, among other works, *The Grapes of Wrath* (1939), a sociological novel that put him in the front rank of twentieth-century American writers. He won the Nobel Prize for Literature in 1962.

---

1 I have often wondered at the savagery and thoughtlessness with which our early settlers approached this rich continent. They came at it as though it were an enemy, which of course it was. They burned the forests and changed the rainfall; they swept the buffalo from the plains, blasted the streams, set fire to the grass, and ran a reckless scythe through the virgin and noble timber. Perhaps they felt that it was limitless and could never be exhausted and that a man could move on to new wonders endlessly. Certainly there are many examples to the contrary, but to a large extent the early people pillaged the country as though they hated it, as though they held it temporarily and might be driven off at any time.

2 This tendency toward irresponsibility persists in very many of us today; our rivers are poisoned by reckless dumping of sewage and toxic industrial wastes, the air of our cities is filthy and dangerous to breathe from the belching of uncontrolled products from combustion of coal, coke, oil, and gasoline. Our towns are girdled with wreckage and the debris of our toys—our automobiles and our packaged pleasures. Through uninhibited spraying against one enemy we have destroyed the natural balances our survival requires. All these evils can and must be overcome if America and Americans are to survive; but many of us still conduct ourselves as our ancestors did, stealing from the future for our clear and present profit. . . .

3 On the East Coast, and particularly in New England, the colonists farmed meager lands close to their communities and to safety.

Every man was permanently on duty for the defense of his family and his village; even the hunting parties went into the forest in force, rather like raiders than hunters, and their subsequent quarrels with the Indians, resulting in forays and even massacres, remind us that the danger was very real. A man took his gun along when he worked the land, and the women stayed close to their thick-walled houses and listened day and night for the signal of alarm. The towns they settled were permanent, and most of them exist today with their records of Indian raids, of slaughter, of scalpings, and of punitive counter-raids. The military leader of the community became the chief authority in time of trouble, and it was a long time before danger receded and the mystery could be explored.

4 After a time, however, brave and forest-wise men drifted westward to hunt, to trap, and eventually to bargain for the furs which were the first precious negotiable wealth America produced for trade and export. Then trading posts were set up as centers of collection and the exploring men moved up and down the rivers and crossed the mountains, made friends for mutual profit with the Indians, learned the wilderness techniques, so that these explorer-traders soon dressed, ate, and generally acted like the indigenous people around them. Suspicion lasted a long time, and was fed by clashes sometimes amounting to full-fledged warfare; but by now these Americans attacked and defended as the Indians did.

5 For a goodly time the Americans were travelers, moving about the country collecting its valuables, but with little idea of permanence; their roots and their hearts were in the towns and the growing cities along the eastern edge. The few who stayed, who lived among the Indians, adopted their customs and some took Indian wives and were regarded as strange and somehow treasonable creatures. As for their half-breed children, while the tribe sometimes adopted them they were unacceptable as equals in the eastern settlements.

6 Then the trickle of immigrants became a stream, and the population began to move westward—not to grab and leave but to settle and live, they thought. The newcomers were of peasant stock, and they had their roots in a Europe where they had been landless, for the possession of land was the requirement and the proof of a higher social class than they had known. In America they found beautiful and boundless land for the taking—and they took it.

7 It is little wonder that they went land-mad, because there was

so much of it. They cut and burned the forests to make room for crops; they abandoned their knowledge of kindness to the land in order to maintain its usefulness. When they had cropped out a piece they moved on, raping the country like invaders. The topsoil, held by roots and freshened by leaf-fall, was left helpless to the spring freshets, stripped and eroded with the naked bones of clay and rock exposed. The destruction of the forests changed the rainfall, for the searching clouds could find no green and beckoning woods to draw them on and milk them. The merciless nineteenth century was like a hostile expedition for loot that seemed limitless. Uncountable buffalo were killed, stripped of their hides, and left to rot, a reservoir of permanent food supply eliminated. More than that, the land of the Great Plains was robbed of the manure of the herds. Then the plows went in and ripped off the protection of the buffalo grass and opened the helpless soil to quick water and slow drought and the mischievous winds that roamed through the Great Central Plains. There has always been more than enough desert in America; the new settlers, like overindulged children, created even more.

Questions About "Words"

1. What is the effect on you of the language "*reckless* scythe" (par. 1), "*helpless* soil" (par. 7), "*mischievous* winds" (par. 7)?
2. What purpose does Steinbeck reveal by his choice of words: "*noble* timber" (par. 1), "*pillaged* the country" (par. 1), "*stealing* from the future" (par. 2), "*raping* the country *like invaders*" (par. 7)?
3. Find examples of metaphor and simile in paragraphs 6 and 7. What is the purpose of these figures of speech?

Questions on Diction and Writing Techniques

1. How, in paragraph 1, does Steinbeck support the idea of "the savagery and thoughtlessness with which our early settlers approached this rich continent"? Would the paragraph be as,

more, or less effective if its third sentence were omitted? Explain. How, in paragraph 2, does the writer explain the generalization, "This tendency toward irresponsibility persists in very many of us today"?

2. How does Steinbeck achieve coherence in paragraph 1?

3. How does "this" help achieve coherence between paragraphs 1 and 2?

4. Find examples of coordination in the first sentence of paragraph 2.

5. How does Steinbeck achieve coherence between paragraphs 3 and 4?

6. Steinbeck uses "then," a word that signals a change in time, in paragraph 4. Find examples of its use in paragraphs 6 and 7. What does the word contribute to order?

For Discussion, Reading, and Writing

1. "This tendency toward irresponsibility persists in very many of us today. . . ." Using one or more of the examples of "irresponsibility" Steinbeck gives in paragraph 2, or any other you are familiar with, write a short essay in which you use specific details to explain your thesis and precise, specific, concrete diction to convey your meaning clearly to your readers.

2. What does Steinbeck mean by "packaged pleasures" (par. 2)? Can you cite examples of some? Why does he say that "our automobiles and our packaged pleasures" are "toys"? Do you agree? Why?

3. Trying to affect and to control the response of your readers by your choice of words, write a short essay about your hometown, using a topic related to this subject: "Our towns are girdled with wreckage and the debris of our toys—our automobiles and our packaged pleasures."

DECLINE AND FALL OF TEACHING HISTORY

Diane Ravitch

Diane Ravitch, a historian of education at Teachers College, Columbia University, is the author of books on American education and its problems.

1 During the past generation, the amount of time devoted to historical studies in American public schools has steadily decreased. About 25 years ago, most public high-school youths studied one year of world history and one of American history, but today, most study only one year of ours. In contrast, the state schools of many other Western nations require the subject to be studied almost every year. In France, for example, all students, not just the college-bound, follow a carefully sequenced program of history, civics and geography every year from the seventh grade through the 12th grade.

2 Does it matter if Americans are ignorant of their past? Does it matter if the general public knows little of the individuals, the events and the movements that shaped our nation? The fundamental premise of our democratic form of government is that political power derives from the informed consent of the people. Informed consent requires a citizenry that is rational and knowledgeable. If our system is to remain free and democratic, citizens should know not only how to judge candidates and their competing claims but how our institutions evolved. An understanding of history does not lead everyone to the same conclusions, but it does equip people with the knowledge to reach independent judgments on current issues. Without historical perspective, voters are more likely to be swayed by emotional appeals, by stirring commercials, or by little more than a candidate's good looks or charisma.

3 Because of my interest as a historian of education in the condition of the study of history, I have been involved during the last year, in collaboration with the National Assessment of Educational Progress, in planning a countrywide study of what 17-year-olds know about American history. In addition, my contacts with college students during the last year and discussions with other historians have led me to believe that there is cause for concern.

4 On the college lecture circuit this past year, I visited some 30 campuses, ranging from large public universities to small private liberal-arts colleges. Repeatedly, I was astonished by questions from able students about the most elementary facts of American history. At one urban Minnesota university, none of the 30 students in a course on ethnic relations had ever heard of the Supreme Court's Brown v. Board of Education decision of 1954, which held racial segregation in public schools unconstitutional. At a university in the Pacific Northwest, a professor of education publicly insisted that high-school students should concentrate on vocational preparation and athletics, since they had the rest of their lives to learn subjects like history "on their own time."

5 The shock of encountering college students who did not recognize the names of eminent figures like Jane Addams or W. E. B. Du Bois led me to conduct an informal, unscientific survey of professors who teach history to undergraduates. "My students are not stupid, but they have an abysmal background in American, or any other kind of, history," said Thomas Kessner, who teaches American history at Kingsborough Community College in Brooklyn. "They never heard of Daniel Webster; don't understand the Constitution; don't know the difference between the Republican and Democratic parties."

6 This gloomy assessment was echoed by Naomi Miller, chairman of the history department at Hunter College in New York. "My students have no historical knowledge on which to draw when they enter college," she said. "They have no point of reference for understanding World War I, the Treaty of Versailles or the Holocaust." More than ignorance of the past, however, she finds an indifference to dates and chronology or causation. "They think that everything is subjective. They have plenty of attitudes and opinions, but they lack the knowledge to analyze a problem." Professor Miller

believes that "we are in danger of bringing up a generation without historical memory. This is a dangerous situation."

Questions About "Words"

1. Does Ravitch use ordinary, everyday words, formal words, or a combination of both? Support your judgment with specific examples.

2. From Ravitch's diction, can you make an educated guess of the audience she wrote this essay for? Support your answer with specific reference to the text.

3. Compare the diction in this essay with that in "The Death of Benny Paret." Use ample examples to support your views.

Questions on Diction and Writing Techniques

1. How does your dictionary define "fundamental," "premise," "perspective," and "charisma" (par. 2); "assessment," "chronology," and "causation" (par. 6)? Use each word in a sentence.

2. Point out, in paragraph 1, three instances of Ravitch's use of transition words. Explain why she made the choices she did. Mark in your text one or more of those words in other paragraphs of this essay. Find in this essay one other transition word.

3. Underline in your text all examples of Ravitch's use of quotations. In each instance, explain how effective quotation is in explaining her ideas and in developing the paragraph containing it.

4. What purpose is served by beginning paragraph 2 with questions?

5. Find in paragraph 2 two examples of a sentence developed by means of coordination. Underline the coordinate elements.

For Discussion, Reading, and Writing

1. Do you agree with the point of view of the professor referred to at the end of paragraph 4? Write a short essay in which you support or take exception to what he says.

2. In a letter to anyone you know attending high school, explain why you are pursuing your present collegiate program. Write a similar letter to the admissions office of any postgraduate school you might attend.

3. If you think one or more of the issues raised by Ravitch might prove of interest to the students on your campus, write to the editor of your college or university newspaper a letter (such as you might like to see published) on a subject suggested by any part of her essay.

4. Write a letter, based on a recent experience in any of your classes, to a younger brother or sister. Underline all colloquial diction and slang expressions. Would alternative formal words be more appropriate? Explain.

3

Sources of Material

Personal Experience

A writer is not so much someone who has something to say as he is someone who has found a process that will bring about new things he would not have thought of if he had not started to say them.

—William Stafford

AT one time or another you very likely have asked yourself, "What do I have to write about?" If so, you've shared the feeling of many beginning writers. Most of them, however, have more to write about than they realize, for on the subject of themselves they are the most knowledgeable. Henry David Thoreau, at the beginning of *Walden,* based on personal experience, put it this way (italics at end added):

> In most books, the *I,* or first person, is omitted; in this it will be retained; that, in respect to egotism, is the main difference. We commonly do not remember that it is, after all, always the first person that is speaking. *I should not talk so much about myself if there were anybody else I knew as well.*

"Personal experience," it might be claimed, is a redundancy because experience means a personal encounter. But, since observation is a variety of experience, it is useful to use the term "personal experience" to differentiate between the two kinds of experience.

"Observation," in my distinction, refers to awareness of what goes on outside of the writer. By "personal experience" I mean what goes on within the mind of the writer: his or her consciousness of thoughts and ideas and involvement with incidents, persons, places, and things. (The distinction is sometimes elusive. We will consider it again in "Observation," pages 125–133.)

Much of what we know is an accumulation in memory of sensory experiences since infancy. This repository of information is a major source of writing material. Here is a paragraph, written many years after the occasion, filled with recollected details:

> By sundown the streets were empty, the curtains had been drawn, the world put to rights. Even the kitchen walls had been scrubbed and now gleamed in the Sabbath candles. On the long white tablecloth were the "company" dishes, filled for some with *gefilte* fish on lettuce leaves, ringed by red horseradish, sour and half-sour pickles, tomato salad with a light vinegar dressing; for others, with chopped liver in a bed of lettuce leaves and white radishes; the long white *khalleh,* the Sabbath loaf; chicken soup with noodles *and* dumplings; chicken, meat loaf, prunes, and sweet potatoes that had been baked all day into an open pie; compote of prunes and quince, apricots and orange rind; applesauce; a great brown nutcake filled with almonds, the traditional *lekakh*; all surrounded by glasses of port wine, seltzer bottles with their nozzles staring down at us waiting to be pressed; a samovar of Russian tea, *svetouchnee* from the little red box, always served in tall glasses, with lemon slices floating on top. My father and mother sipped it in Russian fashion, through lumps of sugar held between the teeth [Alfred Kazin, *A Walker in the City*].

Your earliest experiences are of course those of childhood. Embedded in memory, they await evocation by you now and could be reported as Simone de Beauvoir does hers in *Memoirs of a Dutiful Daughter:*

> I retain only one confused impression from my earliest years: it is all red, and black, and warm. Our apartment was red: the carpet was red, the Renaissance dining room was red, the figured silk hangings over the stained-glass doors were red, and the velvet curtains

> in Papa's study were red too. The furniture in this awesome sanctum was made of black pearwood; I used to creep into the kneehole under the desk and wrap myself in its dusty gloom; it was dark and warm there, and the red of the carpet pleased my eyes. That is how I passed the early days of infancy. Safely sheltered, I watched, I touched, and I took stock of the world.

Here the writer's reminiscence of early childhood, recalled by her in maturity, consists almost entirely of sensory impressions.

Another example of writing based on personal experience illustrates the writer's consciousness of the meaning of a childhood experience:

> Whenever we children came to stay at my grandmother's house, we were put to sleep in the sewing room, a bleak, shabby, utilitarian rectangle, more office than bedroom, more attic than office, that played to the hierarchy of chambers the role of a poor relation. It was a room seldom entered by the other members of the family, seldom swept by a maid, a room without pride; the old sewing machine, some castoff chairs, a shadeless lamp, rolls of wrapping paper, piles of cardboard boxes that might someday come in handy, papers of pins, and remnants of material united with the iron folding cots put out for our use and the bare floor boards to give an impression of intense and ruthless temporality. Thin white spreads, of the kind used in hospitals and charity institutions, and naked blinds at the windows reminded us of our orphaned condition and of the ephemeral character of our visit; there was nothing here to encourage us to consider this our home [Mary McCarthy, *Memories of a Catholic Girlhood*].

Like Simone de Beauvoir, Mary McCarthy is describing a place that made an impression on her as a child. But McCarthy conveys more meaning and makes a poignant comment on her childhood by making the sewing room in her grandmother's house—"that played to the hierarchy of chambers the role of a poor relation"—symbolic of her and her brother's orphaned condition.

Many people are so busy *doing,* they have little or no time for reflection. And yet men and women, uniquely, are contemplative animals embarked on a continuing search for meaning. When writing about a personal experience, you have the opportunity to review the thing experienced and your response to it with the intention of finding, perhaps for the first time, its importance to you and, going beyond that, its possible significance to others.

Such a viewing of one's past is exemplified by a passage from *A Man Called White* by Walter White, who describes himself in the book's beginning: "I am a Negro. My skin is white, my eyes are blue, my hair is blond. The traits of my race are nowhere upon me." On a day in September 1906, when he was thirteen, he and his family were about to be attacked in their home in Atlanta during a race riot:

> In the flickering light the mob swayed, paused, and began to flow toward us. In that instant there opened up within me a great awareness; I knew then who I was. I was a Negro, a human being with an invisible pigmentation which marked me a person to be hunted, hanged, abused, discriminated against, kept in poverty and ignorance, in order that those whose skin was white would have readily at hand a proof of their superiority, a proof patent and inclusive, accessible to the moron and the idiot as well as to the wise man and the genius. No matter how low a white man fell, he was superior to two-thirds of the world's population, for those two-thirds were not white.

After commenting on his mental response to the threat of the mob —a sudden insight about his own status in Atlanta—the writer, at the end of this passage, makes a more generally significant observation about the cause of race riots.

Since most of us live uneventfully, what occurs to us and our responses to it may seem humdrum and not worthy of reporting. Yet, if we can find meaning in our lives for ourselves, we can make out of seemingly ordinary experiences effective essays.

In an essay based on your personal experiences, you have an opportunity to review your past, to evaluate it in order to discover its significance to you, and in doing so to make your past interesting to your readers. However you evaluate it, whether explicitly or implicitly, you should be aware that personal experience is a major source of the essay writer's material. This source is like a well that never runs dry. It is a reservoir that is replenished daily. It requires no trips to the library, no research. What you have experienced thus far today, or even in the last hour, may provide you all the ideas you need for an essay. And, in the well of your past, there is a large supply of material waiting to be drawn upon.

THE VALUE OF UNORIGINAL REMARKS

S. I. Hayakawa

S. I. Hayakawa was a professor of English and president of San Francisco State College and also U.S. senator from California.

---

1 An incident in my own experience illustrates how necessary it sometimes is to give people the opportunity to agree. Early in 1942, a few weeks after the beginning of the war and at a time when rumors of Japanese spies were still widely current, I had to wait two or three hours in a railroad station in Oshkosh, Wisconsin, a city in which I was a stranger. I became aware as time went on that the other people waiting in the station were staring at me suspiciously and feeling uneasy about my presence. One couple with a small child were staring with special uneasiness and whispering to each other. I therefore took occasion to remark to the husband that it was too bad that the train should be late on so cold a night. The man agreed. I went on to remark that it must be especially difficult to travel with a small child in winter when train schedules were so uncertain. Again the husband agreed. I then asked the child's age and remarked that the child looked very big and strong for his age. Again agreement—this time with a slight smile. The tension was relaxing.

2 After two or three more exchanges, the man asked, "I hope you don't mind my bringing it up, but you're Japanese, aren't you? Do you think the Japs have any chance of winning this war?"

3 "Well," I replied, "your guess is as good as mine. I don't know any more than I read in the papers. (This was true.) But the way I figure it, I don't see how the Japanese, with their lack of coal and steel and oil and their limited industrial capacity, can ever beat a powerfully industrialized nation like the United States."

4 My remark was admittedly neither original nor well informed. Hundreds of radio commentators and editorial writers were saying exactly the same thing during those weeks. But just because they were, the remark *sounded familiar* and was *on the right side,* so that it was easy to agree with. The man agreed at once, with what seemed like genuine relief. How much the wall of suspicion had broken down was indicated in his next question. "Say, I hope your folks aren't over there while the war is going on."

5 "Yes, they are. My father and mother and two young sisters are over there."

6 "Do you ever hear from them?"

7 "How can I?"

8 "Do you mean you won't be able to see them or hear from them till after the war is over?" Both he and his wife looked troubled and sympathetic.

9 There was more to the conversation, but the result was that within ten minutes after it had begun they had invited me to visit them in their city and have dinner with them in their home. And the other people in the station, seeing me in conversation with people who *didn't* look suspicious, ceased to pay any attention to me and went back to reading their papers and staring at the ceiling.

Questions About "Personal Experience"

1. What conclusion does Hayakawa draw from his experience?
2. Can you justify placing elsewhere in this essay Hayakawa's comment about the significance he attaches to his experience?
3. What is Hayakawa's purpose in this essay? Does he achieve this purpose? Explain.

Questions on Diction and Writing Techniques

1. What is the function of "therefore" in paragraph 1?
2. Point out the words relating to time that Hayakawa uses to order chronologically the events related in paragraph 1.

3. How do "Japanese" and "Japs" (par. 2) differ?
4. What does Hayakawa achieve by using dialogue?

For Discussion, Reading, and Writing

1. Using dialogue as much as possible, write a short essay beginning with "An incident in my own experience illustrates. . . ."
2. After visiting any public place—a bus station, museum, sports stadium, chess club, department store—and speaking with one or more persons there, report the incident in a short essay that states explicitly or shows by implication the significance of the experience.

MY FIRST LESSON IN HOW TO LIVE AS A NEGRO

Richard Wright

Richard Wright (1908–1960), author of *Native Son* (1940), is among the most important twentieth-century American novelists.

---

1 My first lesson in how to live as a Negro came when I was quite small. We were living in Arkansas. Our house stood behind the railroad tracks. Its skimpy yard was paved with black cinders. Nothing green ever grew in that yard. The only touch of green we could see was far away, beyond the tracks, over where the white folks lived. But cinders were good enough for me and I never missed the green growing things. And anyhow cinders were fine weapons. You could always have a nice hot war with huge black cinders. All

you had to do was crouch behind the brick pillars of a house with your hands full of gritty ammunition. And the first woolly black head you saw pop out from behind another row of pillars was your target. You tried your very best to knock it off. It was great fun.

2 I never fully realized the appalling disadvantages of a cinder environment till one day the gang to which I belonged found itself engaged in a war with the white boys who lived beyond the tracks. As usual we laid down our cinder barrage, thinking that this would wipe the white boys out. But they replied with a steady bombardment of broken bottles. We doubled our cinder barrage, but they hid behind trees, hedges, and the sloping embankments of their lawns. Having no such fortifications, we retreated to the brick pillars of our homes. During the retreat a broken milk bottle caught me behind the ear, opening a deep gash which bled profusely. The sight of blood pouring over my face completely demoralized our ranks. My fellow-combatants left me standing paralyzed in the center of the yard, and scurried for their homes. A kind neighbor saw me and rushed me to a doctor, who took three stitches in my neck.

3 I sat brooding on my front steps, nursing my wound and waiting for my mother to come from work. I felt that a grave injustice had been done me. It was all right to throw cinders. The greatest harm a cinder could do was leave a bruise. But broken bottles were dangerous; they left you cut, bleeding, and helpless.

4 When night fell, my mother came from the white folks' kitchen. I raced down the street to meet her. I could just feel in my bones that she would understand. I knew she would tell me exactly what to do next time. I grabbed her hand and babbled out the whole story. She examined my wound, then slapped me.

5 "How come yuh didn't hide?" she asked me. "How come yuh awways fightin'?"

6 I was outraged, and bawled. Between sobs I told her that I didn't have any trees or hedges to hide behind. There wasn't a thing I could have used as a trench. And you couldn't throw very far when you were hiding behind the brick pillars of a house. She grabbed a barrel stave, dragged me home, stripped me naked, and beat me till I had a fever of one hundred and two. She would smack my rump with the stave, and, while the skin was still smarting, impart to me gems of Jim Crow wisdom. I was never to throw cinders any more. I was never to fight any more wars. I was never,

never, under any conditions, to fight *white* folks again. And they were absolutely right in clouting me with the broken milk bottle. Didn't I know she was working hard every day in the hot kitchens of the white folks to make money to take care of me? When was I ever going to learn to be a good boy? She couldn't be bothered with my fights. She finished by telling me that I ought to be thankful to God as long as I lived that they didn't kill me.

7 All that night I was delirious and could not sleep. Each time I closed my eyes I saw monstrous white faces suspended from the ceiling, leering at me.

8 From that time on, the charm of my cinder yard was gone. The green trees, the trimmed hedges, the cropped lawns grew very meaningful, became a symbol. Even today when I think of white folks, the hard, sharp outlines of white houses surrounded by trees, lawns, and hedges are present somewhere in the background of my mind. Through the years they grew into an overreaching symbol of fear.

Questions About "Personal Experience"

1. What is Wright's purpose in writing paragraph 8? Would this piece be more, less, or equally effective if the paragraph were left out? Explain.

Questions on Diction and Writing Techniques

1. What alternative language might Wright have chosen in lieu of "pop out" and "knock it off" (par. 1)? Which verbs are more vivid?

2. What is the main idea of paragraph 2? Does Wright give you enough information to convince you of its validity? Explain.

3. In paragraph 1, writing about the fight between his gang and other black children, Wright uses "weapons," "ammunition," "target." Find similar diction in paragraph 2. Do these words help convey to you his personal experience? Explain.

4. What does "Jim Crow" (par. 6) denote (see page 84)? What is its derivation? Why does Wright call his mother's advice "Jim Crow wisdom"?

For Discussion, Reading, and Writing

1. Rewrite paragraph 6, incorporating in your version as much dialogue as possible.
2. Filling the blank spaces with language reflecting your own experience, write a short essay beginning with "My first lesson in . . . came when I was. . . ." End the essay with a fitting conclusion drawn from the experience.
3. Using personal experience as your source of material, write an essay about an incident that shaped or helped shape your present attitude toward a person, a class of people, an institution, God, or anything else.
4. Write a short essay that relates an incident or series of events that occurred in your childhood and that might be of interest to others. Try to tell about the experience as you perceived it then. If it seems humorous now, try to make your readers see it that way.

A BULL TERRIER NAMED MACKEREL

Roger Caras

Roger A. Caras, naturalist, film producer, and radio and TV commentator on the world of nature, is the author of forty-odd books and numerous articles on wild and domesticated animals, including his most recent, *A Celebration of Dogs* (1982).

---

1 When I was a boy growing up in Methuen, Massachusetts (or at least trying to), there was a man down the street who had a bull terrier named Mackerel. The unusual name, I believe, came from his shiny coat and some rather peculiar brindle marks along his sides. Mack, as we called him, was kept in a fenced yard, and everyone just assumed that he was a positive terror. We were led to believe, as most people were, that his was a killer breed on a par with the much-maligned doberman pinscher. Poor Mack watched kids stream by on the other side of the fence going to and from school, but nobody would stop to talk to him. We had been warned. There was even a padlock on his gate. Mack had long since given up barking at the kids going by. He just looked dejected and lonely. When he was taken out for a walk it was on a heavy chain lead, and if you encountered his burly owner with dog on a public thoroughfare you crossed the street.

2 One morning the yard was empty, the padlock was missing; Mack was gone. At just about the same time a Boston terrier that lived down the street, the passionately beloved pet of a terrible old lady who had to be twice as mean as Mack, no matter how mean he was supposed to be, vanished, too. That Boston played in its backyard without a fence. Clearly Mack had killed it. The scenario was clear to see. Some psychopath had opened Mack's gate, and when he had been turned out from his normally secure yard he, ever the killer, had gone on the hunt.

3 The police were called immediately. We were told by our parents that they had orders to shoot Mack on sight. There would be no trial. Guilt was assumed.

4 Things got very much worse two days later when another pet in the neighborhood vanished without a trace. It was a cross, as I recall, of a cocker spaniel and something fairly indistinct. Mack the killer dog was obviously still in the area, still killing, and the hunt intensified. Some people put loaded guns near their windows and doors. Kids were walked to and from approved play areas, particularly the smaller kids. Who knew where Mack would stop?

5 Then, about five days after he had vanished, Mack reappeared with his two friends, the Boston and the cocker-whatever mix in tow, in a playground. A woman who immediately went into something like total hysteria encountered a bunch of kids surrounding the three dogs, patting and hugging them. Mack was nearly wiggling

his tail end off with joy. He loved kids and had been so benignly persuasive a leader of his own kind that he had been able to lure the other two dogs out of their yards to follow him on a perfectly harmless spree that lasted several days. The woman's screams triggered a series of phone calls, and the police arrived and actually approached the melee of kids and dogs with guns drawn. Because of the children, and for no other reason, I am certain, no shots were fired. Mack's owner arrived and took his pet home. The other dogs, cuddled and scolded, were carried off the field, and the kids finally settled back down to their ball game.

6 Things were never the same with Mack after that. Kids donated half their sandwiches as they passed. Hands were thrust through the fence, and Mack wiggled himself silly with the attention he got. Every morning and every afternoon he waited for his friends to come by. On Saturdays and Sundays we often went over just to see Mack. He began getting a tad chubby on peanut butter and jelly and bologna, and his owner could be seen watching from behind a lace curtain. Strangely, I don't think he felt he had gained status by Mack's now universal acceptance in the town. He may, in fact, have lost a little. No one seemed to know very much about him except the man who owned the hardware store, who said he bought an awful lot of tools and hardware supplies. No one knew what he did in that house, but outside of it he seemed to have lost a little something in his walk. He wasn't very fearsome himself, although he was very large. Mack made him fearsome, which is why, I am sure, he never did anything to dispel the terrifying mystique that had grown up around his dog. Mystique grows easily in small towns. Mack, I heard long after we had moved away, lived to a ripe old age and never lost his touch with the kids heading to and from Central Grammar School. The Boston terrier that Mack was presumed to have eaten eventually bit some kid. There had been a rabies scare a few weeks before when a wildly yapping dog had been shot on a landing on the school's staircase while kids huddled with their teachers behind closed classroom doors. The police finally got to shoot their dog, but it wasn't Mack. It was some unknown passer-through desperately ill with a dread disease more commonly encountered then than now. The Boston terrier, however, was put to sleep, and the extraordinarily mean old lady died shortly after that. Mack, wiggling his husky, muscled bottom to the end, outlived them all.

I have always considered this story one of the nicer memories of my childhood in Methuen.

Questions About "Personal Experience"

1. Mark in your text those details that make clear to you that Caras' essay is based on personal experience.

Questions on Diction and Writing Techniques

1. How does your dictionary define "brindle" and "maligned" (par. 1), "scenario" and "psychopath" (par. 2), "benignly" and "melee" (par. 5), "mystique" (par. 6)? Use each word in a sentence.
2. Show, with specific examples, how Caras tries to control your attitude ("*poor* Mack," for instance) toward Mack and toward the persons mentioned in this essay.
3. What we have here is basically narration (see pages 176–180). Mark in your text the words Caras chooses to establish chronological order in his storytelling.
4. Does Caras make any judgment, explicit or implied? If it were your essay, would you include a statement such as that of Hayakawa at the beginning of "The Value of Unoriginal Remarks" (page 116)? Explain.

For Discussion, Reading, and Writing

1. If you have fond (or not so fond) memories of a pet, write a short essay about them.
2. James Thurber (1894–1961) was a dog lover who often wrote about dogs and, humorously, from the dog's point of view (see, for example, page 28 above). Write a short essay about people as you imagine some pet in your life might see them.
3. Animal lovers talk of a bonding, a special rapport, that arises between owner and pet. If this has been your experience, write a short essay explaining how bonding with your pet developed.

Observation

The first thing writers look for in their drafts is information. *They know that a good piece of writing is built from specific, accurate, and interesting information. The writer must have an abundance of information from which to construct a readable piece of writing.*

—Donald M. Murray

WRITERS for whom personal experience is a major source of material can increase the effectiveness of their writing by reporting in detail what they perceive, but the emphasis in such writing is on what goes on *within* the writer. In contrast, the emphasis in writing for which observation is a major source of material is on what goes on *outside* the writer.

Through the senses—hearing, sight, smell, taste, and touch—we become aware of the world around us: the ring of a telephone, the flicker of a flame, the aroma of fresh bread, the taste of chewing gum, the coldness of an ice cube. Our awareness of the elements of our environment varies. We are likely to be most perceptive when highly motivated: to identify a strange sound when bedded down outdoors at night in unfamiliar surroundings; to find an item of jewelry lost on a beach; to detect a friend on an arriving train; to discover the ingredients of a dish prepared by a fine cook; to savor the bouquet of an unusual wine.

Training also increases one's ability to notice more. A hunter, a botanist, or a bird watcher is likely to be more aware of the environment on a walk through the woods than is someone who is not initiated in the lore of nature. A doctor, a sailor, a farmer, an orchestra conductor, an editor, an automobile mechanic—each, in his or her specialty, is likely to see details that others might not observe. You surely see things keenly in your fields of interest. To be an effective writer, you must train yourself by practice to be more observant, with all your senses, more of the time.

A good exercise in observation is to place a notebook and pencil beside you on the table while having a meal in any eating place and to jot down in a word, phrase, or sentence what you perceive with your five senses, including snatches of conversation. Or take notes of what you observe at a party, during a class, in a locker room. Better yet, do one of these exercises with a friend, together or separately, and then compare notes.

There is a correlation between careful observation and good writing. Consider the effect on you of the specific details in this passage; count the number of them the writer observed and reports to his readers:

> It was in Burma, a sodden morning of the rains. A sickly light, like yellow tinfoil, was slanting over the high walls into the jail yard. We were waiting outside the condemned cells, a row of sheds fronted with double bars, like small animal cages. Each cell measured about ten feet by ten and was quite bare within except for a plank bed and a pot for drinking water. In some of them brown, silent men were squatting at the inner bars, with their blankets draped around them. These were the condemned men, due to be hanged within the next week or two [George Orwell, "A Hanging"].

I find these specific details:

1. A sodden morning of the rains
2. A sickly light
3. Slanting over the high walls into the jail yard
4. A row of sheds
5. Fronted with double bars
6. Each cell measured about ten feet by ten
7. Quite bare within except for a plank bed

8. And a pot for drinking water
9. Brown, silent men
10. Squatting at the inner bars
11. With their blankets draped around them

By making his writing concrete, the writer makes it more vigorous.

A beginning writer will often settle for a quick impression instead of observing with care and then reporting the specific details on which that impression is based. She might report of her subject, merely: "He looked disreputable." Here, by contrast, is how an attentive writer reported her observations of Stephen Crane, American novelist, poet, and short-story writer:

> He was thin to emaciation, his face was gaunt and unshaven, a thin dark moustache straggled on his upper lip, his black hair grew low on his forehead and was shaggy and unkempt. His gray clothes were much the worse for wear and fitted him so badly it seemed unlikely he had ever been measured for them. He wore a flannel shirt and a slovenly apology for a necktie, and his shoes were dusty and worn gray about the toes and were badly run over at the heel. I had seen many a tramp printer come up the *Journal* stairs to hunt a job, but never one who presented such a disreputable appearance as this storymaker man [Willa Cather, "When I Knew Stephen Crane"].

Cather supports in detail her conclusion that Crane's appearance was "disreputable" and thereby gives her readers the information needed to make it credible.

I have been using the word "observation" so far in the sense of recognizing and noting facts or occurrences. Here are examples of facts:

> John is six feet tall.
>
> Mary weighs one hundred and ten pounds.
>
> This morning the sun rose in London at 6:30 A.M.
>
> An inch of rain fell in Chicago yesterday.

The Yankees scored four runs in the ninth inning of their last game with the Red Sox.

The driver of the green Buick was caught driving in the southbound lane of U.S. Route 1 at 70 m.p.h.

These are statements about what is known. They can be verified. We say that they are *facts.*

"Observation" has another meaning. According to an old chestnut, "Where there's smoke there's fire." We may see smoke, but even without seeing fire we conclude that it must be there. You fail to find your car in a parking lot and say it has been stolen. You hear the sound of a siren and say it comes from an ambulance. You detect the smell of charcoal burning and say your neighbor is having a cookout. You taste a hamburger and say the cook has been too lavish with the salt. In each instance, you are observing, or you are coming to a conclusion, by a process of reasoning called *inferring.* An *inference,* in the words of S. I. Hayakawa, is "a statement about the unknown made on the basis of the known. . . . The common characteristic of inferences is that they are statements about matter which are not directly known, made on the basis on what has been observed."

Much of our knowledge of our environment is the result of inference, conclusion, judgment. Through observation, in both senses of the term, we attain awareness of the real world.

How objective—unaffected by personal feelings or prejudice—can or should we be? (I will return to this question in "Description," pages 205–228.) According to Thoreau:

> There is no such thing as pure *objective* observation. Your observation, to be interesting, *i.e.*, to be significant, must be *subjective.* The sum of what the writer of whatever class has to report is simply some human experience. . . . Senses that take cognizance of outward things merely are of no avail [Henry David Thoreau, *Journal,* May 6, 1854].

In the light of Thoreau's comment, consider this report:

> One afternoon in late August, as the summer's sun streamed into the car and made little jumping shadows on the windows, I sat

gazing out at the tenement-dwellers, who were themselves looking out of their windows from the gray crumbling buildings along the tracks of upper Manhattan. As we crossed into the Bronx, the train unexpectedly slowed down for a few miles. Suddenly from out of my window I saw a large crowd near the tracks, held back by two policemen. Then, on the other side from my window, I saw a sight I would never be able to forget: a little boy almost severed in halves, lying at an incredible angle near the track. The ground was covered with blood, and the boy's eyes were opened wide, strained and disbelieving in his sudden oblivion. A policeman stood next to him, his arms folded, staring straight ahead at the windows of our train. In the orange glow of late afternoon the policeman, the crowd, the corpse of the boy were for a brief moment immobile, motionless, a small tableau to violence and death in the city. Behind me, in the next row of seats, there was a game of bridge. I heard one of the four men say as he looked out at the sight, "God, that's horrible." Another said, in a whisper, "Terrible, terrible." There was a momentary silence, punctuated only by the clicking of the wheels on the track. Then, after the pause, I heard the first man say: "Two hearts" [Willie Morris, *North Toward Home*].

Notice the number of concrete details the objective reporter chooses to make us see and feel the scene he portrays. These, being part of "some human experience" (in Thoreau's words), elicit a subjective response, implied in the last few sentences, that makes the writer's observations interesting and significant: that to the four men in the car the death of a fellow human being is of less concern than a game of cards.

This passage exemplifies the point that the distinction between observation (the awareness of what goes on outside a writer) and personal experience (what goes on within the mind of the writer) is sometimes elusive. There is such a close connection between the world outside of the writer and his or her response to it that often it is difficult to keep the two apart.

Forceful writing depends in large measure on reporting details. Thus the more observant you are, the more effective are your essays likely to be; among the important tools of the successful writer are the five senses. But, as Thoreau suggests, writers—you among them—

are not machines. You have a right to report your unique perception of the world around you and to include in writing that uses observation as your main source of material your feelings and your interpretation of your experience.

CAPTAIN OF HIS SHIP

Bob Greene

Bob Greene is a syndicated columnist for the *Chicago Tribune* and a contributing editor of *Esquire* magazine. He is the author of several books, including the best-selling *Good Morning, Merry Sunshine* (1984).

1 Sometimes, when you're not looking for anything, something comes up and strikes you as clear as daybreak. I had been traveling by bus through corn-and-soybean country for several days; my reasons were personal ones, and I had found what I was looking for, and now I was on my way back to Chicago.

2 I seldom ride interstate buses, but these few days had been enough to convince me that there is little romance to them. As a traveler who usually finds himself in airports, I had become numbed by this week's endless hours in dank, musty buses, heading slowly between places that no other form of public transportation serves.

3 My fellow passengers were not inflation-fighters; they were on the buses because buses are the lowest common denominator of American transportation. There is nothing cheaper; the low price was the only reason that the people were aboard. They were the bottom social stratum of the country's travelers; they needed to get someplace, and the bus was all they could afford.

4 Now I was on the last leg of my journey; the Trailways bus I

was on had started the trip in St. Louis, and was on a nine-hour run through Missouri and Illinois. Several hours into the ride, I began to notice something.

5 It was the driver. He was a young man with a mustache and sideburns; I would have to guess he was in his early thirties. What struck me was the manner of crispness and precision he brought to his job. He was dressed neatly, and he addressed his passengers politely, and at the rest stops he timed his schedule exactly with his wristwatch.

6 When a passenger approached him with a question along the way, the driver did not act as if he were annoyed; he took time to answer in a friendly, informed way. It was, frankly, a lousy route; instead of heading directly to Chicago, the schedule called for him to stop at any number of tiny towns along the way: Clinton, Fullerton, Farmer City, Gibson.

7 Usually there was no bus station in these cities; the driver would pull the coach into a gas station parking lot, or stop in front of a restaurant. One person might get off, or two might get on. It hardly seemed worth his time to be making the detours to serve so few passengers.

8 And yet he carried out his job with class. He welcomed each passenger to the bus; hurried out the door to assist with baggage; made a fresh count of travelers for his logbook at every stop. I got the impression that he was memorizing all of our faces; we might be with him only for one gray autumn day, but we were his passengers and he seemed to be making an effort to take a personal interest in that.

9 He was just a long-haul bus driver heading up some forgotten route in the middle of the country, but for his attitude, this might have been a Boeing 747 on its way to Paris. I found myself wondering what struck me so oddly about this man, and in a second the realization came. This attitude of his—this pride in the work he was doing—was the very thing we have for so long been told has vanished from the American work force.

10 Had the driver taken a lazy and slovenly approach, no one would have ever known; the passengers on an interstate bus aren't the kind of people who have the pull to make trouble. They have no alternative; if they don't like the bus, there's no cheaper way for them to go. Certainly there was no prestige built into the driver's

work. Trailways isn't even the big name in long-haul buses; Greyhound is.

11 But on this ride, it was as if the idea of not doing his job well had never crossed the driver's mind. And a funny thing was happening; because the driver found dignity in his own work, he instilled his load of passengers with a small feeling of dignity, too. Oh, they knew they were riding on an uncomfortable bus with men and women who probably couldn't afford any other means of transportation; but because the driver had pride, the passengers seemed to feel a little better, too.

12 At one toll booth the driver paid the attendant, then leaned out the window to say something. I listened. The driver had seen a car stalled on the side of the highway several miles back, and was advising the toll-booth man to telephone the state police to inform them that there was a traveler in trouble. I hadn't noticed the stalled car, but the driver had, and he obviously considered this part of his job.

13 When we pulled into the station in Chicago's Loop, the driver stood at the bottom of the steps leading out of the bus, helping each passenger depart, saying goodbye to each of us. He stayed there until the bus was empty.

14 It was something to see. Most of the passengers had no one to greet them; they wandered out of the station one by one. In a bus station there is none of that sense of drama you're always getting at a big airport; here the feeling was not of an adventure beginning, but of dreary, uneventful life continuing.

15 And yet, because of his attitude—the way he feels about his work—the driver had, for a few hours, made things different. When I arrived home, I realized something inexcusable: for all the driver's impressiveness, I hadn't even bothered to learn his name. So I called the Trailways dispatcher and found out. It is Ted Litt.

Questions About "Observation"

1. Underline in your text the many examples of the care with which Greene observed his surroundings on the trip by bus he writes about in this essay.

2. Make a list of the details that you find especially effective in portraying the attitude of the driver toward his job.

Questions on Diction and Writing Techniques

1. How does your dictionary define "common denominator" and "stratum" (par. 3), "slovenly" (par. 10), "impressiveness" (par. 15)? Use each of these words in a sentence.
2. Greene might have begun paragraph 5:

   It was the driver, a young man with a mustache and sideburns; I would have to guess he was in his thirties.

   Why did he write the first sentence as he did?
3. What is the effect of sentence 2 of paragraph 12 and of sentence 1 of paragraph 14?
4. What generalizations does Greene make based on his observations? Are they amply supported by those observations? Do the generalizations add meaning to his essay? Explain.

For Discussion, Reading, and Writing

1. Bob Greene wrote, in his introduction to the collection of essays from which this selection was taken:

   I am neither a pundit nor a political philosopher. I try to be a storyteller; I try to go out and explore something that interests me, and then—after hanging around and listening and asking questions—I try to give the reader some sense of what it was like to have been there.

   With a similar purpose in mind, and for an audience such as you take Greene's to have been, observe any person or group of people—at a party, in the lobby of a theater, at the checkout counter of a supermarket, in the locker room of a gym, in your school cafeteria. Jot down, at the time or soon thereafter, as much as possible of what you see and hear. Cull your notes for particularly significant details—those that are most likely to give your readers "some sense of what it was to have been there." Organize your material as you continue your prewriting. Write a draft of an essay based on your observations. Rewrite.

WHEN THE YOUNG HAVE IT GOOD

Robert Ardrey

Robert Ardrey has had a varied career as playwright, screenwriter, and anthropologist.

---

1 The African hunting dog, known in the early days as the Cape hunting dog, is perhaps the world's most successful predator, excluding only man. It is not a dog at all, not even a member of the family *Canidae,* but has four toes on his foot, ears like ping-pong paddles, and bears the scientific name *Lycaon pictus.* It looks like a dog, however, and not a very large one, since it weighs about forty pounds. Its success as a hunter has been based entirely on a capacity to outrun any animal in Africa, together with the superb coordination of its hunting pack. But despite its success, or because of it, the hunting dog is a rare animal today. Since the early times of settlement in the Cape, three hundred years ago, its reputation has been so terrifying that men have hunted it, even poisoned it, as vermin.

2 The hunting dog has terrified not only men but other animals. I have watched Thomson's gazelle graze within two hundred yards of a hungry cheetah, the fastest of land animals. But in 1966, when Eliot Elisofon and I had the chance to photograph a large hunting-dog pack for three days, dawn to dusk, no antelope approached close enough to be identified without binoculars. Within our view was perhaps thirty square miles of flat, open, treeless plain; along the margins animals grazed. Just once four zebras strolled by at a distance of several hundred yards. Since they had the confidence, one must assume that the margin was sufficient for escape. But also the pack was sleeping.

3 At that time a study of one pack, over a period of a few months, was all that science had yet collected in the way of reliable

observation. When I returned to the Serengeti two years later, however, Kruuk and Schaller, as by-products of their hyena and lion specialties, had collected more information on the entire predator community than science had ever possessed before. It is information which, although largely unpublished, I am permitted to use before this investigation closes. Now, in terms of adult-young relations of almost shocking amiability, I wish simply to describe one hunt.

4 Schaller, by the summer of 1968, had followed twenty-two packs. He came by my cottage about four o'clock one afternoon, having spotted a pack which he judged would hunt about five thirty. By four thirty we had found it, sleeping in the midst of a rolling area of plain parched by the dry season, burned black by fire. We animal-watched, waited, talked. There were ten adults and fourteen pups well over half grown. Schaller had known the pack when the pups were born six months earlier and there had been sixteen. They had lost only two. It was an infant mortality rate so low as to be difficult to believe. Finally three adults were stirring, nosing the others to their feet. All went to the pups, and now there was a rolling pell-mell of play, adults and pups together, and the strange twittering sound, like a flock of sparrows, that the dogs make when excited.

5 "War dance," said Schaller. And like a ritual it was, for the dogs when sufficiently excited were all on their feet. The three leaders headed off, other adults behind them, then the pups, and last a disabled adult on three legs. It was precisely five thirty; whether they had heard a factory whistle blow or Schaller earlier had given them instructions, I do not know. One of the most memorable sights in nature, however, is that of a pack strung out in single file almost a quarter of a mile long, headed into the late, gray light with white-tipped tails upraised like beacons to make following easier.

6 They trotted. The hunting dog—like the albatross, the elephant seal, and few other species—has no least fear of men, and one may drive beside the pack as if one were not there. We checked the Land Rover's speedometer, and they were doing fifteen miles an hour. The pups kept the pace with ease, as did the adult on three legs. Now the leaders speeded up to a run. The speedometer read twenty-five miles an hour. Still the pups and the three-legged rear guard kept even. But now the leaders were putting on pressure and a gap was widening between adults and pups.

7 Since game flee an area in which a pack is running, a common tactic is to approach a rise at high speed on the chance of surprising prey on the far side. Such speed for the three leaders, with whom none could keep up, was over forty miles an hour. They outdistanced us, and by the time we reached the rise the three had stopped, the others were catching up, and across the empty valley beyond, Thomson's gazelles were stotting half a mile away. The word was being spread. Hunting dogs kill by surprise in ten or fifteen minutes or have a long search ahead through a forewarned world. Yet 85 percent of all hunts observed by Schaller have been successful, a record to stun a lion pride.

8 The leaders were moving again in a new direction at a modest run, the whole torchlight parade of bouncing white tails reassembled behind them. Then the leaders were digging in at full run and we could see three large wart hogs ahead running at an angle to our left toward their hole. That monstrous machine, the Land Rover, will survive cross-country driving at such speed, but only with difficulty will its human occupants. I lost the wart hogs. Within my view, however, the dogs were beginning one of their notable maneuvers. When prey curves in its flight, each dog in the file sets a separate course so that the pack is like narrowly set spokes in a wheel. They are not following; that is left to the leaders. They are setting courses of interception along the probable curve. But now there was no necessity. The wart hogs had vanished and we thought they had made it underground. But the leaders were struggling, for they had caught the last one by the hind legs and all one could hear was the squealing of the wart hog.

9 "Poor pig," said Schaller. Like a first-class nightmare, one is unlikely to forget a hunting-dog kill, since it does not kill but eats its prey alive. Nothing has so contributed to hunting-dog horror as the long-drawn manner of its prey's death. But in truth the dog cannot kill. He is small, and his teeth are small, even for his size. He has forty-two, and they are designed for slicing, not killing. Only the cats have killing teeth; even the wolf, taking caribou or moose, will proceed as does the hunting dog. And yet, while nature may provide its explanations, the spectacle remains other than nice.

10 I find it a subject for meditation that within my limited career of animal-watching, the two images most horrid and sublime were separated by little over sixty seconds. By now the hundred-pound

wart hog's viscera were torn open and he was finished, though still squealing. Then the fourteen pups arrived, crowding into the living feast. And with their arrival every adult stepped back, none with more than a mouthful of meat. They were undoubtedly hungry, for their bellies were lean. Now and again they would string themselves out in hunting formation at some hint of further prey. But in the hour and fifteen minutes that Schaller and I sat beside the kill, no adult took another mouthful of meat. The food was exclusively for the pups.

11 We sat in the gathering darkness in the middle of a plain emptied of all living creatures by fear of these formidable little beasts. And we discussed what course of natural selection could have produced such inhibition favoring the young. Only a very high adult death rate could place such selective value on the successful raising of young to maturity. I speculated on disability. In the lion pride all cubs eat last, and if kills are few or small, they starve. But the adult lion is very nearly invulnerable. The hunting dog, small and relatively fragile, may suffer a high casualty rate when attacking prey more formidable than wart hogs. Schaller shook his head. "I think disease," he said.

12 When it grew too dark to stay longer, we drove away. And six months later Schaller wrote me that distemper had hit the pack, leaving only nine survivors. When the young have it good, there is a reason somewhere.

Questions About "Observation"

1. Cite three or more specific details that indicate how carefully Ardrey observed his surroundings.
2. What does Ardrey infer from the strolling by of four zebras at a distance of several hundred yards?

Questions Diction and Writing Techniques

1. In paragraph 1 there is an example of simile: "like ping-pong paddles." Find other examples of simile in paragraphs 4, 5, and 9.

2. In paragraphs 4 and 5, Ardrey chooses temporal diction to guide his readers through a time sequence: "finally" (par. 4); "then" and "last" (par. 5). List at least five more examples of his use of such words in the rest of the selection.
3. Ardrey might have written the last sentence in paragraph 5:

   "One of the most memorable sights in nature, however, is that of a pack strung out, headed into the late light with tails upraised."

   Which of the versions of the sentence do you prefer? Why?
4. The paragraphs in this essay might be grouped 1–3, 4–10, and 11–12. What is the function of each group in Ardrey's plan of organization?
5. Does Ardrey give you enough information to make clear to you why the African hunting dog is successful as a hunter? Explain.
6. Does Ardrey make clear to you "what course of natural selection could have produced such inhibition favoring the young" (par. 11)?
7. Does Ardrey give you sufficient specific information for you to accept as valid his general statement "When the young have it good, there is a reason somewhere" (par. 12)? Explain.

For Discussion, Reading, and Writing

1. To what does Ardrey attribute the African hunting dog's success as a hunter?
2. How does Ardrey explain the terror that the African hunting dog holds for other animals?
3. Write a paragraph or two about the adult-young relations of any creatures you have had occasion to observe.
4. Prepare to write a short essay by observing with care any part of your school or other environment. Make notes of what you observe. From your observations, note-taking, and thinking about your subject, find a suitable thesis (such as Ardrey's, "When the young have it good, there is a reason somewhere."). Write the essay.

DEAD HEAT

Dick Cavett

Dick Cavett, best known as a TV personality, is also a contributing editor of *Saturday Review.*

---

1 It's like a bad dream, a man the color of chalk is lying on a table with an oxygen mask over his face. Some sort of monitoring device seems to be checking his vital signs. He is conscious, but the young man on the next table is not and grim-faced emergency-room volunteers are inserting a needle into a vein. A stretcher arrives with an unconscious figure soaked in sweat and shivering, a drip-bottle feeding into his arm.

2 There are long rows of stretchers on the ground, each containing a blanketed victim. Some are being asked where they hurt and others are just lying there looking dazed and disoriented.

3 Where am I? Is this the aftermath of a terrorist bombing? The scene of a passenger train collision? On location for a disaster flick? Or have I been transported in time to the roadside of the Bataan death march?

4 The correct answer is none of the above. I am in dear old Central Park and the occasion is that annual festival of fun and frolic, the New York City Marathon.

5 I had always been out of town on the big day, so I thought it might be fun to don my jogging gear and go over to the area of the finish line, clasp a few hands, give out some cups of water and congratulate the finishers. I hadn't bargained for ending up in what looked like Custer's battlefield after the gunsmoke had cleared.

6 On the way over I had entered into the spirit of the thing, joining in with the self-appointed curbside boosters in shouting "You can do it!" to the numbered runners fighting to keep going. Now,

seeing the carnage, I realize this was akin to yelling "Jump!" to a man on a windowledge.

7 It occurs to me that it's all relatively easy for the early finishers. They only torture themselves for a couple of hours. I am seeing the later arrivals, some of whom have struggled for twice as long and longer.

8 "What does all this have to do with fitness?" I ask a doctor in a tent tersely labeled "Acute." "Not a goddam thing. It makes me sick," he replies. I ask another medic how many people are in shape to run twenty-six miles in this humidity without risk. "Nobody is," he states flatly, and goes on to say that anyone running in this weather is risking heat stroke, a pesky little hazard, one of whose early symptoms is death.

9 Someone reports that they are now "collapsing like flies" as they come off the bridge and I hear an ominous "611" barked into a walkie-talkie. "What's that mean?" I ask reluctantly. "That's how many emergencies we have treated so far. It'll be over a thousand before long. You should have been here earlier. This is the part of the marathon they don't show you."

10 Twenty yards away I can see attractive young girls handing out gaily beribboned "finisher" medals to all who manage to struggle over the line. Overhearing phrases like "dangerously low blood pressure," "acute chest pain" and "defibrillator," I wonder if handing out little dunce caps might be more appropriate. A lady doc says, "Some of the damage will show up months from now." I feel myself suddenly turning against the whole sport and having to remind myself that this is not exercise but excess, a perversion of the idea of fitness. If a teaspoon of medicine is good for you, a tubful must be better.

11 These people are not all dodos by any means, and yet you would think that anyone with an I.Q. at least as high as the day's humidity level (ninety-six) would know the difference between beneficial exercise and masochism. How smart is it to take pride in all this super-macho hitting-the-wall jazz? Wouldn't putting up a real wall and letting people slam into it save a lot of time and be just as much fun?

12 A drenched and zombielike figure wanders by unsteadily, his expression one of sheer taxidermy. "You do this for your health?" I ask, surprised at my sarcasm. "No more," he mutters.

13 What can we say about all this? Might it be time, peradventure, to review the long-term benefits of acute cramping, shin-splints, cartilage damage and the opportunity to have diarrhea in front of millions of fascinated TV viewers? Is there a smidgen of inconsistency in applauding the mother of five who claws her way off the stretcher and drags her exhausted and dehydrated carcass across the painted line, while in other contexts we admonish the young not to abuse their bodies?

14 I realize that only one man dropped dead during the race, and so I am merely *posing* these questions. I certainly wouldn't want to spoil anyone's fun.

Questions About "Observation"

1. Mark in your text the paragraphs and underline the sentences and phrases that make clear to you how well Cavett observed the New York City Marathon. How does careful observation relate to his purpose in writing this essay?

2. In addition to using his eyes, Cavett used his ears. Point out instances of this. What does the information gathered in that way add to the essay?

3. Why, for a writer seeking material for an essay, was the finish line a useful vantage point for viewing the marathon?

Questions on Diction and Writing Techniques

1. How does your dictionary define "aftermath" (par. 3), "carnage" (par. 6), "perversion" (par. 10), "masochism" (par. 12), "taxidermy" and "peradventure" (par. 13)? Use each of these words in a sentence.

2. Underline in your text two or more instances of Cavett's choice of simile to increase the impact of his description of the scene at the finish line.

3. Cavett might have written in paragraph 7:

   They only exert themselves for a couple of hours. I am seeing the later arrivals, some of whom have run for twice as long and longer.

   Why did he choose the verbs he did?

4. Cavett might have begun his essay with a one-sentence paragraph:

   I am in dear old Central Park and the occasion is that annual festival of fun and frolic, the New York City Marathon.

   Why did he start the essay as he did?

5. What is Cavett's purpose in writing two of the sentences in paragraph 13 as rhetorical questions?

6. Evaluate paragraph 14 as a concluding paragraph.

7. Is the thesis of this essay expressed or implied? Explain.

For Discussion, Reading, and Writing

1. Observe carefully any strenuous athletic contest, whether in person or on TV, at its beginning and end, making notes as you do so. Summarize your perceptions in a paragraph of not over one hundred words.

2. There are arguments pro and con running (or jogging) as a form of exercise. Using observation as your primary source of material, write a short essay on the subject. (You might find chatting with a runner a convenient source of useful information; see "Reading and Interviews" pages 154–174.)

3. Be prepared to discuss in class how a change in vantage point can affect one's observation of, for example, the scene of an accident, a crowded bus, a sports event. To better appreciate the effect of a change in vantage point on observation, consider a commonplace event near at hand: a meeting of your English class. Sit (with the permission of your instructor) in the first row one day, in the last row another day).

Diaries and Journals

And so I plowed through the first draft, leaning heavily on the journal entry for data.

—Annie Dillard

A renowned concert pianist is said to have remarked, "When I don't practice one day, I know it. When I miss practice two days, my wife knows it. When I fail to practice three days, my audience knows it." Skill in writing also requires continual practice. One way of achieving it is by keeping a diary or journal.

"Diary" and "journal" are virtually synonymous terms. If there is a useful distinction between them, it is that a diary may be more private, more intimate than a journal and that in a journal the writer is more likely not only to record, but also to reflect on what took place.

If you are among the beginning writers who are self-conscious or hypercritical of their writing, the privacy of a diary may help you to write more freely. In your diary you need not be concerned about grammar, spelling, punctuation, or anything else—such as the possibility of adverse criticism by your composition teacher—that might inhibit putting your ideas on paper.

One reason for keeping a diary is it can be a repository of information that you might incorporate in more formal writing—to fulfill, for example, writing assignments in your courses in college. Thus a diary can be—in addition to a kind of writing—a source of material. In it you might incorporate information and ideas derived from personal experience and observations.

Other reasons for keeping a diary or journal are

1. To keep a record of one's activities
2. To record a personal experience and one's feelings and thoughts about it
3. To evaluate an experience and to discover its significance
4. To train oneself to become more observant
5. To become more reflective

By allowing one to give vent to feelings that might otherwise be bottled up, keeping a diary can also be useful as a sort of therapy.

An entry in Thoreau's *Journal* illustrates the opportunity a journal or diary offers for reflection:

> It occurred to me when I awoke this morning, feeling regret for intemperance of the day before in eating fruit, which had dulled my sensibilities, that man was to be treated as a musical instrument, and if any viol was to be made of sound timber and kept well tuned always, it was he, so that when the bow of events is drawn across him he may vibrate and resound in perfect harmony. A sensitive soul will be continually trying its strings to see if they are in tune. A man's body must be rasped down exactly to a shaving. It is of far more importance than the wood of a Cremona violin [Henry David Thoreau, *Journal,* September 12, 1853].

Thoreau might have written merely

> Woke up today feeling ill. Overindulged the day before.

Instead he mulls over his experience and, illuminating his conclusion with an apt analogy, writes a cogent statement about how one should care for one's body.

When should you write in your diary? As often as appeals to you, during any free time you have. If you're like most people, you probably won't find time unless you make up your mind to write daily or on alternate days at the same time each day.

How much should you write? Consider a few conservative entries Nathaniel Hawthorne made in his journal in August 1850:

> *August 8th*
>
> E. P. Whipple & wife took tea.
>
> *August 12th*
>
> Seven chickens hatched. Afternoon, J. T. Headley and brother called.—Eight chickens.
>
> *August 19th*
>
> Monument Mountain, in the early sunshine; its base enveloped in mist, parts of which are floating in the sky; so that the great hill looks really as if it were founded on a cloud. Just emerging from the mist is seen a yellow field of rye, and above that, forest.
>
> *August 21st (Wednesday)*
>
> Eight more chickens hatched.—Ascended a mountain with wife; a beautiful, mellow, autumnal sunshine.
>
> *August 24th*
>
> In the afternoons, now-a-days, this valley in which I dwell seems like a vast basin, filled with golden sunshine as with wine.

Don't frown upon trivial entries. Anything that comes to mind, however seemingly insignificant, could be included. One reason for this is that your ability to write will improve with any writing you do regularly. (See Peter Elbow's "Freewriting," pp. 339–340.)

Consider these short entries Virginia Woolf made in her diary in 1940:

> *Friday, June 7th*
>
> Just [back] from London this roasting hot evening. The great battle which decides our life or death goes on. Last night an air raid here. Today battle sparks. Up till 2:30 this morning.
>
> *Friday, August 23*
>
> Book flopped. Sales down to 15 a day since air raid on London. Is that the reason? Will it pick up?

> *Monday, September 2nd*
>
> There might be no war, the past two days. Only one air raid warning. Perfectly quiet nights. A lull after the attacks on London.

Entries may be brief notes or essays in miniature.

How factual should one be in a diary? Joan Didion, in "On Keeping a Notebook," wrote: "So the point of my keeping a notebook has never been, nor is it now, to have an accurate factual record of what I have been doing or thinking . . . *How it felt to me:* that is getting closer to the truth about a notebook . . . *Remember what it was to me:* that is always the point." But this is her view of what a notebook (journal or diary) should be like. It need not be yours.

Writing is a useful way for you to clarify your thinking; writing in a diary gives you a chance to do this before an audience that is always handy. Eric Hoffer was a longshoreman when he wrote, "I had to sort things out; to talk to somebody. So . . . I began a diary." He is now a well-known essayist, with several books to his credit. His diary, kept during 1958 and 1959, appeared as *Working and Thinking on the Waterfront.* These are its first entries:

> *June 1, 1958*
>
> 5 A.M. I am getting self-righteous. This usually happens after a long stretch of work. I remember Tolstoi saying somewhere that work makes not only ants but men, too, cruel.
>
> 4 P.M. Went to the dentist to have my teeth cleaned. Lili and the boy met me afterwards and we went to the beach. We had a good, plentiful meal at the Hitchrack. It is long since I tasted such good liver. The boy has learned several dirty words. Lili does not seem alarmed.

Hoffer's entries demonstrate the range of material to be found in diaries—from the trivial ("Went to the dentist to have my teeth cleaned") to the philosophical ("I remember Tolstoi saying somewhere that work makes not only ants but men, too, cruel.").

PAPER IS PATIENT

Anne Frank

Anne Frank (1929–1945) and her family, Jews in hiding from the German secret police in Nazi-occupied Amsterdam, were discovered and arrested on August 4, 1944. Eight months later Anne died in the concentration camp at Bergen-Belsen. Her diary was found by friends and published in the United States in 1952.

Saturday, 20 June, 1942

1 I haven't written for a few days, because I wanted first of all to think about my diary. It's an odd idea for someone like me to keep a diary; not only because I have never done so before, but because it seems to me that neither I—nor for that matter anyone else—will be interested in the unbosomings of a thirteen-year-old schoolgirl. Still, what does that matter? I want to write, but more than that, I want to bring out all kinds of things that lie buried deep in my heart.

2 There is a saying that "paper is more patient than man"; it came back to me on one of my slightly melancholy days, while I sat chin in hand, feeling too bored and limp even to make up my mind whether to go out or stay at home. Yes, there is no doubt that paper is patient and as I don't intend to show this cardboard-covered notebook, bearing the proud name of "diary," to anyone, unless I find a real friend, boy or girl, probably nobody cares. And now I come to the root of the matter, the reason for my starting a diary: it is that I have no such real friend.

3 Let me put it more clearly, since no one will believe that a girl of thirteen feels herself quite alone in the world, nor is it so. I have darling parents and a sister of sixteen. I know about thirty people whom one might call friends—I have strings of boy friends, anxious to catch a glimpse of me and who, failing that, peep at me through

mirrors in class. I have relations, aunts and uncles, who are darlings too, a good home, no—I don't seem to lack anything. But it's the same with all my friends, just fun and joking, nothing more. I can never bring myself to talk of anything outside the common round. We don't seem to be able to get any closer, that is the root of the trouble. Perhaps I lack confidence, but anyway, there it is, a stubborn fact and I don't seem to be able to do anything about it.

4 Hence, this diary. In order to enhance in my mind's eye the picture of the friend for whom I have waited so long, I don't want to set down a series of bald facts in a diary like most people do, but I want this diary itself to be my friend, and I shall call my friend Kitty.

Questions About "Diaries and Journals"

1. What reasons for keeping a diary does Frank give?
2. Explain whether she achieves her purpose of avoiding setting down "a series of bald facts" (par. 4).

Questions on Diction and Writing Techniques

1. What is the derivation of "diary"?
2. How does Frank attain coherence between paragraphs 3 and 4?
3. What is the degree of formality of Frank's writing? Who is her audience? How are the two related?

For Discussion, Reading, and Writing

1. Fill the blanks in this passage from memory to make it intelligible:

   Hence, this ______. In order to enhance in my mind's eye the picture of the ______ for whom I have waited so long. I don't want to set down a series of bald ______ in a diary like most people do, but I want this ______ itself to be my ______, and I shall call my friend Kitty.

   Compare your words with those in paragraph 4.

2. Why does Frank say that it's an odd idea for her to keep a diary?
3. What do you take Frank to mean by "paper is patient" (par. 2)? Do you agree?
4. Do Frank's reasons for keeping a diary apply to you? Whether they do or not, explain in a paragraph or two why you will or will not keep one.
5. Whether or not you keep it up, start a diary and for a week or two make daily entries in it, however brief.
6. Write an entry in a diary in the form of a letter to a real or imaginary person on the subject of friendship.

FROM MAN TO BOY

John Coleman

John R. Coleman, during a sabbatical leave from the presidency of Haverford College, worked at a variety of menial jobs. The diary he kept was published in *Blue-Collar Journal* (1974).

Tuesday, March 27

1 One of the waitresses I find hard to take asked me at one point today, "Are you the boy who cuts the lemons?"

2 "I'm the man who does," I replied.

3 "Well, there are none cut." There wasn't a hint that she heard my point.

4 Dana, who has cooked here for twelve years or so, heard that exchange.

5 "It's no use, Jack," he said when she was gone. "If she doesn't

know now, she never will." There was a trace of a smile on his face, but it was a sad look all the same.

6 In that moment, I learned the full thrust of those billboard ads of a few years ago that said, "BOY. Drop out of school and that's what they'll call you the rest of your life." I had read those ads before with a certain feeling of pride; education matters, they said, and that gave a lift to my field. Today I saw them saying something else. They were untrue in part; it turns out that you'll get called "boy" if you do work that others don't respect even if you have a Ph.D. It isn't education that counts, but the job in which you land. And the ads spoke too of a sad resignation about the world. They assumed that some people just won't learn respect for others, so you should adapt yourself to them. Don't try to change them. Get the right job and they won't call *you* boy any more. They'll save it for the next man.

7 It isn't just people like this one waitress who learn slowly, if at all. Haverford College has prided itself on being a caring, considerate community in the Quaker tradition for many long years. Yet when I came there I soon learned that the cleaning women in the dormitories were called "wombats" by all the students. No one seemed to know where the name came from or what connection, if any, it had with the dictionary definition. *The American College Dictionary* says a wombat is "any of three species of burrowing marsupials of Australia . . . somewhat resembling ground hogs." The name was just one of Haverford's unexamined ways of doing things.

8 It didn't take much persuasion to get the name dropped. Today there are few students who remember it at all. But I imagine the cleaning women remember it well.

9 Certainly I won't forget being called a boy today.

Questions About "Diaries and Journals"

1. How does Coleman bring personal experience and observation to bear on this journal entry?
2. What conclusion does he arrive at?
3. Would his writing be as effective if he had not tried to find significance in the waitress's question? Explain.

Questions on Diction and Writing Techniques

1. Instead of reporting in the third person what the waitress and cook said, Coleman uses dialogue. Why?
2. What does he signal to you by using "but" (par. 6)? Find another instance of his use of this word in this essay for a similar reason.
3. What is the function of "yet" (par. 7)?
4. To better understand how Coleman organized his essay, divide it into parts consisting of one or more paragraphs and explain the function of each part.

For Discussion, Reading, and Writing

1. Why, according to Coleman, were the billboards in part untrue?
2. How, according to Coleman, were the students at Haverford College like the waitress?
3. Jot down notes, as in a journal entry, based on your recollection of an incident that you experienced or observed today. Think about the incident, considering its significance. Expand your notes into a draft of an essay. Develop them into a finished essay that you might want others to read.

HELP ME BUILD THIS BRIDGE

Sylvia Plath

Sylvia Plath (1932–1963) was an American poet, much of whose intensely personal writing (some published posthumously) presaged an early death by her own hand.

Excerpt from a letter to Richard Sassoon
December 11

1 What concerns me among multitudes and multitudes of other sad questions which one had better try to lure aside with parfaits and sunshine, is that there is a certain great sorrow in me now, with as many facets as a fly's eye, and I must give birth to this monstrosity before I am light again. Otherwise I shall resemble a dancing elephant. . . . I am tormented by the questions of the devils which weave my fibers with grave-frost and human dung, and have not the ability or genius to write a big letter to the world about this. When one makes of one's own heavens and hells a few hunks of neatly typewritten paper and editors are very polite and reject it, one is, in whimsy, inclined to identify editors with god's ministers. This is fatal.

2 Perhaps when we find ourselves wanting everything it is because we are dangerously near to wanting nothing. There are two opposing poles of wanting nothing: When one is so full and rich and has so many inner worlds that the outer world is not necessary for joy, because joy emanates from the inner core of one's being. When one is dead and rotten inside and there is nothing in the world.

3 I feel now as if I were building a very delicate intricate bridge quietly in the night, across the dark from one grave to another while the giant is sleeping. Help me build this O so exquisite bridge.

4 I want to live each day for itself like a string of colored beads, and not kill the present by cutting it up in cruel little snippets to fit some desperate architectural draft for a Taj Mahal in the future.

Questions About "Diaries and Journals"

1. This entry is an excerpt from a letter to Plath's boyfriend. Is a diary an appropriate repository for one's letters? Explain.
2. How does an intimate letter differ from a diary entry?
3. What does this entry reveal about Plath at the time she wrote it?

Questions on Diction and Writing Techniques

1. Define "facets" and "whimsy" (par. 1), "poles" and "emanates" (par. 2). Use each word in a sentence.
2. Underline in your text all figures of speech in this selection. What do they contribute to your understanding Plath's ideas?
3. Compare the tone of this selection with that of the diary entries of Anne Frank and John Coleman.

For Discussion, Reading, and Writing

1. Confide in a journal entry your innermost feelings, whether joyful or morbid.
2. Write an intimate letter, of any length, to someone dear to you.
3. For use in someday writing a descriptive essay, make notes, as in a journal entry, of the appearance of the place you are in now. Be sure to observe carefully and to include in your jottings all vivid and significant details.

Reading and Interviews

Interviewing is where the fun begins, and where you may uncover information that is accessible in no other way.

—Jessica Mitford

FROM the time when someone first reads to us as children we receive information secondhand. From the printed page, whether reading randomly or purposefully, we get much information not otherwise available. Everything we read—in books, magazines, newspapers—adds to our knowledge of the world. The accumulation of information so attained is greater by far than that achieved by our own experiences and observations, however great these may be. Consider how much you have learned from books and other writings since you first began to read, on subjects as diverse as literature, history, geography, biology, mathematics, and religion. Reading is an important source of a writer's material.

In college, you probably read more thoughtfully than before—to acquire information and to achieve understanding. When you read for information, you are seeking facts. When you read for understanding, you are looking beyond the facts to their significance. Your reading is particularly purposeful when you read for immediate uses and toward a specific goal: to increase your knowledge of a subject in preparation for writing an essay, a report, or a research paper, or for taking an exam. The experience of a writer from Hartford, Connecticut, will illustrate this purposefulness.

Mary Smith (or so we'll call her), while interviewing a bridge engineer in the Connecticut Highway Department to get material for a proposed essay on covered bridges, learned by chance that the engineer had an interest in whales and a concern for them as an endangered species. The engineer, Mary learned, was a member of the Connecticut Cetacean Society, whose purpose is to preserve the order *Cetacea* (aquatic, chiefly marine animals, including whales, dolphins, and porpoises). Its members were to go on their annual whale-watching trip in Cape Cod Bay in the middle of May, then three months away. That whales stopped off the coast of Massachusetts during their migrations was a surprise to Mary. Seeing in the whale-watching trip an occasion for a weekend outing and the subject of an essay, she started to prepare herself by gathering information about whales.

First she turned to the *Encyclopaedia Britannica* (1967 edition) where she found a 10½-page illustrated article on whales with sections such as "Whales in Legend and Literature," "Feeding Adaptations and Food," "Breeding and Reproduction," and "Migrations," and a bibliography of general and special references; a three-page article on whaling with sections such as "Early Whaling," "Modern Whaling," "Whale and Sperm Oils," and "Regulation"; and, in a long article on wildlife conservation, a short section on whales, giving a brief history of the measures taken to conserve them, including the creation of the International Whaling Commission (IWC). Then, for regional information about whales and whaling, Mary browsed through and read sections of books and pamphlets in the library of the Connecticut Historical Society in Hartford.

For up-to-date information about whales, she consulted *The New York Times Index,* where she discovered references to recent *Times* articles about whales and their conservation, and *The Readers' Guide to Periodical Literature,* where she found references to recent magazine articles on her subject.

On the weekend of May 13–14, Mary sailed from Provincetown on two four-hour trips in Cape Cod Bay on board *Dolphin III.* Sunday afternoon she spent at the whale and whaling exhibit at the Provincetown Museum and at the National Park Service building a few miles away, where she found and bought a useful slender volume, *Whale Fishery of New England.* Mary's reading and interviews (about which, more later), plus of course her personal experience and observations, resulted in an essay of about 1,250 words. I reproduce it here, complete:

Watching the Great Whales

May is the time of year when the biggest animals on planet Earth visit southern New England. Offshore, sometimes within a mile of land, one may encounter creatures from 30 to 60 feet long, weighing from 30 to 60 tons—the great whales.

Great whales is a term used to designate the ten largest cetaceans (from *cetus,* Latin for whale). They range in length from the 30-foot-long minke to the 100-foot blue whale and are among the 80 or so species of the order *Cetacea,* which includes porpoises and dolphins, the smaller members of the whale family.

Whales are migratory animals. Some travel eight thousand miles each year, from feeding grounds to calving grounds and back. Genuses of the Northern Hemisphere make an annual pilgrimage north in the late winter and spring, some from tropical to polar latitudes where planktonic food proliferates in the summer. On their way north in the spring and again en route to the Caribbean and the equator in the fall, a number of them stop over in southern New England waters, using them as a picnic area where for a few weeks they enjoy a regional fare of plankton, herring, and the 3- to 4-inch-long sand lance or sand eel.

On a recent weekend a group of ninety Connecticut residents from many parts of the state, including New Britain, Glastonbury, Rocky Hill, Avon, and Hartford, went hunting for these whales in Cape Cod Bay on a trip sponsored by the Children's Museum of Hartford and led by its administrative director, Frank Gardner. These modern Queequegs—cameras in hand instead of harpoons—shipped out on two successive days on four-hour whale-watching trips aboard a latter-day *Pequod:* the trim, broad-beamed, 90-foot steel-hulled fisherman, *Dolphin III* out of Provincetown, Albert Avellar, Captain.

Most of them are members of the Connecticut Cetacean Society (CCS), a conservation organization founded in 1973 that now has over seven hundred members, two hundred of them from out of state, and that is the only state organization of its kind in the country. Perhaps best known for its promotion of the successful campaign to have the sperm whale designated by the state legislature in 1975 as the official animal of Connecticut, the Society has the aim of preserving members of the order *Cetacea* by seeking the abolition of the killing of all whales.

This attitude toward whales is a far cry from that of Connecticut Yankees of other years.

Interest in whaling, in Connecticut, goes back to the colonial period. For more than half a century, until the early 1700s, whaling by Nutmeggers, on a relatively modest scale, was concentrated offshore and in Long Island Sound, where whales often appeared. In 1712, a ship whaling in Nantucket Sound Shoals was blown during a storm far out to sea, where its captain sighted a school of sperm whales. This species' oil of exceptional quality, used to make fine candles, lured New England whalers farther and farther away from the mainland and ultimately all over the Seven Seas.

At the height of whaling in America, the middle third of the last century, New London—which in its whaling heyday is said to have had more millionaires than any other town or city in the country—was the third most active whaling port, after only New Bedford, by far the biggest, and Nantucket. In one year its shipping included seventy whalers. At least 820 whaling voyages originated there from 1784 to 1876.

In Connecticut, second to New London, with 130 sailings from 1830 to 1860, was Stonington; third, with 105 whaling sailings, was Mystic, whose seaport now permanently berths—for us and later generations to inspect—the *Charles W. Morgan*, the last of the great American whaling vessels. Other Connecticut ports such as East Haddam, New Haven, and Bridgeport also from time to time cleared whaling ships.

After the Civil War, in part due to the discovery of petroleum, whose by-product kerosene first supplanted candles for illumination, the New England whaling industry, and with it Connecticut's, declined. The last whaling voyage to originate in Connecticut started in New London in 1909.

Nonetheless, whaling on a large scale, with modern whale catchers and factory ships, has continued. It has been estimated that more whales were killed in the last fifty years than in all of whaling history going back to the ninth century. The right whale, one of the great whales, may have been hunted to the verge of extinction; it is rarely sighted today.

Concern for the future of whaling and for whales led to the creation in 1946 of the International Whaling Commission, whose purpose is to pool statistics and to set limits on whale catches. But policing of the whaling nations' observance of quotas is difficult. Conservationists are, understandably, disturbed.

Thus the organizing of CCS, some of whose members, led by Dr. Robbins Barstow, its executive director, were among the whale watchers on board the *Dolphin III* when its crew cast off her lines at Macmillan pier in Provincetown harbor to search for whales in Cape Cod Bay.

The Connecticut whale watchers sighted from twenty to thirty fin (finback) whales at different times and in different parts of the bay, some as long as 60 feet. The more distant ones were first identified by their spouts only. When these were spotted, one would hear from some of the landlubbers the proverbial "Thar she blows!" Captain Avellar eased his ship as close to the whales as he could, generally within 50 to 250 feet. Two whales, one of them a 60-ton finback, crossed within 30 feet of the bow of *Dolphin III*.

With the help of marine biologist Dr. Charles "Stormy" Mayo of U. Mass., one minke whale was identified. But, neither a humpback nor any of the other great whales—except finbacks—that have been seen in Cape Cod Bay in recent years made an appearance.

However, at the end of the first day's search Captain Avellar sighted a school of hundreds of white-sided dolphins about a mile off the hook of Provincetown, between Wood's End and Long Point Lighthouse. An endangered species themselves, the dolphins were feeding, as is nature's way, on schools of tiny sand lance.

Captain Avellar guided his ship among them, and the Connecticut whale watchers had the opportunity of seeing these cetaceans put on a spectacular marine acrobatic performance, as from time to time, while pursuing their evening meal, the 6- to 8-foot-long dolphins leaped out of the water, for a moment hung suspended in air, and then slowly slid back into the sea.

The reaction of those on board ship to the display was summed up by Eunice Wallace, of Hartford: "It was dramatically thrilling, like a ballet. Baryshnikov couldn't have done better."

While on board the *Dolphin III*, Mary made notes of what she saw and of what she heard in conversations with the ship's first mate and members of CCS. She listened carefully and recorded in a notebook the gist of a brief introductory talk by Dr. Mayo. She jotted down information that the marine biologist gave intermittently over a loudspeaker in his reports of and comments on his sightings of whales. Mary also introduced herself to Mr. Gardner and Dr. Barstow (who in turn introduced her to Dr. Mayo), asked them questions that came to mind about whales, and asked each if she might visit them in Hartford for an interview. Both readily and cordially agreed.

Back in Hartford, Mary decided to write a first draft of her essay before phoning to make appointments with Mr. Gardner and Dr. Barstow because (1) she had enough information to get started, (2) she could already see how to organize what material she had, and (3) the questions to be put to them would, she thought, be more specific and more thorough after she discovered in the course of writing a first draft what information she still needed to make her essay complete.

Mary made appointments over the phone to see Dr. Barstow at his place of work and Mr. Gardner at the Children's Museum. She then borrowed a tape recorder from the audiovisual department of her college. Having completed a first draft of her essay and through it having found what gaps in her knowledge of her subject seemed to remain, she made a list of questions she would ask the executive director of CCS, among them:

When was the CCS organized?

Who were its founders?

What prompted them to start it?

How many members did it start out with?

How many does CCS have now?

When did you join it? Why?

What is CCS's purpose?

How well is it fulfilling that aim?

Why are you concerned about the fate of the cetaceans?

Mary's list of questions for the administrative director of the Children's Museum, for the purpose of rounding out the information garnered previously, included:

Why do whales stop off in Cape Cod Bay during their migrations?

We saw during the weekend one minke and a number of finbacks. Has the humpback or any other of the great whales been sighted there in recent years?

What do whales feed on in Cape Cod Bay?

How many dolphins do you estimate we saw on Saturday?

How big do you think they were?

What were they feeding on?

Is there a rule for estimating the weight of a whale? If so, what is it?

Dr. Barstow and Mr. Gardner were not only willing, but eager to talk about their favorite subject in detail and at length. In addition to using the tape recorder, Mary jotted down notes on her sheet of questions, in part to remind herself to pursue lines of inquiry suggested by some of the responses and new ideas presented by the two men. Dr. Barstow gave her copies of recent issues of the CCS monthly bulletin and a copy of a little book that he and the president of CCS, Don Stineti, who did the artwork, had put together—*Meet the Great Ones: An Introduction to Whales and Other Cetaceans.* In response to Mary's final question, both men interviewed said, "Yes, if you need any more information, please don't hesitate to phone."

The interview is not often utilized in college writing. Yet it is a handy and fruitful source of material for a writer. From it you can get firsthand information and opinions on almost any subject, often from experts whose knowledge is invaluable. People like to talk about themselves and their concerns, and they enjoy being called upon to give information, whether specialized or not, and to state their opinions. They are generally flattered by being interviewed, willing to answer questions, and almost always cooperative.

The more you learn about your subject before the interview, the more definitive will your questions be. It is a good idea to bring to an interview a list of carefully prepared questions phrased to plug the gaps in your knowledge and a scheme—however tentative—for the organization of your material in a proposed essay. Nevertheless, you may find that the interview may take a turn that you did not anticipate. This may be all to the good, for the person interviewed may introduce material about which you did not have, and perhaps could not have had, prior knowledge. But if you want to control the direction the interview takes, it is best to follow as closely as possible the sequence of your prepared questions.

Note taking is always useful, but too much of it—especially if it delays proceedings—may distract the person interviewed and cause her or his interest to wane. In any case, a tape recorder—if the interviewee does not object to your using one—will be beneficial because of the ease and completeness with which it records conversation.

Even with carefully prepared questions and reasonably good responses, you may find, when you start to incorporate into your writing the information gathered in an interview, unexpected gaps in your knowledge. More likely than not, a phone call to the person you interviewed will get you the needed information.

The results make the interview worthwhile. It is indispensable when the information you seek is nowhere else available. Also, direct quotation—which must be done carefully and accurately—of an interviewee, even when the information is neither essential nor unique, is likely to sound more convincing than your own words. Knowledge given firsthand by the interviewee is likely to seem to your reader more immediate, vivid, and authoritative than your transcription of it.

JAILBREAK MARRIAGE

Gail Sheehy

Gail Sheehy is an award-winning reporter, essayist, and frequent contributor to magazines. Her books include *Passages* (1976), the source of this selection, which is about the "predictable crises of adult life."

---

1 Although the most commonplace reason women marry young is to "complete" themselves, a good many spirited young women gave another reason: "I did it to get away from my parents." Particularly for girls whose educations and privileges are limited, a *jailbreak marriage* is the usual thing. What might appear to be an act of rebellion usually turns out to be a transfer of dependence.

2 A lifer: that is how it felt to be Simone at 17, how it often feels for girls in authoritarian homes. The last of six children, she was caught in the nest vacated by the others and expected to "keep the family together." Simone was the last domain where her mother could play out the maternal role and where her father could exercise full control. That meant good-bye to the university scholarship.

3 Although the family was not altogether poor, Simone had tried to make a point of her independence by earning her own money since the age of 14. Now she thrust out her bankbook. Would two thousand dollars in savings buy her freedom?

4 "We want you home until you're 21."

5 Work, her father insisted. But the job she got was another closed gate. It was in the knitting machine firm where her father worked, an extension of his control. Simone knuckled under for a year until she met Franz. A zero. An egocentric Hungarian of pointless aristocracy, a man for whom she had total disregard. Except for one attraction. He asked her to marry him. Franz would be the getaway vehicle in her jailbreak marriage scheme: "I decided the

best way to get out was to get married and divorce him a year later. That was my whole program."

6 Anatomy, uncontrolled, sabotaged her program. Nine months after the honeymoon, Simone was a mother. Resigning herself, she was pregnant with her second child at 20.

7 One day, her husband called with the news, the marker event to blast her out of the drift. His firm had offered him a job in New York City.

8 "Then and there, I decided that before the month was out I would have the baby, find a lawyer, and start divorce proceedings." The next five years were like twenty. It took every particle of her will and patience to defeat Franz, who wouldn't hear of a separation, and to ignore the ostracism of her family.

9 At the age of 25, on the seventh anniversary of her jailbreak marriage (revealed too late as just another form of entrapment), Simone finally escaped her parents. Describing the day of her decree, the divorcée sounds like so many women whose identity was foreclosed by marriage: "It was like having ten tons of chains removed from my mind, my body—the most exhilarating day of my life."

Questions About "Reading and Interviews"

1. What evidence is there in this piece that Sheehy used interviews as a source of her material?
2. What is Sheehy's purpose in this essay? How does the use of interviews help her achieve that purpose?
3. What impact does Sheehy's use of interview material have on you?
4. Rewrite one or two of Simone's remarks in the third person. Compare the effect on you of this method of reporting an interview with that of direct quotation, which Sheehy uses.

Questions on Diction and Writing Techniques

1. Define and use in sentences "domain" (par. 2) and "egocentric" (par. 5).

2. Comment on whether "jailbreak marriage" (par. 1) is an apt phrase. Find two other metaphors (see pages 88–89) that are consistent with "jailbreak."

3. Sheehy might have written the first sentence of paragraph 2 like this: "To Simone at 17 it felt like being a lifer, the way it often feels for girls in authoritarian homes." What was the writer's purpose in writing the sentence the way she did?

4. What is the derivation of "good-bye" (par. 2)?

5. Sheehy might have written the first sentence of paragraph 5 like this: "Her father insisted that she work." Why did she choose the inverted word order?

6. Combine sentences 3 ("Simone knuckled under . . .") through 7 (ending with "to marry him") of paragraph 5 into one sentence. Which version do you prefer? Why?

7. What words might Sheehy have chosen as alternatives to "sabotage" (par. 6)? Which verb do you prefer? Why?

For Discussion, Reading, and Writing

1. This essay is mainly about (circle one):

   A. Simone's marriage to Franz.

   B. Simone's distaste for Franz.

   C. Simone's attempt to find her own identity.

   D. why some women marry young.

   E. why some women run away from home.

2. Using the interview as your major source of material, write a paragraph or two about "an act of rebellion" (par. 1) by any person you know.

3. Interview young couples to gather your material and then write an essay on a restricted subject having to do with marriage.

4. Write an essay, based on interviews with your parents, grandparents, teachers, or any other older persons, on some aspect of

   birth control

   motherhood without marriage

   premarital sex

   trial marriage

   abortion

THROW-AWAY SOCIETY

Alvin Toffler

Alvin Toffler, editor, correspondent, and lecturer, is best known as a social thinker. In *Future Shock* (1970), the source of this excerpt, he writes about our system of values, about changes in our industrial society and how we adapt to them.

---

1 "Barbie," a twelve-inch plastic teen-ager, is the best-known and best-selling doll in history. Since its introduction in 1959, the Barbie doll population of the world has grown to 12,000,000—more than the human population of Los Angeles or London or Paris. Little girls adore Barbie because she is highly realistic and eminently dress-upable. Mattel, Inc., makers of Barbie, also sells a complete wardrobe for her, including clothes for ordinary daytime wear, clothes for formal party wear, clothes for swimming and skiing.

2 Recently Mattel announced a new improved Barbie doll. The new version has a slimmer figure, "real" eyelashes, and a twist-and-turn waist that makes her more humanoid than ever. Moreover,

Mattel announced that, for the first time, any young lady wishing to purchase a new Barbie would receive a trade-in allowance for her old one.

3 What Mattel did not announce was that by trading in her old doll for a technologically improved model, the little girl of today, citizen of tomorrow's super-industrial world, would learn a fundamental lesson about the new society: that man's relationships with *things* are increasingly temporary.

4 The ocean of man-made physical objects that surrounds us is set within a larger ocean of natural objects. But increasingly, it is the technologically produced environment that matters for the individual. The texture of plastic or concrete, the iridescent glisten of an automobile under a streetlight, the staggering vision of a cityscape seen from the window of a jet—these are the intimate realities of his existence. Man-made things enter into and color his consciousness. Their number is expanding with explosive force, both absolutely and relative to the natural environment. This will be even more true in super-industrial society than it is today.

5 That man-thing relationships are growing more and more temporary may be illustrated by examining the culture surrounding the little girl who trades in her doll. This child soon learns that Barbie dolls are by no means the only physical objects that pass into and out of her young life at a rapid clip. Diapers, bibs, paper napkins, Kleenex, towels, non-returnable soda bottles—all are used up quickly in her home and ruthlessly eliminated. Corn muffins come in baking tins that are thrown away after one use. Spinach is encased in plastic sacks taht can be dropped into a pan of boiling water for heating, and then thrown away. TV dinners are cooked and often served on throw-away trays. Her home is a large processing machine through which objects flow, entering and leaving, at a faster and faster rate of speed. From birth on, she is inextricably embedded in a throw-away culture.

6 The idea of using a product once or for a brief period and then replacing it, runs counter to the grain of societies or individuals steeped in a heritage of poverty. Not long ago Uriel Rone, a market researcher for the French advertising agency Publicis, told me: "The French housewife is not used to disposable products. She likes to keep things, even old things, rather than throw them away.

We represented one company that wanted to introduce a kind of plastic throw-away curtain. We did a marketing study for them and found the resistance too strong." This resistance, however, is dying all over the developed world.

7 Thus a writer, Edward Maze, has pointed out that many Americans visiting Sweden in the early 1950's were astounded by its cleanliness. "We were almost awed by the fact that there were no beer and soft drink bottles by the roadsides, as, much to our shame, there were in America. But by the 1960's, lo and behold, bottles were suddenly blooming along Swedish highways . . . What happened? Sweden had become a buy, use and throw-away society, following the American pattern." In Japan today throw-away tissues are so universal that cloth handkerchiefs are regarded as old fashioned, not to say unsanitary. In England for sixpence one may buy a "Dentamatic throw-away toothbrush" which comes already coated with toothpaste for its one-time use. And even in France, disposable cigarette lighters are commonplace. From cardboard milk containers to the rockets that power space vehicles, products created for short-term or one-time use are becoming more numerous and crucial to our way of life.

8 The recent introduction of paper and quasi-paper clothing carried the trend toward disposability a step further. Fashionable boutiques and working-class clothing stores have sprouted whole departments devoted to gaily colored and imaginatively designed paper apparel. Fashion magazines display breathtakingly sumptuous gowns, coats, pajamas, even wedding dresses made of paper. The bride pictured in one of these wears a long white train of lace-like paper that, the caption writer notes, will make "great kitchen curtains" after the ceremony.

9 We develop a throw-away mentality to match our throw-away products. This mentality produces, among other things, a set of radically altered values with respect to property. But the spread of disposability through the society also implies decreased durations in man-thing relationships. Instead of being linked with a single object over a relatively long span of time, we are linked for brief periods with the succession of objects that supplant it.

Questions About "Reading and Interviews"

1. Point out what material in this essay Toffler derived from interviews and what from reading.
2. How might Toffler have secured the information contained in paragraph 1?
3. How do the writer's sources of material in this essay relate to his purpose in writing it?

Questions on Diction and Writing Techniques

1. What does the amount of detailed information in paragraph 1 contribute to its effectiveness as an opening paragraph?
2. Define and use in sentences "humanoid" (par. 2), "boutiques" (par. 8), "sumptuous" (par. 8).
3. What purpose is served by "moreover" (par. 2), "however" (par. 6), "thus" (par. 7), "but" (par. 9)?
4. Find an example of metaphor in paragraph 4 and another in paragraph 5.
5. Toffler might have written sentence 3 of paragraph 4 like this: "The intimate realities of his existence are the texture of plastic or concrete, the iridescent glisten of an automobile under a streetlight, the staggering vision of a cityscape seen from the window of a jet." Which version better emphasizes the main idea he wants to convey to you?
6. What is the main idea of paragraph 5? Is any information that you need in order to understand and accept the idea not given?
7. What is the topic sentence of paragraph 7? Can you justify placing it elsewhere in the paragraph? Comment on whether it is well explained.
8. What words might Toffler have chosen instead of "sprouted" (par. 8)? Which do you prefer? Why?
9. What is an essay's thesis (see pages 2–9)? Where does the writer of this essay digress? Is the essay unified? Explain.

For Discussion, Reading, and Writing

1. Which of these statements, according to Toffler, are true (T), which false (F)?

   A. ______ Little girls like Barbie because she is unbreakable.

   B. ______ The new, improved Barbie doll is more humanoid than ever.

   C. ______ Our relationships with things are increasingly temporary.

   D. ______ Products created for short-term or one-time use are good for business.

   E. ______ We develop a throw-away mentality to match our throw-away products.

2. Might there be a correlation between "decreased durations in man-thing relationships" (par. 9) and decreased duration in man-woman relations? If this subject interests you, write an essay about it based on interviews with married, divorced, or single persons you know.

3. What benefit, if any, is there in "being linked with a single object over a relatively long span of time" (par. 9)? Write a short essay on the subject.

4. Using the textbooks in a course you are taking or have taken as your main source of material, write an essay explaining a thesis related to the topic "The Throw-Away Society."

5. Using reading, interviews, or both as your chief sources of material, write a short essay on disposable clothing, throw-away drink containers, automobile junkyards, garbage dumps, or any other product or by-product of "the throw-away society."

THE PROBLEM THAT HAS NO NAME

Betty Friedan

Betty Friedan, American writer and social reformer, is active in the feminist movement. Her popular *The Feminine Mystique* (1963) helped draw attention to American women's lack of fulfillment as childbearers and housewives.

---

1 Gradually I came to realize that the problem that has no name was shared by countless women in America. As a magazine writer I often interviewed women about problems with their children, or their marriages, or their houses, or their communities. But after a while I began to recognize the telltale signs of this other problem. I saw the same signs in suburban ranch houses and split-levels on Long Island and in New Jersey and Westchester County; in colonial houses in a small Massachusetts town; on patios in Memphis; in suburban and city apartments; in living rooms in the Midwest. Sometimes I sensed the problem, not as a reporter, but as a suburban housewife, for during this time I was also bringing up my own three children in Rockland County, New York. I heard echoes of the problem in college dormitories and semi-private maternity wards, at PTA meetings and luncheons of the League of Women Voters, at suburban cocktail parties, in station wagons waiting for trains, and in snatches of conversations overheard at Schrafft's. The groping words I heard from other women, on quiet afternoons when children were at school or on quiet evenings when husbands worked late, I think I understood first as a woman long before I understood their larger social and psychological implications.

2 Just what was this problem that has no name? What were the words women used when they tried to express it? Sometimes a woman would say, "I feel empty somehow . . . incomplete." Or she would say, "I feel as if I don't exist." Sometimes she blotted out the

feeling with a tranquilizer. Sometimes she thought the problem was with her husband, or her children, or that what she really needed was to redecorate her house, or move to a better neighborhood, or have an affair, or another baby. Sometimes, she went to a doctor with symptoms she could hardly describe: "A tired feeling . . . I get so angry with the children it scares me . . . I feel like crying without any reason." (A Cleveland doctor called it "the housewife's syndrome.") A number of women told me about great bleeding blisters that break out on their hands and arms. "I call it the housewife's blight," said a family doctor in Pennsylvania. "I see it so often lately in these young women with four, five and six children who bury themselves in their dishpans. But it isn't caused by detergent and it isn't cured by cortisone."

3 Sometimes a woman would tell me that the feeling gets so strong she runs out of the house and walks through the streets. Or she stays inside her house and cries. Or her children tell her a joke, and she doesn't laugh because she doesn't hear it. I talked to women who had spent years on the analyst's couch, working out their "adjustment to the feminine role," their blocks to "fulfillment as a wife and mother." But the desperate tone in these women's voices, and the look in their eyes, was the same as the tone and the look of other women, who were sure they had no problem, even though they did have a strange feeling of desperation.

4 A mother of four who left college at nineteen to get married told me:

> I've tried everything women are supposed to do—hobbies, gardening, pickling, canning, being very social with my neighbors, joining committees, running PTA teas. I can do it all, and I like it, but it doesn't leave you anything to think about—any feeling of who you are. I never had any career ambitions. All I wanted was to get married and have four children. I love the kids and Bob and my home. There's no problem you can even put a name to. But I'm desperate. I begin to feel I have no personality. I'm a server of food and a putter-on of pants and a bedmaker, somebody who can be called on when you want something. But who am I?

5 A twenty-three-year-old mother in blue jeans said:

I ask myself why I'm so dissatisfied. I've got my health, fine children, a lovely new home, enough money. My husband has a real future as an electronics engineer. He doesn't have any of these feelings. He says maybe I need a vacation, let's go to New York for a weekend. But that isn't it. I always had this idea we should do everything together. I can't sit down and read a book alone. If the children are napping and I have one hour to myself I just walk through the house waiting for them to wake up. I don't make a move until I know where the rest of the crowd is going. It's as if ever since you were a little girl, there's always been somebody or something that will take care of your life: your parents, or college, or falling in love, or having a child, or moving to a new house. Then you wake up one morning and there's nothing to look forward to.

6 A young wife in a Long Island development said:

I seem to sleep so much. I don't know why I should be so tired. This house isn't nearly so hard to clean as the cold-water flat we had when I was working. The children are at school all day. It's not the work. I just don't feel alive.

Questions About "Reading and Interviews"

1. How did Friedan find out about "the problem that has no name"?
2. What does the information in paragraph 2 add to what Friedan writes in paragraph 1?
3. Why does the writer include the quotations in paragraphs 2 through 6? Without the quotations, could she have set forth the ideas in those paragraphs as convincingly as she does with them? Explain. How are the paragraphs related to the writer's thesis?
4. Explain whether, and to what extent, your understanding of "the problem" is enhanced by Friedan's explanation of it in this piece.

Questions on Diction and Writing Techniques

1. Define "telltale" (par. 1) and use the word in a sentence.
2. What is the effect on you of the repetition of "problem that has no name" and of "problem" (par. 1)? Does the repetition contribute to the coherence of the selection? Explain.
3. What is Friedan's purpose in writing "Or" in paragraph 2? Find another instance in this essay of her use of this conjunction for the same reason.

For Discussion, Reading, and Writing

1. Friedan's conclusion in this essay is (circle one):

   A. Bringing up her own three children was crucial to Friedan's understanding the problem that has no name.

   B. Of the women interviewed by Friedan, the suburban housewives are the most unfulfilled.

   C. Women in rural America are happier than those elsewhere.

   D. The Equal Rights Amendment is the only solution to the problem that Friedan identifies.

   E. The problem that has no name was shared by countless women in America.

2. Using information in this essay or from other sources, including interviews, explain in a paragraph or two whether the proper place of a woman is in the home.
3. In 1869 John Stuart Mill wrote in "The Subjection of Women" (italics added): "The principle which regulates the existing social relations between the two sexes—the legal subordination of one sex to the other—is wrong in itself, and now one of the chief hindrances to human improvement; . . . *it ought to be replaced by a principle of perfect equality, admitting no power or privilege on the one side, nor disability on the other.*" Using specific details and recommendations, write a short essay that explains clearly your views on the italicized portion of Mill's statement.

4. Using as your main source of material interviews of your mother, aunts, sisters, or any other women you know well, write a short essay that explains the frustration or the success of some woman or women in making their lives interesting, satisfying, purposeful. (You may be able to borrow a tape recorder from the audiovisual department of your college to record your interviews.)

4

Types of Essays

Narration

Careful observation, significant details, characterization, insight into a character or a situation—all these can be as much a part of good factual writing as they are of fiction. And the basic techniques of both are and always have been the same: exposition, description, and narration.

—Lillian Ross

THE information that a writer gathers from the various sources of material discussed in Part Three may be used in one or another of four types of essays: narration, description, exposition, and argumentation. (Narration, description, and exposition are discussed in the three sections of Part Four. Argumentation will be treated separately, following Part Five.) Although for convenience we will examine them one at a time, an essay may contain elements of two or more types, in any combination. An expository essay–whose purpose is to explain–might narrate, might describe, and might argue a point to convince readers to accept the writer's beliefs. Langston Hughes' "Salvation" (pages 188–190) is an essay containing elements of more than one type of composition. To be sure, it does tell a story. But it also describes the scene in the church, and it explains why Langston was not really saved.

The placement of selections in this and the next two sections is not inevitable. I have placed each as I have because, in my view, the essay chosen better exemplifies one type of composition than another. What I have just said about the placement of selections in Part Four also applies to the essays in the other parts of the book. For example, the pieces in Part Three that illustrate the use of personal experience as a source of material are also examples of narration. They tell about events.

We all have stories to tell and the desire to tell them—in conversation, diaries, and letters. Some are about events we have experienced; some have been related to us by others; some may be about imagined occurrences. The type of composition called *narration* gives an account of events or experiences in *time.* (A *description,* in contrast, gives an account of observed details in *space*; see pages 205–228.)

Here are some things to keep in mind when you use the narrative form:

1. *Be sure your story has a point.* If you ask yourself *why* you are telling a story, you are likely to discover that it is because the events seemed significant to you; often they made you more aware of yourself, of others, of your surroundings, and of your thoughts.

   Some beginning writers either see no meaning in their stories or fail to communicate the meaning to their readers. Have you ever heard a story told by a person to whom you felt like saying or did say, "Okay, so what's your point?" It's a valid question because, except for stories told just to entertain, writers tell stories for a reason.

   In some narration, writers make their points explicitly, although usually not quite so explicitly as in this fable—a short tale that teaches a practical lesson:

   In the woods of the Far West there once lived a brown bear who could take it or let it alone. He would go into a bar where they sold mead, a fermented drink made of honey, and he would have just two drinks. Then he would put some money on the bar and say, "See what the bears in the back room will have," and he would go home. But finally he took to drinking by himself most of the day. He would reel home at night, kick over the umbrella stand, knock down the bridge lamps, and ram his elbows through the windows. Then he would collapse on the floor and lie there until he went to sleep. His wife was greatly distressed and his children were very frightened.

   At length the bear saw the error of his ways and began to

reform. In the end he became a famous teetotaller and a persistent temperance lecturer. He would tell everybody that came to his house about the awful effects of drink, and he would boast about how strong and well he had become since he gave up touching the stuff. To demonstrate this, he would stand on his head and on his hands and he would turn cartwheels in the house, kicking over the umbrella stand, knocking down the bridge lamps, and ramming his elbows through the windows. Then he would lie down on the floor, tired by his healthful exercise, and go to sleep. His wife was greatly distressed and his children were very frightened.

Moral: You might as well fall flat on your face as lean over too far backward [James Thurber, *Fables for Our Time*].

A story will often imply the point the writer wants to make. This is the method Willie Morris uses in his account of an accident on the train tracks in upper Manhattan (pages 128–129). But, whether implied or made explicit, the point of any story included in an essay should be clear to readers.

See how George Orwell achieves this purpose in "A Hanging":

It was about forty yards to the gallows. I watched the bare brown back of the prisoner marching in front of me. He walked clumsily with his bound arms, but quite steadily, with that bobbing gait of the Indian who never straightens his knees. At each step his muscles slid neatly into place, the lock of hair on his scalp danced up and down, his feet printed themselves on the wet gravel. And once, in spite of the men who gripped him by each shoulder, he stepped slightly aside to avoid a puddle in the path.

It is curious; but till that moment I had never realized what it means to destroy a healthy, conscious man. When I saw the prisoner step aside to avoid the puddle I saw the mystery, the unspeakable wrongness, of cutting a life short when it is in full tide. . . .

Having had a sudden insight into the wrongness of capital punishment, Orwell makes a significant generalization about the events he relates in his essay. This evaluation of his experience is the point he wants to make in his account of a hanging. Your evaluation of your experiences—expressing the significance you discover in them—will make your stories more effective too.

2. *Be sure the time sequence is clear.* You can readily impose order on your story by narrating the events in the sequence in which they occurred—by telling the story in *chronological order.* The natural order of events—beginning, middle, and end—is narration's simplest and most-used arrangement. You may choose, however, to start your story at any important point in the sequence of events to be narrated, especially if by doing so you can better arrest the attention of your readers. You can then go back in time—like flashbacks in movies—to tell about the early incidents of your story.

   Chronological order can readily be assured by the use of words pertaining to time, as in this passage from John James Audubon's *Ornithological Autobiography* (italics added):

   > *As soon as* the Pigeons discover a sufficiency of food to entice them to alight, they fly round in circles, reviewing the country below. *During* their evolutions, *on such occasions,* the dense mass which they form exhibits a beautiful appearance, *as it changes its direction, now* displaying a glistening sheet of azure, *when* the backs of the birds come simultaneously into view, *and anon, suddenly* presenting a mass of rich deep purple. They *then* pass lower, over the woods, and *for a moment* are lost among the foliage, but *again* emerge, and are seen gliding aloft. They *now* alight, but *the next moment,* as if *suddenly* alarmed, they take to wing, producing by the flappings of their wings a noise like the roar of distant thunder, and sweep through the forests to see if danger is near. Hunger, however, *soon* brings them to the ground. *When* alighted, they are seen industriously throwing up the withered leaves in quest of the fallen mast. The rear ranks are continually rising, passing over the main-body, and alighting in front, *in such rapid succession,* that the whole flock seems still on wing. The quantity of ground thus swept is astonishing, and so completely has it been cleared, that the gleaner who might follow in their rear would find his labour completely lost. *Whilst* feeding, their avidity is at times so great that in attempting to swallow a large acorn or nut, they are seen gasping for a *long while,* as if in the agonies of suffocation.

3. *Use dialogue whenever possible.* The reporting of conversation between two or more persons is a useful method of moving a story forward. It also helps to make the story seem more authentic and more immediate. Finally, dialogue is an effective way to characterize persons in a story, as it is in a play. Needless to say, the conversation in your narration should sound natural and be appropriate to the speaker.

4. *Select details carefully.* Good storytelling requires the purposeful selection of details. Some beginning writers include either the wrong details or more details than the effective relating of the events requires. In your narrative writing you should select details that help you to convey to your readers the point of your essay. This is what Orwell did in the passage from "A Hanging" just quoted. The detail of the condemned man avoiding the puddle of water related to Orwell's purpose in telling the story and to the meaning he saw in it.

5. *Choose a point of view.* In everyday usage, "point of view" means an opinion or attitude. In writing, the term has other meanings:

   a. One definition of point of view is the relation of the writer to a story, whether as a participant in the events being narrated, that is, as a first-person narrator, using "I" or "we," or as a reporter of events other people have experienced, using "he," "she," or "they," as in Maya Angelou's "Cotton-Picking Time" (pages 236–238).

   b. Point of view also means the physical place from which the writer views the events in a story.

   c. Point of view means, as well, the perception of the observer through whose eyes the events narrated are seen. A parent and child walking in the woods would not view the environment in the same way. The writer has the option of describing the scene as seen by (from the viewpoint of) the child, the parent, or, alternately, both.

To avoid confusing readers, your point of view within a single piece must be consistent.

MEAN STREETS AND MEAN PEOPLE

Willard Gaylin

Willard Gaylin is a psychoanalyst and professor of psychiatry at the Columbia College of Physicians and Surgeons as well as a frequent contributor to journals and a writer of books relating to his specialty. This selection is the prologue to *The Rage Within: Anger in Modern Life* (1984).

---

1 East 96th Street is the unofficial border that separates "the fashionable Upper East Side" of Manhattan, to the south, from Harlem, on the north. When hailing a cab to Harlem it is an unwritten street principle that you stand on the proper side of the avenue, clearly indicating the direction in which you will be traveling.

2 A New York taxi driver, whether he is a hired employee or a small entrepreneur operating his own cab, is licensed to operate, and thereby earn his living, by the city. One of the rules in the taxi code stipulates that the cabdriver must take his customer to any point within the city limits that the rider requests. Never mind that the driver makes more money operating in Manhattan; is lost when he enters the precincts of Brooklyn; is frightened by the prospect of a trip to Harlem at night. The rules are clear. He must go where the customer asks.

3 Many cabdrivers *are* frightened by trips into Harlem. While statistics will support the fact that people travel safely in Harlem all the time, those same statistics will indicate that the risks are greater in ghetto neighborhoods than in middle-class neighborhoods. For those who travel little, the statistics can be ignored. For those who travel day in and day out, week in and week out statistics can be a threat to existence.

4 Some taxi drivers will refuse to go into Harlem. When the

rider requests such a service the driver finds himself in double jeopardy: to take even a middle-class woman to a large public facility in Harlem may be seen as a potential risk, for as she leaves the cab, another, more threatening person may enter and direct him into an area more remote from public view, deeper into the ghetto, distant from the safety and security of public movement and public surveillance. To refuse, of course, is to run another risk, particularly if the rider is an impatient, white, middle-class commuter, who in his outrage and frustration at missing his train is more likely than others to take the time to report the cabby for his violation of the code.

5 Despite his trepidation the driver will usually take you wherever you ask. Once you are in the car, the power relationship shifts perceptibly; he now takes charge. The rage he feels toward you for his intimidation and "humiliation" will be manifested, either explicitly or in the manner of his driving. He can make a ten-minute cab drive up Madison Avenue an absolute hell.

6 To avoid such confrontation, to mitigate the constant abrasive anger that is the grit of current urban life, one masters specific maneuvers aimed at oiling the machinery; one contrives an array of prophylactic devices. One such is proper advance communication. Your signal to the cabby must indicate the maximum possible information. Since I regularly commute to my suburban home from the 125th Street station in Harlem, I understand the rules of the game and play by them.

7 That was precisely what I had done this particular afternoon. The cabby saw my hail while waiting for the light at 96th Street. He nodded in my direction, thereby sealing the contract between us. The light changed; he cut across two lanes of traffic from west to east on the one-way street and screeched to a stop right alongside me.

8 On entering the cab I picked up my copy of *The New York Times.* The newspaper is an important commuter's device. Most city-wise people accept this signal as readily as they would a "No trespass" or "Do not enter" sign. Some, however, interpret it simply as an indication that the reader is not inclined to speak. They assume their freedom to address the reader with the understanding that they may get no response. In the seven to ten minutes it takes to get from my office to the train I want no discussion. I certainly do not want argument. I have learned to be stubbornly mute. The

cabdriver often prattles for his own purposes, undismayed by my lack of response. This driver was a talker.

9 As soon as I entered this cab I knew I was in for one standard political tirade that I am forced to endure at infrequent but not rare intervals. The major thesis is that the "fuckin niggers" have ruined the city. It is often embellished with details of having grown up "right there around the corner on 114th Street and Third Avenue," with nostalgic and romantic details of what a wonderful neighborhood it had been "just a few years ago." In my salad days, I would demur, defend, debate, leave the cab or find other means to dissociate myself from the imposed point of view; but years in the city have taught me a more effective device. I simply extinguish this oral assault from perception as I do the smells of the garbage and the sight of the graffiti.

10 It was obviously not the first time the cabdriver had made this presentation. That should not suggest that it was a passionless or tired replay. It was told with barely controlled rage, through clenched teeth, interspersed with expletives, gestures and all the signs of chronic anger now crystallized into hatred. I had braced myself for seven unpleasant, but not atypical, minutes of city life when chance dictated a confrontation with another example of urban rage.

11 Jaywalking is not a serious offense. Most New Yorkers do usually cross with the green, if only for purposes of survival. Nonetheless, the pace and urgency of the city demand that when safety allows, everyone walk—at the red, at the green and in between; it matters not. This I would call utilitarian jaywalking. The law against this particular offense is rarely enforced; one runs little risk of punishment, and the pressure of time and space is such in the city as to encourage violation.

12 This is a crime of convenience, not a statement of political action. There is, however, another kind of jaywalking that represents an act of defiance, whose purpose is to announce contempt for the rules. In my short daily trip between 96th and 125th streets I have seen it performed with great style. It is practiced with particular flair by adolescents. Here jaywalking is a statement. It is often a slow, mannered and leisurely saunter across Madison Avenue against the light. The jaywalker dares the oncoming driver to either hit him or else suffer the humiliation of being forced to swerve.

The gesture is extraordinarily reminiscent of the casual air of the matador who asserts his ascendancy over the bull by walking slowly and disdainfully as the bull passes within inches of him at full charge. It is one of the variant urban forms of "Chicken," and as such is intended to be a statement of independence, defiance and manhood.

13 On this particular day one such saunterer was unaware of the nature of the raging bull he was about to meet. Sitting in the back seat, I was alerted by some change in tone or temperament in the driver. Looking up from my paper, I saw a defiant jaywalker slowly cutting across the four lanes of Madison Avenue. The actual event that I am about to describe took less time than is necessary to tell about it, but it was sufficient to raise the level of adrenaline circulating through my body and to cause me to sweat perceptibly.

14 The driver was on a collision course with the jaywalker. He seemed determined not to swerve but if anything, to accelerate and adjust course to ensure impact. He did not want to miss. I had visions of a dead boy hurled into the air by the taxi. The boy crossing the street became aware that his challenge was being met in a different way this time, and rose to that challenge by slowing his course. At the very moment the impact seemed inevitable, the jaywalker—finally frightened—made a quick jump out of the way of the oncoming taxi, thus saving his life. The driver let out an indecipherable articulation of sheer triumph, while the jaywalker in a rage of defeat and humiliation smashed his fist on the back of the car while screaming obscenities.

15 The cabdriver, now ecstatic, abandoned his routine speech, and chuckled and chortled over his triumph the rest of the way to the 125th Street station. With constraint I paid the fare and left the cab. The cabby—now in an ebullient mood—thanked me as he locked the cab doors and flicked on his off-duty sign to discourage any Harlem riders. Still unsettled, I walked to the ticket counter and asked for a ticket to Hastings. For some reason the clerk misheard me and gave me a ticket to Greystone. I said, "You made a mistake. I said Hastings, not Greystone." He answered, mean-eyed and mean-mouthed, "You asked for Greystone and you got Greystone." What I answered was ugly and uncivil and protected by editorial privilege. Eight minutes elapsed between my hailing the cab and my finally getting my ticket to Hastings.

16 What purpose was served by this anger? What was this anger about? With whom were these people angry?

17 The cabdriver was presumably angry with blacks. But why? And with all blacks? How is one angry with an entire population? Had he suffered some specific injury by a member of this group? Not necessarily; but even if so, how is that so generally transferable? What sustains that anger? What are its limits?

18 With whom was the teenage jaywalker angry? No one? Everyone? Car owners? His position, or lack of it? Was this a game? A sign of contempt, independence, manhood, pride, courage? Was he angry or bored? What private purposes were served by his defiant behavior? What are *its* limits?

19 What prompted the anger of the ticket clerk? How had I offended him? Did he resent me? All commuters? His work? His life? Was this his typical demeanor, or had I been the unfortunate recipient of an anger generated by an employer or a wife, displaced to a convenient and less threatening individual? And what about me? What about my anger? Here, at least, we can go beyond mere conjecture. The surliness of the clerk was surely not the "cause" of my anger. We city dwellers are inured to the minor rudenesses of urban life. Boorishness in the city, like insect and bird sounds in the country, passes unnoticed, protected from observation by its very ubiquity. My response was a final common pathway for my anger with the racism of the cabby; my disappointment in and anger with myself for tolerating it; my anger with the teenager for foolishly and recklessly risking his life and beyond all that my disgust with the degradation of public life, and my fear of some potential consequences of this social anger and the anomie it portends.

20 Each participant carried into each of these interchanges a set of unresolved frustrations and angers barely contained. Each may have utilized this encounter as an end point for an anger rooted in a myriad of ill-defined and trivial psychological assaults reinforced by unrecognized or uncontrollable sociological frustrations.

21 Modern life seems designed to generate quantities of anger while, perversely, limiting the effectiveness of the anger response. Anger, an emotion specifically engineered to protect us against physical threats to our survival, continues to be generated in conditions where the threats, even when real, are rarely physical, and even when physical are rarely resolved by our own physical responses.

Our biological anger response, inbred in precivilized times to protect us against specific, identifiable, physical threats, now, when the sources of danger are symbolic, abstract and cumulative, serves only to increase our vulnerability. In becoming civilized, we have made our biologically programmed anger mechanism obsolete.

22 We have learned, therefore, to contain the anger response constantly generated by the multiple assaults of modern life on self-pride and self-confidence. We have trained ourselves to endure frustrations as the inevitable price of a technological society.

23 In this complex society we have created, we have lost control over the elements that shape our work and our pleasure. And we feel impotent and vulnerable. We are frightened and angered by signs of disorder, but even more by the recognition that what order may or may not exist seems beyond our control or design.

24 Beyond real misery—and surely that exists for too many—are the ever-present existential frustrations of modern life; the constant mundane humiliations; the minor indignities that corrode our self-worth. And each assault on pride and confidence increases our sense of vulnerability and generates a quantum of now useless anger. So we learn to restrict the anger mechanism, but in so doing we dangerously lower our flash point, and we suffer the physiology of a repressed and maladaptive anger.

25 To walk the streets of any large city is to see anger everywhere. To live in the city is to be in a state of inexplicable anger much of the time. The short fuse is a way of life in the city today, and the city today is not just New York, but Detroit, Toledo and even Middletown. And the city today is a portent of a rural mood barely one pace behind. We no longer lead lives of quiet desperation. We are for the most part in a state of contained anger.

Questions About "Narration"

1. Mark in your text all the evidence you can find of Gaylin's use of storytelling.

2. How much of what you find is based on personal experience? Be specific.

3. How relevant to the main idea of his essay is Gaylin's storytelling?
4. To what extent does narration explain the essay's main idea? Does it effectively clarify the abstract words and ideas of the essay? Explain.

Questions on Diction and Writing Techniques

1. How does your dictionary define "entrepreneur" and "stipulates" (par. 2), "surveillance" (par. 4); "trepidation" (par. 5), "mitigate" and "prophylactic" (par. 6), "salad days" (par. 9), "utilitarian" (par. 11), "indecipherable" (par. 14); "ubiquity" (par. 19), "existential" and "quantum" (par. 24)? Use each word or phrase in a sentence.
2. What is Gaylin's purpose, in paragraph 8, in writing "however"? Find another instance of his choosing that word for the same reason.
3. Show, with reference to the text, how Gaylin uses examples to support one or more generalizations (see "Illustration," pp. 252–270).
4. To better understand the organization of this essay, divide it into groups of paragraphs. Explain the function of each. Write a summary of the essay in a paragraph of not over seventy-five words.

For Discussion, Reading, and Writing

1. In a short essay about anger, use narration as your main expository technique.
2. Find in your personal experience at least one incident that you can use to explain any view you may have about anger. Relate that incident in a short essay.
3. Use storytelling to support any topic based on an abstract idea such as love, togetherness, empathy, loneliness, communication, adulthood.
4. Are you ever aware of rage within yourself? Respond to the question in a short essay.

SALVATION

Langston Hughes

Langston Hughes (1902–1967), American writer and poet, was among the first to urge his fellow black artists to use their distinctive experiences as the material for their works.

---

1 I was saved from sin when I was going on thirteen. But not really saved. It happened like this. There was a big revival at my Auntie Reed's church. Every night for weeks there had been much preaching, singing, praying, and shouting, and some very hardened sinners had been brought to Christ, and the membership of the church had grown by leaps and bounds. Then just before the revival ended, they held a special meeting for children, "to bring the young lambs to the fold." My aunt spoke of it for days ahead. That night I was escorted to the front row and placed on the mourners' bench with all the other young sinners, who had not yet been brought to Jesus.

2 My aunt told me that when you were saved you saw a light, and something happened to you inside! And Jesus came into your life! And God was with you from then on! She said you could see and hear and feel Jesus in your soul. I believed her. I had heard a great many old people say the same thing and it seemed to me they ought to know. So I sat there calmly in the hot, crowded church, waiting for Jesus to come to me.

3 The preacher preached a wonderful rhythmical sermon, all moans and shouts and lonely cries and dire pictures of hell, and then he sang a song about the ninety and nine safe in the fold, but one little lamb was left out in the cold. Then he said: "Won't you come? Won't you come to Jesus? Young lambs, won't you come?" And he held out his arms to all us young sinners there on the

mourners' bench. And the little girls cried. And some of them jumped up and went to Jesus right away. But most of us just sat there.

4 A great many old people came and knelt around us and prayed, old women with jet-black faces and braided hair, old men with work-gnarled hands. And the church sang a song about the lower lights are burning, some poor sinners to be saved. And the whole building rocked with prayer and song.

5 Still I kept waiting to *see* Jesus.

6 Finally all the young people had gone to the altar and were saved, but one boy and me. He was a rounder's son named Westley. Westley and I were surrounded by sisters and deacons praying. It was very hot in the church, and getting late now. Finally Westley said to me in a whisper: "God damn! I'm tired o' sitting here. Let's get up and be saved." So he got up and was saved.

7 Then I was left all alone on the mourners' bench. My aunt came and knelt at my knees and cried, while prayers and songs swirled all around me in the little church. The whole congregation prayed for me alone, in a mighty wail of moans and voices. And I kept waiting serenely for Jesus, waiting, waiting—but he didn't come. I wanted to see him, but nothing happened to me. Nothing! I wanted something to happen to me, but nothing happened.

8 I heard the songs and the minister saying: "Why don't you come? My dear child, why don't you come to Jesus? Jesus is waiting for you. He wants you. Why don't you come? Sister Reed, what is this child's name?"

9 "Langston," my aunt sobbed.

10 "Langston, why don't you come? Why don't you come and be saved? Oh, Lamb of God! Why don't you come?"

11 Now it was really getting late. I began to be ashamed of myself, holding everything up so long. I began to wonder what God thought about Westley, who certainly hadn't seen Jesus either, but who was now sitting proudly on the platform, swinging his knickerbockered legs and grinning down at me, surrounded by deacons and old women on their knees praying. God had not struck Westley dead for taking his name in vain or for lying in the temple. So I decided that maybe to save further trouble, I'd better lie, too, and say that Jesus had come, and get up and be saved.

12 So I got up.

13 Suddenly the whole room broke into a sea of shouting, as

they saw me rise. Waves of rejoicing swept the place. Women leaped in the air. My aunt threw her arms around me. The minister took me by the hand and led me to the platform.

14 When things quieted down, in a hushed silence, punctuated by a few ecstatic "Amens," all the new young lambs were blessed in the name of God. Then joyous singing filled the room.

15 That night, for the last time in my life but one—for I was a big boy twelve years old—I cried. I cried, in bed alone, and couldn't stop. I buried my head under the quilts, but my aunt heard me. She woke up and told my uncle I was crying because the Holy Ghost had come into my life, and because I had seen Jesus. But I was really crying because I couldn't bear to tell her that I had lied, that I had deceived everybody in the church, that I hadn't seen Jesus, and that now I didn't believe there was a Jesus any more, since he didn't come to help me.

Questions About "Narration"

1. The aunt, by "see," meant "see . . . Jesus in your soul" (par. 2). The boy, however, uses the word literally: "Still I kept waiting to *see* Jesus" (par. 5). What other evidence is there in this essay that Hughes wrote it from the point of view of a twelve-year-old?
2. What does the writer's reporting the boy's reaction in bed to the way he resolved his dilemma in church contribute to the impression on you of the story he relates?
3. In a sentence of not over twenty-five words, state the point Hughes makes in his essay.
4. Make a list of five or more specific details Hughes uses to make his story real and vivid.

Questions on Diction and Writing Techniques

1. How do the first two sentences help paragraph 1 to fulfill the requirements of an introductory paragraph (see page 33)?
2. Why does the writer use "but" in the last sentence of paragraph 3?

3. Why does Hughes make the sentences of paragraph 5 and 12 separate paragraphs?
4. Are "sea of shouting" and "waves of rejoicing" (par. 13) apt phrases? Explain.
5. What is the effect on you of the short sentences in paragraph 13?
6. By what technique for expanding a sentence (see pages 57–68) does Hughes increase the density of the last sentence of his essay?

For Discussion, Reading, and Writing

1. Fill the blanks in this passage from memory to make it intelligible:

   My aunt told me that when you were _____ you saw a _____, and something _____ to you inside. And Jesus came into your life! And God was with you from then on! She said you could see and hear and _____ Jesus in your soul. I _____ her.

   Compare your words with those in paragraph 2.
2. If, as happened to young Langston Hughes, pressures of one kind or another ever forced you to be hypocritical, write in a paragraph or two the story of that experience, making sure to explain to your reader its effect on you.
3. Evoking memories of your childhood, tell in the first person, from the point of view of yourself as a child, the story of an insightful religious experience.
4. In his autobiography, the Irish poet William Butler Yeats said about an early disillusioning experience that it was "the first breaking of the dream of childhood." If you ever were disillusioned similarly, write a short essay showing how, selecting vivid, specific details to convey your story to your reader.

38 WHO SAW MURDER DIDN'T CALL THE POLICE

Martin Gansberg

Martin Gansberg, a reporter and editor of *The New York Times* for many years, is also a contributor to several magazines and a teacher at Fairleigh Dickinson University.

---

1 For more than half an hour 38 respectable, law-abiding citizens in Queens watched a killer stalk and stab a woman in three separate attacks in Kew Gardens.

2 Twice the sound of their voices and the sudden glow of their bedroom lights interrupted him and frightened him off. Each time he returned, sought her out and stabbed her again. Not one person telephoned the police during the assault; one witness called after the woman was dead.

3 That was two weeks ago today. But Assistant Chief Inspector Frederick M. Lussen, in charge of the borough's detectives and a veteran of 25 years of homicide investigations, is still shocked.

4 He can give a matter-of-fact recitation of many murders. But the Kew Gardens slaying baffles him—not because it is a murder, but because the "good people" failed to call the police.

5 "As we have reconstructed the crime," he said, "the assailant had three chances to kill this woman during a 35-minute period. He returned twice to complete the job. If we had been called when he first attacked, the woman might not be dead now."

6 This is what the police say happened beginning at 3:20 A.M. in the staid, middle-class, tree-lined Austin Street area:

7 Twenty-eight-year-old Catherine Genovese, who was called Kitty by almost everyone in the neighborhood, was returning home from her job as manager of a bar in Hollis. She parked her red Fiat in a lot adjacent to the Kew Gardens Long Island Rail Road Station,

facing Mowbray Place. Like many residents of the neighborhood, she had parked there day after day since her arrival from Connecticut a year ago, although the railroad frowns on the practice.

8 She turned off the lights of her car, locked the door and started to walk the 100 feet to the entrance of her apartment at 82-70 Austin Street, which is in a Tudor building, with stores on the first floor and apartments on the second.

9 The entrance to the apartment is in the rear of the building because the front is rented to retail stores. At night the quiet neighborhood is shrouded in the slumbering darkness that marks most residential areas.

10 Miss Genovese noticed a man at the far end of the lot, near a seven-story apartment house at 82-40 Austin Street. She halted. Then, nervously, she headed up Austin Street toward Lefferts Boulevard, where there is a call box to the 102d Police Precinct in nearby Richmond Hill.

'He Stabbed Me!'

11 She got as far as a street light in front of a bookstore before the man grabbed her. She screamed. Lights went on in the 10-story apartment house at 82-67 Austin Street, which faces the bookstore. Windows slid open and voices punctured the early-morning stillness.

12 Miss Genovese screamed: "Oh, my God, he stabbed me! Please help me! Please help me!"

13 From one of the upper windows in the apartment house, a man called down: "Let that girl alone!"

14 The assailant looked up at him, shrugged and walked down Austin Street toward a white sedan parked a short distance away. Miss Genovese struggled to her feet.

15 Lights went out. The killer returned to Miss Genovese, now trying to make her way around the side of the building by the parking lot to get to her apartment. The assailant stabbed her again.

16 "I'm dying!" she shrieked. "I'm dying!"

A City Bus Passed

17 Windows were opened again, and lights went on in many apartments. The assailant got into his car and drove away. Miss

Genovese staggered to her feet. A city bus, Q-10, the Lefferts Boulevard line to Kennedy International Airport, passed. It was 3:35 A.M.

18 The assailant returned. By then, Miss Genovese had crawled to the back of the building, where the freshly painted brown doors to the apartment house held out hope of safety. The killer tried the first door; she wasn't there. At the second door, 82-62 Austin Street, he saw her slumped on the floor at the foot of the stairs. He stabbed her a third time—fatally.

19 It was 3:50 by the time the police received their first call, from a man who was a neighbor of Miss Genovese. In two minutes they were at the scene. The neighbor, a 70-year-old woman and another woman were the only persons on the street. Nobody else came forward.

20 The man explained that he had called the police after much deliberation. He had phoned a friend in Nassau County for advice and then he had crossed the roof of the building to the apartment of the elderly woman to get her to make the call.

21 "I didn't want to get involved," he sheepishly told the police.

Suspect Is Arrested

22 Six days later, the police arrested Winston Moseley, a 29-year-old business-machine operator, and charged him with the homicide. Moseley had no previous record. He is married, has two children and owns a home at 133-19 Sutter Avenue, South Ozone Park, Queens. On Wednesday, a court committed him to Kings County Hospital for psychiatric observation.

23 When questioned by the police, Moseley also said that he had slain Mrs. Annie May Johnson, 24, of 146-12 133d Avenue, Jamaica, on Feb. 29 and Barbara Kralik, 15, of 174-17 140th Avenue, Springfield Gardens, last July. In the Kralik case, the police are holding Alvin L. Mitchell, who is said to have confessed that slaying.

24 The police stressed how simple it would have been to have gotten in touch with them. "A phone call," said one of the detectives, "would have done it." The police may be reached by dialing "O" for operator or SPring 7-3100.

25 The question of whether the witnesses can be held legally responsible in any way for failure to report the crime was put to the Police Department's legal bureau. There, a spokesman said:

26 "There is no legal responsibility, with few exceptions, for any citizen to report a crime."

Statutes Explained

27 Under the statutes of the city, he said, a witness to a suspicious or violent death must report it to the medical examiner. Under state law, a witness cannot withhold information in a kidnapping.

28 Today witnesses from the neighborhood, which is made up of one-family homes in the $35,000 to $60,000 range with the exception of the two apartment houses near the railroad station, find it difficult to explain why they didn't call the police.

29 Lieut. Bernard Jacobs, who handled the investigation by the detectives, said:

30 "It is one of the better neighborhoods. There are few reports of crimes. You only get the usual complaints about boys playing or garbage cans being turned over."

31 The police said most persons had told them they had been afraid to call, but had given meaningless answers when asked what they had feared.

32 "We can understand the reticence of people to become involved in an area of violence," Lieutenant Jacobs said, "but where they are in their homes, near phones, why should they be afraid to call the police?"

33 He said his men were able to piece together what happened—and capture the suspect—because the residents furnished all the information when detectives rang doorbells during the days following the slaying.

34 "But why didn't someone call us that night?" he asked unbelievingly.

35 Witnesses—some of them unable to believe what they had allowed to happen—told a reporter why.

36 A housewife, knowingly if quite casual, said, "We thought it was a lover's quarrel." A husband and wife both said, "Frankly, we were afraid." They seemed aware of the fact that events might have been different. A distraught woman, wiping her hands in her apron, said, "I didn't want my husband to get involved."

37 One couple, now willing to talk about that night, said they

heard the first screams. The husband looked thoughtfully at the bookstore where the killer first grabbed Miss Genovese.

38 "We went to the window to see what was happening," he said, "but the light from our bedroom made it difficult to see the street." The wife, still apprehensive, added: "I put out the light and we were able to see better."

39 Asked why they hadn't called the police, she shrugged and replied: "I don't know."

40 A man peeked out from a slight opening in the doorway to his apartment and rattled off an account of the killer's second attack. Why hadn't he called the police at the time? "I was tired," he said without emotion. "I went back to bed."

41 It was 4:25 A.M. when the ambulance arrived for the body of Miss Genovese. It drove off. "Then," a solemn police detective said, "the people came out."

Questions About "Narration"

1. What purpose, aside from reciting the story of a murder, does Gansberg have in writing this essay? In your answer make specific reference to your text.
2. What do Gansberg's opening paragraphs contribute to the dominant impression he leaves you with?
3. How else and where in his essay does he reinforce that impression?
4. What does dialogue contribute to the point he makes? To the effectiveness of the narration?
5. To better understand Gansberg's purpose and how he succeeds in making this an effective essay, divide the essay into logical units and explain the function of each.

Questions on Diction and Writing Techniques

1. Gansberg might have written sentence 2 of paragraph 7: "She parked her car near a Long Island Rail Road station." Which version of the sentence is preferable? Why?

2. He might have written the second sentence of paragraph 9: "At night the neighborhood is dark." Why did he write the sentence the way he did?
3. What are Gansberg's sources of material?
4. What do the kind of words, sentences, and paragraphs Gansberg chooses contribute to the readability of his essay?

For Discussion, Reading, and Writing

1. Why was Inspector Lussen shocked?
2. What reasons did people give for not helping Miss Genovese?
3. If you had been one of the thirty-eight citizens, what would you have done?
4. Relate in a short essay an event or series of events that illustrates people's inhumanity toward or love for others. Consider organizing your essay the way Gansberg organized his.

A HANGING

George Orwell

George Orwell (1903–1950), British novelist and essayist, reports in this essay a personal experience in Burma where, as a young man, he served with the Indian imperial police.

---

1 It was in Burma, a sodden morning of the rains. A sickly light, like yellow tinfoil, was slanting over the high walls into the jail yard. We were waiting outside the condemned cells, a row of sheds

fronted with double bars, like small animal cages. Each cell measured about ten feet by ten and was quite bare within except for a plank bed and a pot of drinking water. In some of them brown silent men were squatting at the inner bars, with their blankets draped round them. These were the condemned men, due to be hanged within the next week or two.

2 One prisoner had been brought out of his cell. He was a Hindu, a puny wisp of a man, with a shaven head and vague liquid eyes. He had a thick, sprouting moustache, absurdly too big for his body, rather like the moustache of a comic man on the films. Six tall Indian warders were guarding him and getting him ready for the gallows. Two of them stood by with rifles and fixed bayonets, while the others handcuffed him, passed a chain through his handcuffs and fixed it to their belts, and lashed his arms tight to his sides. They crowded very close about him, with their hands always on him in a careful, caressing grip, as though all the while feeling him to make sure he was there. It was like men handling a fish which is still alive and may jump back into the water. But he stood quite unresisting, yielding his arms limply to the ropes, as though he hardly noticed what was happening.

3 Eight o'clock struck and a bugle call, desolately thin in the wet air, floated from the distant barracks. The superintendent of the jail, who was standing apart from the rest of us, moodily prodding the gravel with his stick, raised his head at the sound. He was an army doctor, with a grey toothbrush moustache and a gruff voice. "For God's sake hurry up, Francis," he said irritably. "The man ought to have been dead by this time. Aren't you ready yet?"

4 Francis, the head jailer, a fat Dravidian in a white drill suit and gold spectacles, waved his black hand. "Yes, sir, yes sir," he bubbled. "All iss satisfactorily prepared. The hangman iss waiting. We shall proceed."

5 "Well, quick march, then. The prisoners can't get their breakfast till this job's over."

6 We set out for the gallows. Two warders marched on either side of the prisoner, with their rifles at the slope; two others marched close against him, gripping him by arm and shoulder, as though at once pushing and supporting him. The rest of us, magistrates and the like, followed behind. Suddenly, when we had gone ten yards, the procession stopped short without any order or warning. A

dreadful thing had happened—a dog, come goodness knows whence, had appeared in the yard. It came bounding among us with a loud volley of barks, and leapt round us wagging its whole body, wild with glee at finding so many human beings together. It was a large woolly dog, half Airedale, half pariah. For a moment it pranced round us, and then, before anyone could stop it, it had made a dash for the prisoner, and jumping up tried to lick his face. Everyone stood aghast, too taken aback even to grab at the dog.

7 "Who let that bloody brute in here?" said the superintendent angrily. "Catch it, someone!"

8 A warder, detached from the escort, charged clumsily after the dog, but it danced and gambolled just out of his reach, taking everything as part of the game. A young Eurasian jailer picked up a handful of gravel and tried to stone the dog away, but it dodged the stones and came after us again. Its yaps echoed from the jail walls. The prisoner, in the grasp of the two warders, looked on incuriously, as though this was another formality of the hanging. It was several minutes before someone managed to catch the dog. Then we put my handkerchief through its collar and moved off once more, with the dog still straining and whimpering.

9 It was about forty yards to the gallows. I watched the bare brown back of the prisoner marching in front of me. He walked clumsily with his bound arms, but quite steadily, with that bobbing gait of the Indian who never straightens his knees. At each step his muscles slid neatly into place, the lock of hair on his scalp danced up and down, his feet printed themselves on the wet gravel. And once, in spite of the men who gripped him by each shoulder, he stepped slightly aside to avoid a puddle on the path.

10 It is curious, but till that moment I had never realised what it means to destroy a healthy, conscious man. When I saw the prisoner step aside to avoid the puddle, I saw the mystery, the unspeakable wrongness, of cutting a life short when it is in full tide. This man was not dying, he was alive just as we were alive. All the organs of his body were working—bowels digesting food, skin renewing itself, nails growing, tissues forming—all toiling away in solemn foolery. His nails would still be growing when he stood on the drop, when he was falling through the air with a tenth of a second to live. His eyes saw the yellow gravel and the grey walls, and his brain still remembered, foresaw, reasoned—reasoned even about

puddles. He and we were a party of men walking together, seeing, hearing, feeling, understanding the same world; and in two minutes, with a sudden snap, one of us would be gone—one mind less, one world less.

11 The gallows stood in a small yard, separate from the main grounds of the prison, and overgrown with tall prickly weeds. It was a brick erection like three sides of a shed, with planking on top, and above that two beams and a crossbar with the rope dangling. The hangman, a grey-haired convict in the white uniform of the prison, was waiting beside his machine. He greeted us with a servile crouch as we entered. At a word from Francis the two warders, gripping the prisoner more closely than ever, half led, half pushed him to the gallows and helped him clumsily up the ladder. Then the hangman climbed up and fixed the rope round the prisoner's neck.

12 We stood waiting, five yards away. The warders had formed in a rough circle round the gallows. And then, when the noose was fixed, the prisoner began crying out on his god. It was a high, reiterated cry of "Ram! Ram! Ram! Ram!", not urgent and fearful like a prayer or a cry for help, but steady, rhythmical, almost like the tolling of a bell. The dog answered the sound with a whine. The hangman, still standing on the gallows, produced a small cotton bag like a flour bag and drew it down over the prisoner's face. But the sound, muffled by the cloth, still persisted, over and over again: "Ram! Ram! Ram! Ram! Ram!"

13 The hangman climbed down and stood ready, holding the lever. Minutes seemed to pass. The steady, muffled crying from the prisoner went on and on, "Ram! Ram! Ram!" never faltering for an instant. The superintendent, his head on his chest, was slowly poking the ground with his stick; perhaps he was counting the cries, allowing the prisoner a fixed number—fifty, perhaps, or a hundred. Everyone had changed colour. The Indians had gone grey like bad coffee, and one or two of the bayonets were wavering. We looked at the lashed, hooded man on the drop, and listened to his cries—each cry another second of life; the same thought was in all our minds: oh, kill him quickly, get it over, stop that abominable noise!

14 Suddenly the superintendent made up his mind. Throwing up his head he made a swift motion with his stick. "Chalo!" he shouted almost fiercely.

15 There was a clanking noise, and then dead silence. The prisoner

had vanished, and the rope was twisting on itself. I let go of the dog, and it galloped immediately to the back of the gallows; but when it got there it stopped short, barked, and then retreated into a corner of the yard, where it stood among the weeds, looking timorously out at us. We went round the gallows to inspect the prisoner's body. He was dangling with his toes pointed straight downwards, very slowly revolving, as dead as a stone.

16 The superintendent reached out with his stick and poked the bare body; it oscillated slightly. "*He's* all right," said the superintendent. He backed out from under the gallows, and blew out a deep breath. The moody look had gone out of his face quite suddenly. He glanced at his wrist-watch. "Eight minutes past eight. Well, that's all for this morning, thank God."

17 The warders unfixed bayonets and marched away. The dog, sobered and conscious of having misbehaved itself, slipped after them. We walked out of the gallows yard, past the condemned cells with their waiting prisoners, into the big central yard of the prison. The convicts, under the command of warders armed with lathis, were already receiving their breakfast. They squatted in long rows, each man holding a tin pannikin, while two warders with buckets marched round ladling out rice; it seemed quite a homely, jolly scene, after the hanging. An enormous relief had come upon us now that the job was done. One felt an impulse to sing, to break into a run, to snigger. All at once everyone began chattering gaily.

18 The Eurasian boy walking beside me nodded towards the way we had come, with a knowing smile: "Do you know, sir, our friend (he meant the dead man), when he heard his appeal had been dismissed, he pissed on the floor of his cell. From fright.—Kindly take one of my cigarettes, sir. Do you not admire my new silver case, sir? From the boxwallah, two rupees eight annas. Classy European style."

19 Several people laughed—at what, nobody seemed certain.

20 Francis was walking by the superintendent, talking garrulously: "Well, sir, all hass passed off with the utmost satisfactoriness. It wass all finished—flick! like that. It iss not always so—oah, no! I have known cases where the doctor wass obliged to go beneath the gallows and pull the prisoner's legs to ensure decease. Most disagreeable!"

21 "Wriggling about, eh? That's bad," said the superintendent.

22 "Ach, sir, it iss worse when they become refractory! One man,

I recall, clung to the bars of hiss cage when we went to take him out. You will scarcely credit, sir, that it took six warders to dislodge him, three pulling at each leg. We reasoned with him. 'My dear fellow,' we said, 'think of all the pain and trouble you are causing to us!' But no, he would not listen! Ach, he wass very troublesome!"

23 I found that I was laughing quite loudly. Everyone was laughing. Even the superintendent grinned in a tolerant way. "You'd better all come out and have a drink," he said quite genially. "I've got a bottle of whisky in the car. We could do with it."

24 We went through the big double gates of the prison, into the road. "Pulling at his legs!" exclaimed a Burmese magistrate suddenly, and burst into a loud chuckling. We all began laughing again. At that moment Francis's anecdote seemed extraordinarily funny. We all had a drink together, native and European alike, quite amicably. The dead man was a hundred yards away.

Questions About "Narration"

1. In a paragraph of not over one hundred words, narrate in your own words the sequence of events Orwell reports in this essay.
2. Why did he choose to include in the essay the incident of the dog?
3. What other incident seemed to Orwell to be significant? Why?
4. Is paragraph 10 a digression from Orwell's storytelling? Explain.

Questions on Diction and Writing Techniques

1. Mark in your text those words that, though new to you, you understood from their context. Define them in your own words. Compare your definitions with those in your dictionary. Look up in your dictionary any other words that are new to you. Use the words in both groups in sentences.
2. Identify five or more similes in this essay.
3. Orwell might have written "sounded" instead of "floated" (par. 3). What alternative verbs might he have chosen in lieu of "marched,"

"bounding," and "pranced" (par. 6)? Which–Orwell's or your alternative words–are more vivid? Explain.

4. In lieu of the last sentence of paragraph 8 Orwell might have written "Then we put my handkerchief through its collar and moved off once more, with the dog still hassling." Which version of the sentence do you prefer? Why?

5. Orwell might have written sentence 4 of paragraph 10 "All the organs of his body were working, all toiling away in solemn foolery." Which version of the sentence conveys more meaning? Explain.

6. Orwell might have written the next-to-last sentence in paragraph 24 "We all had a drink together, quite amicably, native and European alike." How, in the rewritten sentence, is emphasis changed?

7. What does dialogue contribute to Orwell's portrayal of the characters in this essay? To the effectiveness of his storytelling?

8. What is the purpose and the effect of the last sentence in Orwell's essay?

9. Find, in addition to the details listed on pages 126–127, ten or more specific details in this essay that make it evident that Orwell was a careful observer.

For Discussion, Reading, and Writing

1. Making specific reference to the text, explain why the superintendent was impatient.

2. Nowhere in his essay does Orwell tell you what the offense of the prisoner was. Is this omission significant? Why or why not?

3. What went through Orwell's mind when he realized what it means to kill a fellow human being?

4. For the punishment of what crime(s) would you recommend or condone capital punishment?

5. Attend a trial in a criminal court in your area, or any other public event that interests you. In preparation for writing a

short essay on the subject, make a list of details—as you observe them and again just before writing your first draft—that will help you to relate the event effectively. In a second draft,

replace inapt and general words with words that are appropriate (when in doubt consult your dictionary) and concrete and thus will more clearly tell your story;

add as much imagery as may be appropriate to the purpose of your story;

revise your sentences, where necessary, to convey more meaning or to shift emphasis to their main ideas; and

add dialogue wherever appropriate.

Description

If those who have studied the art of writing are in accord on any one point, it is this: the surest way to arouse and hold the attention of the reader is by being specific, definite, and concrete. The greatest writers—Homer, Dante, Shakespeare—are effective largely because they deal in particulars and report the details that matter. Their words call up pictures.

—*The Elements of Style*

"THE artistic aim when expressing itself in written words must make its appeal through the senses. . . . My task which I am trying to achieve is, by the power of the written word to make you hear, to make you feel—it is, before all, to make you *see*." Although when Joseph Conrad wrote this he had in mind his work as a writer of fiction, what he says applies to the writing of description in nonfiction prose.

The purpose of description is to give an account of observed details in *space*. The aim is to make the reader see. The appeal is to the mind's eye. Photographers reproduce their subjects on photographic paper; painters may do likewise on canvas. Writers, in contrast, must create their subjects in their readers' minds. Their medium is words. Whether the thing to be depicted is as small as a lemon or as extensive as a landscape, through language writers transform the objects of their attention into mental images.

In this context, "see" means to perceive with all our senses—hearing, sight, smell, taste, and touch. Thus it follows that writers of description, in transposing their perceptions into words, will mention details that appeal to one or more of the five senses. Such language is called *sensory diction.* Writers will report that a peach, for example, is a combination of *yellows, pinks,* and *reds*; that its skin feels *velvety*; that it tastes *sweet.* They will write about a campfire that the *moist* logs burn with a *hiss* and a *crackle,* of giving off a *piny* odor and casting on the *cold, rough* ground *wavering, black* shadows. Words that refer to sensory experiences evoke sensory images; by reporting as many sensory details as practicable, writers can more readily make their readers see what they saw.

Description is of two kinds: objective or factual and subjective or personal. *Objective description* attempts to represent things as they are, as in the report of a scientist. Writers striving for objectivity exclude their own feelings about their subject; they stay detached, personally uninvolved. *Subjective description* is quite different. The subjective writer reports his or her view of the subject and includes personal feelings and opinions.

Here is an example of objective description:

> Shark, member of a group of almost exclusively marine and predaceous fishes. Sharks are heavy fishes, possessing neither lungs nor swim bladders. Their skeletons are made of cartilage rather than bone, and this, along with large deposits of fat, partially solves their weight problem; nevertheless, most sharks must keep moving in order to breathe and to stay afloat. They are good swimmers; the wide spread of the pectoral fins and the upward curve of the tail fin provide lift, and the sweeping movements of the tail provide drive. Their tough hides are studded with minute, toothlike structures called denticles. Sharks have pointed snouts; their crescent-shaped mouths are set on the underside of the body and contain several rows of sharp, triangular teeth. . . .

This description, from *The New Columbia Encyclopedia,* is scientific, factual, objective. Nowhere in it do the writer's feelings or opinions intrude. Contrast it with this description:

> His entire form is fluid, weaving from side to side; his head moves slightly from left to right, right to left, timed to the rhythm of his motion through the water. Only the eye is fixed, focused on me, circling within the orbit of the head, in order not to lose sight for a fraction of a second of his prey or, perhaps, of his enemy. . . .

> There is no threat, no movement of aggression. Only a sort of nonchalant suspicion is apparent in the movements and attitudes of the shark, and yet he generates fear. Amazed and startled, filled with apprehension, circling with movements as slow and silent as possible, I try to keep him constantly in front of me.
>
> There is something of the miraculous in the suddenness of his appearance as well as in his infinite grace; the surface of the water is far above and its absence contributes to the magical quality of the moment. He turns once more, and the sphere he encompasses expands or contracts, in accordance with his own primitive impulses or the subtle changes of the current. His silent circling is a ballet governed by untraceable mechanisms. The blue tranquillity of his form surrounds me with the sensation of a web of murderous and yet beautiful force. I have the feeling that I have accompanied his circular voyage since the beginning of time. His configuration is perfect. Suddenly, the idea that he deserves killing comes to me like a shock and instantly shatters the spell. Murder is the real function of this ideal form, of this icy-blue camouflage, and of that enormous, powerful tail. . . .
>
> The great blue shark continues his approach toward me in the unchanging manner which has been that of his race throughout its existence. He is really a superb animal, almost seven feet in length, and I know, since I have often seen them before, that his jaws are lined with seven rows of teeth, as finely honed as the sharpest razor [Jacques-Yves Cousteau, *The Shark*].

Notice that Cousteau refers to the shark not as "it," but, more personally, as "he." At the outset the writer makes us aware of his presence ("the eye is fixed, focused on *me*"), of his feelings about his subject ("*he generates fear*"), and of his own behavior in response to it ("Amazed and startled, filled with apprehension, *circling with movements as slow and silent as possible, I try to keep him constantly in front of me*").

Cousteau's choice of adjectives also reveals a subjective reaction —an emphasis on the observer and a personal appraisal of his subject: "There is something of the *miraculous* in the suddenness of his appearance"; "*magical* quality of the moment"; "*superb* animal." Moreover, Cousteau doesn't hesitate to state an opinion, with a play on words: "Murder is the *real* function of this *ideal* form. . . ."

Finally, the writer uses figures of speech to call forth visual images: "His silent circling is a *ballet*"; "The blue tranquillity of his form surrounds me with the sensation of *a web* of murderous and yet beautiful force"; "his jaws are lined with seven rows of teeth, *as finely boned as the sharpest razor*."

Unlike the writing in *The New Columbia Encyclopedia,* which focuses exclusively on the shark, Cousteau's description includes himself. It not only reports the writer's responses to the shark; it tries to affect the reader's as well.

Even photography is not purely objective: What a camera records on film is determined by the direction the photographer chooses to aim it, by the operator's choice of lens, composition, aperture stop, speed, film, and by the photographer's purpose and bias. Your observations of the world around you are affected by your background, training, point of view, and sharpness of senses. Other people, with different attributes and experiences, observe the world differently. None of the views, yours or theirs, is purely objective. Each description will reflect dissimilar biases and varying responses.

Your purpose in writing description will be to recreate in the mind of your reader a place, person, or thing that you have seen. Thus the process of description begins with observation.

Here are two suggestions for writing description:

1. *Select details carefully.* Choose details that will best delineate the thing described. These details must be arranged methodically. If you were to describe the place where you are now, you would choose details not at random, but in some logical order, such as from left to right, from one consistent physical point of view. If you were to describe a thing in motion, you could impose order on your subject by describing the sequence of its movements.

2. *Be sure your diction is apt.* To convey clearly what you saw, you must use diction that is specific (words that refer to individual things) rather than general language (words that include all of a group or a class). Specific words convey to readers a precise mental picture (see the discussion of specific and general words on pages 86–87.)

The ultimate effect of successful description is to make on the reader a harmonious, vivid impression, as Mark Twain does in this descriptive passage from *Roughing It:*

> As the sun was going down, we saw the first specimen of an animal known familiarly over two thousand miles of mountain and desert—from Kansas clear to the Pacific Ocean—as the "jackass rabbit." He is well named. He is just like any other rabbit, except that he is from one-third to twice as large, has longer legs in proportion to his size, and has the most preposterous ears that ever were mounted on any creature *but* a jackass. When he is sitting quiet, thinking about his sins, or is absent-minded or unapprehensive of danger, his majestic ears project above him conspicuously; but the breaking of a twig will scare him nearly to death, and then he tilts his ears back gently and starts for home. All you can see, then, for the next minute, is his long gray form stretched out straight and "streaking it" through the low sage-brush, head erect, eyes right, and ears just canted a little to the rear, but showing you where the animal is, all the time, the same as if he carried a jib. Now and then he makes a marvelous spring with his long legs, high over the stunted sage-brush, and scores a leap that would make a horse envious. Presently, he comes down to a long, graceful "lope," and shortly he mysteriously disappears. He has crouched behind a sage-brush, and will sit there and listen and tremble until you get within six feet of him, when he will get under way again. But one must shoot at this creature once, if he wishes to see him throw his heart into his heels, and do the best he knows how. He is frightened clear through, now, and he lays his long ears down on his back, straightens himself out like a yardstick every spring he makes, and scatters miles behind him with an easy indifference that is enchanting.

SUMMER BEYOND WISH

Russell Baker

Russell Baker is one of America's most highly regarded humorists (see pages 20–22).

---

1 A long time ago I lived in a crossroads village of northern Virginia and during its summer enjoyed innocence and never knew boredom, although nothing of consequence happened there.

2 Seven houses of varying lack of distinction constituted the community. A dirt road meandered off toward the mountain where a bootleg still supplied whiskey to the men of the countryside, and another dirt road ran down to the creek. My cousin Kenneth and I would sit on the bank and fish with earthworms. One day we killed a copperhead which was basking on a rock nearby. That was unusual.

3 The heat of summer was mellow and produced sweet scents which lay in the air so damp and rich you could almost taste them. Mornings smelled of purple wisteria, afternoons of the wild roses which tumbled over stone fences and evenings of honeysuckle.

4 Even by standards of that time it was a primitive place. There was no electricity. Roads were unpaved. In our house there was no plumbing. The routine of summer days was shaped by these deficiencies. Lacking electric lights, one went early to bed and rose while the dew was still in the grass. Kerosene lamps were cleaned and polished in an early-morning hubbub of women, and children were sent to the spring for fresh water.

5 This afforded a chance to see whether the crayfish population had multiplied. Later, a trip to the outhouse would afford a chance to daydream in the Sears, Roebuck catalog, mostly about shotguns and bicycles.

6 With no electricity, radio was not available for pacifying the young. One or two people did have radios that operated on mail-order batteries about the size of a present-day car battery, but these were not for children, though occasionally you might be invited in to hear "Amos 'n' Andy."

7 All I remember about "Amos 'n' Andy" at that time is that it was strange hearing voices come out of furniture. Much later I was advised that listening to "Amos 'n' Andy" was racist and was grateful that I hadn't heard much.

8 In the summer no pleasures were to be had indoors. Everything of delight occurred in the world outside. In the flowers there were hummingbirds to be seen, tiny wings fluttering so fast that the birds seemed to have no wings at all.

9 In the heat of midafternoon the women would draw the blinds, spread blankets on the floor for coolness and nap, while in the fields the cattle herded together in the shade of spreading trees to escape the sun. Afternoons were absolutely still, yet filled with sounds.

10 Bees buzzed in the clover. Far away over the fields the chug of an ancient steam-powered threshing machine could be faintly heard. Birds rustled under the tin of the porch roof.

11 Rising dust along the road from the mountains signaled an approaching event. A car was coming. "Car's coming," someone would say. People emerged from houses. The approaching dust was studied. Guesses were hazarded about whom it might contain.

12 Then—a big moment in the day—the car would cruise past.

13 "Who was it?"

14 "I didn't get a good look."

15 "It looked like Packy Painter to me."

16 "Couldn't have been Packy. Wasn't his car."

17 The stillness resettled itself as gently as the dust, and you could wander past the henhouse and watch a hen settle herself to perform the mystery of laying an egg. For livelier adventure there was the field that contained the bull. There, one could test his courage by seeing how far he dared venture before running back through the fence.

18 The men drifted back with the falling sun, steaming with heat and fatigue, and washed in tin basins with water hauled in buckets from the spring. I knew a few of their secrets, such as who kept his whiskey hidden in a Mason jar behind the lime barrel, and what

they were really doing when they excused themselves from the kitchen and stepped out into the orchard and stayed out there laughing too hard.

19 I also knew what the women felt about it, though not what they thought. Even then I could see that matters between women and men could become very difficult and, sometimes, so difficult that they spoiled the air of summer.

20 At sunset people sat on the porches. As dusk deepened, the lightning bugs came out to be caught and bottled. As twilight edged into night, a bat swooped across the road. I was not afraid of bats then, although I feared ghosts, which made the approach of bedtime in a room where even the kerosene lamp would quickly be doused seem terrifying.

21 I was even more afraid of toads and specifically of the toad which lived under the porch steps and which everyone assured me would, if touched, give me warts. One night I was allowed to stay up until the stars were in full command of the sky. A woman of great age was dying in the village and it was considered fit to let the children stay abroad into the night. As four of us sat there we saw a shooting star and someone said, "Make a wish."

22 I did not know what that meant. I didn't know anything to wish for.

Questions About "Description"

1. Mark in your text and enumerate the images by means of which Baker achieves the dominant impression of his boyhood that this essay makes on you.

2. Show how Baker's description helps him attain his expository purpose.

3. Underline in your text as many descriptive details as you can find. How many of them are expressed in sensory words? List those words in groups: sense of smell, sight, etc.

4. Find in this essay a few examples of subjective description.

Questions on Diction and Expository Techniques

1. What synonyms might Baker have chosen, in paragraph 11, in lieu of "event"? Why, in the context of this essay, is his choice of word apt?
2. How, in paragraph 4, does Baker support the idea in the first sentence of the paragraph?
3. How does the idea in the first sentence of paragraph 5 relate to the idea in the last sentence of paragraph 4? Explain the relationship of the ideas in paragraphs 4, 5, and 6.
4. What expository technique does Baker signal in paragraph 18 with "such as"?
5. What words immediately establish coherence between paragraphs 18 and 19? Between paragraphs 20 and 21?
6. Find a paragraph in the essay in which Baker helps achieve coherence with chronological order.
7. To what extent does Baker use narration to achieve his expository purpose? Support your answer with specific reference to the text.
8. What would this essay lose in effectiveness if the dialogue in paragraphs 11 and 13–16 were omitted?
9. Where in this essay is the point of view not that of Baker the man but of Baker the boy? What effect does such treatment of Baker's material have on you?

For Discussion, Reading, and Writing

1. Is Baker contradictory when he writes "Afternoons were absolutely still, yet filled with sounds"? Explain.
2. He says also that "nothing of consequence happened." If this is true, how could he never have known boredom?
3. Whether or not your childhood was as idyllic as Baker says his was, describe any portion of it in a short essay.

THEY ALSO WAIT WHO STAND AND SERVE THEMSELVES

Andrew Ward

Andrew Ward is a short-story writer and the author of humorous essays that have appeared in a variety of journals.

1 Anyone interested in the future of American commerce should take a drive sometime to my neighborhood gas station. Not that it is or ever was much of a place to visit. Even when I first moved here, five years ago, it was shabby and forlorn: not at all like the garden spots they used to feature in the commercials, where trim, manicured men with cultivated voices tipped their visors at your window and asked what they could do for you.

2 Sal, the owner, was a stocky man who wore undersized, popped-button shirts, sagging trousers, and oil-spattered work shoes with broken laces. "Gas stinks" was his motto, and every gallon he pumped into his customers' cars seemed to take something out of him. "Pumping gas is for morons," he liked to say, leaning indelibly against my rear window and watching the digits fly on the pump register. "One of these days I'm gonna dump this place on a Puerto Rican, move to Florida, and get into something nice, like hero sandwiches."

3 He had a nameless, walleyed assistant who wore a studded denim jacket and, with his rag and squeegee, left a milky film on my windshield as my tank was filling. There was a fume-crazed, patchy German shepherd, which Sal kept chained to the air pump, and if you followed Sal into his cluttered, overheated office next to the service bays, you ran a gauntlet of hangers-on, many of them Sal's brothers and nephews, who spent their time debating the

merits of the driving directions he gave the bewildered travelers who turned into his station for help.

4 "I don't know," one of them would say, pulling a bag of potato chips off the snack rack, "I think I would have put 'em onto 91, gotten 'em off at Willow, and then—Bango!—straight through to Hamden."

5 Sal guarded the rest room key jealously and handed it out with reluctance, as if something in your request had betrayed some dismal aberration. The rest room was accessible only through a little closet littered with tires, fan belts, and cases of oil cans. Inside, the bulb was busted and there were never any towels, so you had to dry your hands on toilet paper—if Sal wasn't out of toilet paper, too.

6 The soda machine never worked for anyone except Sal, who, when complaints were lodged, would give it a contemptuous kick as he trudged by, dislodging warm cans of grape soda which, when their pop-tops were flipped, gave off a fine purple spray. There was, besides the snack rack in the office, a machine that dispensed peanuts on behalf of the Sons of Garibaldi. The metal shelves along the cinder-block wall were sparsely stocked with cans of cooling system cleaner, windshield de-icer, antifreeze, and boxed head lamps and oil filters. Over the battered yellow wiper case, below the Coca Cola clock, and half hidden by a calendar from a janitorial supply concern, hung a little brass plaque from the oil company, awarded in recognition of Salvatore A. Castallano's ten-year business association.

7 I wish for the sake of nostalgia that I could say Sal was a craftsman, but I can't. I'm not even sure he was an honest man. I suspect that when business was slow he may have cheated me, but I never knew for sure because I don't know anything about cars. If I brought my Volvo in because it was behaving strangely, I knew that as far as Sal was concerned it could never be a simple matter of tightening a bolt or re-attaching a hose. "Jesus," he'd wearily exclaim after a look under the hood. "Mr. Ward, we got problems." I usually let it go at that and simply asked him when he thought he could have it repaired, because if I pressed him for details he would get all worked up. "Look, if you don't want to take my word for it, you can go someplace else. I mean, it's a free country, you know? You got spalding on your caps, which means your dexadrometer isn't charging, and pretty soon you're gonna have hairlines in your flushing

drums. You get hairlines in your flushing drums and you might as well forget it. You're driving junk."

8 I don't know what Sal's relationship was with the oil company. I suppose it was pretty distant. He was never what they call a "participating dealer." He never gave away steak knives or NFL tumblers or stuffed animals with his fill-ups, and never got around to taping company posters on his windows. The map rack was always empty, and the company emblem, which was supposed to rotate thirty feet above the station, had broken down long before I first laid eyes on it, and had frozen at an angle that made it hard to read from the highway.

9 If, outside of television, there was ever such a thing as an oil company service station inspector, he must have been appalled by the grudging service, the mad dog, the sepulchral john. When there was supposed to have been an oil shortage a few years ago, Sal's was one of the first stations to run out of gas. And several months ago, during the holiday season, the company squeezed him out for good.

10 I don't know whether Sal is now happily sprinkling olive oil over salami subs somewhere along the Sun Belt. I only know that one bleak January afternoon I turned into his station to find him gone. At first, as I idled by the no-lead pump, I thought the station had been shut down completely. Plywood had been nailed over the service bays, Sal's name had been painted out above the office door, and all that was left of his dog was a length of chain dangling from the air pump's vacant mast.

11 But when I got out of the car I spotted someone sitting in the office with his boots up on the counter, and at last caught sight of the "Self-Service Only" signs posted by the pumps. Now, I've always striven for a degree of self-sufficiency. I fix my own leaky faucets and I never let the bellboy carry my bags. But I discovered as I squinted at the instructional sticker by the nozzle that there are limits to my desire for independence. Perhaps it was the bewilderment with which I approach anything having to do with the internal combustion engine; perhaps it was my conviction that fossil fuels are hazardous; perhaps it was the expectation of service, the sense of helplessness, that twenty years of oil company advertising had engendered, but I didn't want to pump my own gas.

12 A mongrel rain began to fall upon the oil-slicked tarmac as I

followed the directions spelled out next to the nozzle. But somehow I got them wrong. When I pulled the trigger on the nozzle, no gas gushed into my fuel tank, no digits flew on the gauge.

13 "Hey, buddy," a voice sounded out of a bell-shaped speaker overhead. "Flick the switch."

14 I turned toward the office and saw someone with Wild Bill Hickok hair leaning over a microphone.

15 "Right. Thanks," I answered, and turned to find the switch. There wasn't one. There was a bolt that looked a little like a switch, but it wouldn't flick.

16 "The switch," the voice crackled in the rain. "Flick the switch."

17 I waved back as if I'd finally understood, but I still couldn't figure out what he was talking about. In desperation, I stuck the nozzle back into my fuel tank and pulled the trigger. Nothing.

18 In the office I could see that the man was now angrily pulling on a slicker. "What the hell's the matter with you?" he asked, storming by me. "All you gotta do is flick the switch."

19 "I couldn't find the switch," I told him.

20 "Well, what do you call this?" he wanted to know, pointing to a little lever near the pump register.

21 "A lever," I told him.

22 "Christ," he muttered, flicking the little lever. The digits on the register suddenly formed neat rows of zeros. "All right, it's set. Now you can serve yourself," the long-haired man said, ducking back to the office.

23 As the gas gushed into my fuel tank and the fumes rose to my nostrils, I thought for a moment about my last visit to Sal's. It hadn't been any picnic: Sal claimed to have found something wrong with my punting brackets, the German shepherd snapped at my heels as I walked by, and nobody had change for my ten. But the transaction had dimension to it: I picked up some tips about color antennas, entered into the geographical debate in the office, and bought a can of windshield wiper solvent (to fill the gap in my change). Sal's station had been a dime a dozen, but it occurred to me, as the nozzle began to balk and shudder in my hand, that gas stations of its kind were going the way of the village smithy and the corner grocer.

24 I got a glob of grease on my glove as I hung the nozzle back on the pump, and it took me more than a minute to satisfy myself

that I had replaced the gas cap properly. I tried to whip up a feeling of accomplishment as I headed for the office, but I could not forget Sal's dictum: Pumping gas is for morons.

25 The door to the office was locked, but a sign directed me to a stainless steel teller's drawer which had been installed in the plate glass of the front window. I stood waiting for a while with my money in hand, but the long-haired man sat inside with his back to me, so at last I reached up and hesitantly knocked on the glass with my glove.

26 The man didn't hear me or had decided, in retaliation for our semantic disagreement, to ignore me for a while. I reached up to knock again, but noticed that my glove had left a greasy smear on the window. Ever my mother's son, I reflexively reached into my pocket for my handkerchief and was about to wipe the grease away when it hit me: at last the oil industry had me where it wanted me —standing in the rain and washing its windshield.

Questions About "Description"

1. Ward tells us that his neighborhood gas station was "shabby and forlorn." With his choice of what specific details does he show us that this is so?

2. With what details does Ward portray Sal? Explain whether Sal's behavior and utterances are part of this portrayal.

3. Mark in your text the descriptive details with which Ward portrays the new attendant of the gas station. What does Ward's reporting of the man's utterances and movements contribute to that portrayal?

Questions on Diction and Writing Techniques

1. How does your dictionary define "walleyed" (par. 3), "aberration" (par. 5), "contemptuous" (par. 6), "nostalgia" (par. 7), "sepulchral" (par. 9), "retaliation" and "semantic" (par. 26)? Use each word in a sentence.

2. What part does narration play in the development of this essay? Be specific.

3. How does Ward's use of comparison (see pages 271–290) control your attitude toward his experiences and toward his evaluation of them?

4. What idea(s) that he develops later in the essay does Ward introduce in paragraph 1?

5. Show how individual paragraphs and/or groups of paragraphs contribute toward the achievement of Ward's purpose in writing this essay.

6. Ward might have concluded his essay with paragraph 24. Why did he add paragraphs 25–26?

For Discussion, Reading, and Writing

1. Paragraph 6 is chock-full of descriptive details. Look about you in the place where you are sitting now and write a similar paragraph of description.

2. Write a short descriptive essay about your neighborhood (or any other) gas station.

3. Describe in a short essay any public place you are familiar with —a supermarket, cafeteria, bookstore, record shop, whatever— and at least one of its employees.

4. Being as fanciful as you please, write a short essay about a gas station—or any other public place where goods and/or services are sold—from the point of view of an attendant or any other employee. Be sure to develop your essay with telling descriptive details. Dialogue might be effective too.

EMPEROR NORTON I

Joan Parker

Joan Parker is a freelance writer who has a special interest in memorabilia of the American West. Her articles have appeared in various journals.

1 During the Gold Rush of 1849 and the years that followed, San Francisco attracted more than any city's fair share of eccentrics. But among all the deluded and affected that spilled through the Golden Gate in those early days, one man rose to become perhaps the most successful eccentric in American history: Norton I, Emperor of the United States and Protector of Mexico.

2 Joshua Abraham Norton, an English Jew, arrived in San Francisco on the steamer *Franzika* in 1849 from Algoa bay, Cape of Good Hope, with $40,000. With that stake, he proceeded to make a fortune. He was an astute agent for several mercantile houses, a broker, and an energetic land speculator. In a few years Norton had become a respected citizen worth a quarter of a million dollars. But in 1853 he overextended himself in one grand effort to corner every grain of rice already in the city or on its way there. When unexpected shiploads sailed into port, prices crashed, and with them toppled the fortunes of Norton and several friends who had trusted his advice. During the long, excruciating lawsuit resulting from default on his contract, Norton's fine mind began to warp. Ruined, he dropped from the city's life—only to emerge a few years later in the guise of an emperor.

3 In September of 1859 a dignified, stocky man appeared in the offices of the San Francisco *Evening Bulletin* and solemnly submitted a proclamation that began: "At the peremptory request and desire of a large majority of the citizens of these United States, I, Joshua Norton . . . declare and proclaim myself Emperor of these United

States. . . ." Amused by this unusual feature story, the editor ran it without comment, but few people in the busy boom town paid much attention—even when the subsequent proclamations abolished Congress and the state supreme court for fraud and corruption. However, when Norton began appearing in the streets in a gaudy uniform given him by the commander of the Presidio, San Francisco's army garrison, the citizenry began to take notice. There was, of course, some jeering, and rival newspapers ridiculed the Emperor. He riposted in the *Bulletin*, which he now used as his official publication, against "certain scurrilous and untrue articles attacking our right and propriety . . . in one or two insignificant papers . . . and the portions of a community whose taste can be pampered by low and improper articles," and decreed that the "good sense and honesty of purpose of the nations . . . not be insulted by such trash."

4 Resplendent in his large gold epaulets, garrison cap, and saber, Norton applied himself to the business of being an emperor as diligently as he had to being an entrepreneur. He joined the promenade along Montgomery and Kearney streets to show himself to his people, and accepted the ironic bows of his subjects with the serenity befitting his new profession. He faithfully attended public gatherings of all kinds and continued to issue proclamations for the progress and justice of his empire.

5 His unfeigned concern for his people, his inherent dignity, and his tact (he never stayed long enough during his many calls to be considered a bore) soon won over the city completely. For twenty years the citizens of San Francisco cheerfully supported him in his delusion. His imperial bonds—usually issued in the amount of fifty cents—were honored, and the modest taxes he levied were paid. He ate and drank free at the best restaurants and saloons and was invited to speak at political rallies. When the state legislature met, a large upholstered chair was always reserved for him. The city directory listed him as "Norton, Joshua, Emperor." And when the genuine Emperor Dom Pedro II of Brazil visited the city in 1876, San Francisco proudly presented its own to him with fitting pomp and circumstance.

6 When Norton's uniform wore out, a public subscription bought him a new one. On a similar occasion the board of supervisors voted city funds. Tailors who made and contributed uniforms proudly

announced themselves on window cards "by appointment to His Majesty." His loyal subjects gave him a variety of hats, a magnificent walking stick, and a big tricolored Chinese umbrella to keep his imperial self dry on rainy days. When an inevitable do-gooder attempted to have him committed, the judge dismissed the inquiry into the Emperor's sanity with the curt remark that Norton was "just about the best going in the king line."

7 Norton I, Emperor of the United States (he had earlier shed his original title of Protector of Mexico, declaring it impossible to protect such an unsettled nation), died in January, 1880. As he lay in the morgue, a crowd began to gather. "The general interest felt in the deceased was soon manifest," reported the San Francisco *Chronicle* in an article headed "LE ROI EST MORT." By noon the crush was so large that the police were called. All classes were represented, from "capitalist to pauper, clergyman, pickpocket, well-dressed ladies and social outcasts, the aged and children." "He is dead," mourned the *Morning Call*, "and no citizen of San Francisco could have been taken away who would be more generally missed." A kind of innocence had been taken away, and would indeed be missed.

8 A reported thirty thousand San Franciscans attended his first funeral. But more than fifty years later, there was another. In 1934, when the still growing city engulfed the Masonic Cemetery, the Emperor's remains were dug up and reburied at Woodlawn. Norton remained so alive in the imagination of his city even then that Mayor Angelo J. Rossi placed a wreath on the grave, the municipal band played, and the Third Batallion, 159th Infantry, fired three volleys. A fine granite monument was set in place; it read: NORTON I, EMPEROR OF THE UNITED STATES, PROTECTOR OF MEXICO, JOSHUA A. NORTON 1819–1880. And as one historian has noted, there were no quotation marks around the inscription.

Questions About "Description"

1. Mark in your text the specific details that Parker reports to make clear to you the eccentricity of Norton. Indicate with an A or a B which of these details relate to Norton's appearance, which to his behavior.

2. Does Parker explain sufficiently and clearly how Norton became an eccentric and how the citizens of San Francisco supported him in his delusion? Explain, making specific reference to your text.

Questions on Diction and Writing Techniques

1. Underline in your text those words that are new to you, but whose meaning you inferred from their context. Define them in your own words. Compare your definitions with those in your dictionary. Look up in your dictionary any other words that are new to you. Use the words in both groups in sentences.
2. Did paragraph 1 engage your attention and thereby make you want to read on? Why or why not?
3. Parker might have written "came" or "sailed" instead of "spilled" (par. 1). Why did she choose the verb she did?
4. Why did Parker write "perhaps" (par. 1)?
5. Sentence 1 of paragraph 5 is an example of the joining of grammatical elements of identical construction in pairs or series—coordination. To better understand what this means, consider this diagram of the sentence (omitting, to simplify, the portion of the sentence in parentheses):

   His unfeigned concern for his people,
   his inherent dignity, and
   his tact

   soon won over the
   city completely.

   The coordinate elements are the nouns *concern, dignity,* and *tact.* There is, in paragraph 6, another sentence with coordinate elements. Find the sentence and diagram it.

For Discussion, Reading, and Writing

1. How old was Norton when he arrived in San Francisco?
2. Fill the blanks in this passage from memory to make it intelligible:

   During the ______ ______ of 1849 and the ______ that followed, San Francisco attracted more than any city's fair share of ______. But among all the deluded and affected that ______ through the Golden Gate in those early years, one ______ rose to become perhaps the most successful ______ in American history: Norton I, ______ of the United States and Protector of ______.

3. In a short essay, describe an eccentric or any other person you know, using narration to round out your portrayal.

THE SANTA ANA

Joan Didion

Joan Didion is a novelist and the author of collections of essays, among them *Slouching Towards Bethlehem* (1968) and *The White Album* (1979).

---

1 There is something uneasy in the Los Angeles air this afternoon, some unnatural stillness, some tension. What it means is that tonight a Santa Ana will begin to blow, a hot wind from the northeast whining down through the Cajon and San Gorgonio Passes, blowing up sandstorms out along Route 66, drying the hills and the nerves to the flash point. For a few days now we will see smoke back in the canyons, and hear sirens in the night. I have neither heard nor read that a Santa Ana is due, but I know it, and almost everyone I have seen today knows it too. We know it because we feel it. The baby frets. The maid sulks. I rekindle a waning argument with the telephone company, then cut my losses and lie down, given over to whatever it is in the air. To live with the Santa Ana is

to accept, consciously or unconsciously, a deeply mechanistic view of human behavior.

[2] I recall being told, when I first moved to Los Angeles and was living on an isolated beach, that the Indians would throw themselves into the sea when the bad wind blew. I could see why. The Pacific turned ominously glossy during a Santa Ana period, and one woke in the night troubled not only by the peacocks screaming in the olive trees but by the eerie absence of surf. The heat was surreal. The sky had a yellow cast, the kind of light sometimes called "earthquake weather." My only neighbor would not come out of her house for days, and there were no lights at night, and her husband roamed the place with a machete. One day he would tell me that he had heard a trespasser, the next a rattlesnake.

[3] "On nights like that," Raymond Chandler once wrote about the Santa Ana, "every booze party ends in a fight. Meek little wives feel the edge of the carving knife and study their husbands' necks. Anything can happen." That was the kind of wind it was. I did not know then that there was any basis for the effect it had on all of us, but it turns out to be another of those cases in which science bears out folk wisdom. The Santa Ana, which is named for one of the canyons it rushes through, is a *foehn* wind, like the *foehn* of Austria and Switzerland and the *hamsin* of Israel. There are a number of persistent malevolent winds, perhaps the best known of which are the mistral of France and the Mediterranean sirocco, but a *foehn* wind has distinct characteristics: it occurs on the leeward slope of a mountain range and, although the air begins as a cold mass, it is warmed as it comes down the mountain and appears finally as a hot dry wind. Whenever and wherever a *foehn* blows, doctors hear about headaches and nausea and allergies, about "nervousness," about "depression." In Los Angeles some teachers do not attempt to conduct formal classes during a Santa Ana, because the children become unmanageable. In Switzerland the suicide rate goes up during the *foehn,* and in the courts of some Swiss cantons the wind is considered a mitigating circumstance for crime. Surgeons are said to watch the wind, because blood does not clot normally during a *foehn.* A few years ago an Israeli physicist discovered that not only during such winds, but for the ten or twelve hours which precede them, the air carries an unusually high ratio of positive to negative ions. No one seems to know exactly why that should be; some talk

about friction and others suggest solar disturbances. In any case the positive ions are there, and what an excess of positive ions does, in the simplest terms, is make people unhappy. One cannot get much more mechanistic than that.

4 Easterns commonly complain that there is no "weather" at all in Southern California, that the days and the seasons slip by relentlessly, numbingly bland. That is quite misleading. In fact the climate is characterized by infrequent but violent extremes: two periods of torrential subtropical rains which continue for weeks and wash out the hills and send subdivisions sliding toward the sea; about twenty scattered days a year of the Santa Ana, which, with its incendiary dryness, invariably means fire. At the first prediction of a Santa Ana, the Forest Service flies men and equipment from northern California into the southern forests, and the Los Angeles Fire Department cancels its ordinary nonfirefighting routines. The Santa Ana caused Malibu to burn the way it did in 1956, and Bel Air in 1961, and Santa Barbara in 1964. In the winter of 1966–67 eleven men were killed fighting a Santa Ana fire that spread through the San Gabriel Mountains.

5 Just to watch the front-page news out of Los Angeles during a Santa Ana is to get very close to what it is about the place. The longest single Santa Ana period in recent years was in 1957, and it lasted not the usual three or four days but fourteen days, from November 21 until December 4. On the first day 25,000 acres of the San Gabriel Mountains were burning, with gusts reaching 100 miles an hour. In town, the wind reached Force 12, or hurricane force, on the Beaufort Scale; oil derricks were toppled and people ordered off the downtown streets to avoid injury from flying objects. On November 22 the fire in the San Gabriels was out of control. On November 24 six people were killed in automobile accidents, and by the end of the week the Los Angeles *Times* was keeping a box score of traffic deaths. On November 26 a prominent Pasadena attorney, depressed about money, shot and killed his wife, their two sons, and himself. On November 27 a South Gate divorcee, twenty-two, was murdered and thrown from a moving car. On November 30 the San Gabriel fire was still out of control, and the wind in town was blowing eighty miles an hour. On the first day of December four people died violently, and on the third the wind began to break.

6 It is hard for people who have not lived in Los Angeles to realize

how radically the Santa Ana figures in the local imagination. The city burning is Los Angeles's deepest image of itself: Nathanael West perceived that, in *The Day of the Locust*; and at the time of the 1965 Watts riots what struck the imagination most indelibly were the fires. For days one could drive the Harbor Freeway and see the city on fire, just as we had always known it would be in the end. Los Angeles weather is the weather of catastrophe, of apocalypse, and, just as the reliably long and bitter winters of New England determine the way life is lived there, so the violence and the unpredictability of the Santa Ana affect the entire quality of life in Los Angeles, accentuate its impermanence, its unreliability. The wind shows us how close to the edge we are.

Questions About "Description"

1. List the sensory details that Didion chooses in paragraph 1 to describe the Santa Ana and its physical effects. What other kind of effect does it have? What examples of this effect does Didion give in paragraph 1?
2. What does the information in paragraph 2 add to Didion's description of the Santa Ana?
3. How, in paragraph 3, does Didion tell you what kind of wind the Santa Ana is?
4. What characteristic of the Santa Ana is stressed in paragraph 4?
5. Explain the purpose and effect of the information in paragraph 5.

Questions on Diction and Writing Techniques

1. Mark in your text those words that are new to you, but whose meaning you inferred from their context. Define them in your own words. Compare your definitions with those in your dictionary. Look up in your dictionary any other words that are new to you. Use the words in both groups in sentences.
2. What is Didion's purpose in making the comparison with New England weather?

For Discussion, Reading, and Writing

1. How does Didion know that a Santa Ana will begin to blow?
2. How does Didion come to believe what she was told about the Indians?
3. How long is the usual Santa Ana period? What was the longest single Santa Ana period in recent years?
4. Recall and jot down bits of information about a phenomenon of nature that you have experienced. Using both objective and subjective description, write a short essay about your experience and its significance.

Exposition

I use "expository writing" as an umbrella term to mean simply writing that explains. In that sense, it includes various kinds of writing that are sometimes considered separate modes. But in practice they are not separate. Expository writing tends to be an amalgam. We sometimes explain by narrating, by describing, by defining, by reasoning, and, in the course of writing, perhaps arguing and persuading. Thus, in these terms, expository writing includes prose from factual reporting to personal reminiscence.

—William F. Irmscher

"EXPOSITION" means explanation. It is the type of composition you probably will write most often in college—in reports, term papers, research papers, critical essays, exams.

The main objective of narration is to tell a story, and the main objective of description is to create vivid images. The main objective of exposition is to expose—to set forth and explain—information and ideas. This is not to say that expository writing may not utilize the techniques of narration, description, and argumentation to achieve its goal. We will examine exposition separately, as we do the others, for convenience merely.

This introduction to exposition is itself exposition—a setting forth of information college students will need to know to write expository essays. How I present this information depends on my audience—you, your classmates, and other students like you. Were my readers different—high school freshmen, graduate students, teachers of composition—my choice of material, my arrangement of it, and the extent of my explanation would be different. My purpose with each group would be the same: to present sufficient information to allow my readers to understand how to write exposition. But my writing would vary, in that I might—depending on the group—set forth different material, more or less information, simpler or more complex, shorter or more extensive explanations. There is a connection between purpose and audience. By "purpose" I mean the result a writer intends to achieve with a given group of readers. The purpose in writing exposition is to communicate to readers what they need to know to understand a subject. Keeping them in mind helps the writer to choose appropriate material and to arrange it effectively.

Since knowing how a writer explains a subject to readers may be useful to you when you write, let's consider an expository paragraph:

> Watch your grip on the handle closely when you are learning to saw. It should be held firm but not tight. The saw should run freely. A tight grip prevents the free running of the saw and tends to swerve the blade away from the line. The thumb should be against the left side of the handle. Keep the index finger extended along the right side of the handle to help guide the blade. If the blade starts to cut into the marked line or to move too far away from it, twist the handle slightly in order to draw it back to the correct position [Alfred P. Morgan, *Tools and How to Use Them*].

This paragraph is a response to the question: How do you use a handsaw?

Any expository paragraph or essay gives answers to questions: What? Where? When? Who? How? Why? Most of the essays in this text (though in different sections to illustrate a variety of subjects) are expository, as some of their titles indicate:

"What I Have Lived For," in which Bertrand Russell explains *what* his personal philosophy is

"Who Killed Benny Paret?" in which Norman Mailer explains *who* should be blamed for deaths in professional boxing

"Jailbreak Marriage," in which Gail Sheehy explains *why* some young women marry

You will find it helpful to consider an expository essay as the answer to a question.

Let's assume that you want to write an essay about women in America. Instead of this general subject you would turn your attention to restricted subjects (see pages 2–9) such as day-care centers for the children of working mothers, battered women, or the Equal Rights Amendment. These and related ideas for an essay could be put in the form of questions:

How do day-care centers help working mothers to be independent?

What legal remedies are there for battered women?

Why should the Equal Rights Amendment be adopted?

Why should male-oriented words be revised?

Who was Margaret Fuller?

Why were the women in America granted suffrage?

What is male chauvinism?

Why are there relatively few women medical doctors in the United States?

Asking What? Where? When? Who? How? or Why? has several advantages. The question you ask will emphasize the need for an explanation that will satisfy your readers. If the question is specific, it will restrict your broad subject and narrow the search for information required to convince your readers of the validity of your thesis.

Here are a few additional things to keep in mind when you write expository prose:

1. *Choose your sources of material carefully.* What sources you use will depend on your subject. In an essay with a restricted subject you might find all the information you need in your personal experience, in your observations of others, or in notes in your diary. Or you might seek it in reading or interviews. Whatever your sources of material (see Part Three), you will want to know as much about your topic as its nature demands and time will permit.

2. *Know your purpose.* Keep your readers in mind when assembling your material so that you will be able to communicate to them what they need to know to understand your explanation of your restricted subject. The ultimate question about the success of an expository essay is: "Did the writer, having engaged the readers' attention, make them understand?"

3. *Organize your material to achieve your purpose.* Beginning writers generally find exposition more difficult to write than narration and description. In narration, a sequence of events suggests a proper arrangement of the writer's material. In description, order can be achieved by arranging details methodically, from a consistent physical point of view. In exposition, quite often, a method of organization is less immediately apparent. In Part Five, we will examine in detail techniques for imposing order on expository paragraphs and essays—illustration, comparison and contrast, definition, division and classification, process, and causal analysis.

ELIXIRS OF DEATH

Rachel Carson

Rachel Carson writes here in specific terms and in detail on the general subject "A Fable for Tomorrow" (see pages 46–48).

---

1 For the first time in the history of the world, every human being is now subjected to contact with dangerous chemicals, from the moment of conception until death. In the less than two decades

of their use, the synthetic pesticides have been so thoroughly distributed throughout the animate and inanimate world that they occur virtually everywhere. They have been recovered from most of the major river systems and even from streams of groundwater flowing unseen through the earth. Residues of these chemicals linger in soil to which they may have been applied a dozen years before. They have entered and lodged in the bodies of fish, birds, reptiles, and domestic and wild animals so universally that scientists carrying on animal experiments find it almost impossible to locate subjects free from such contamination. They have been found in fish in remote mountain lakes, in earthworms burrowing in soil, in the eggs of birds—and in man himself. For these chemicals are now stored in the bodies of the vast majority of human beings, regardless of age. They occur in the mother's milk, and probably in the tissues of the unborn child.

2 All this has come about because of the sudden rise and prodigious growth of an industry for the production of man-made or synthetic chemicals with insecticidal properties. This industry is a child of the Second World War. In the course of developing agents of chemical warfare, some of the chemicals created in the laboratory were found to be lethal to insects. The discovery did not come by chance: insects were widely used to test chemicals as agents of death for man.

3 The result has been a seemingly endless stream of synthetic insecticides. In being man-made—by ingenious laboratory manipulation of the molecules, substituting atoms, altering their arrangement—they differ sharply from the simpler inorganic insecticides of prewar days. These were derived from naturally occurring minerals and plant products—compounds of arsenic, copper, lead, manganese, zinc, and other minerals, pyrethrum from the dried flowers of chrysanthemums, nicotine sulphate from some of the relatives of tobacco, and rotenone from leguminous plants of the East Indies.

4 What sets the new synthetic insecticides apart is their enormous biological potency. They have immense power not merely to poison but to enter into the most vital processes of the body and change them in sinister and often deadly ways. Thus, as we shall see, they destroy the very enzymes whose function is to protect the body from harm, they block the oxidation processes from which the body receives its energy, they prevent the normal functioning of

various organs, and they may initiate in certain cells the slow and irreversible change that leads to malignancy.

5 Yet new and more deadly chemicals are added to the list each year and new uses are devised so that contact with these materials has become practically worldwide. The production of synthetic pesticides in the United States soared from 124,259,000 pounds in 1947 to 637,666,000 pounds in 1960—more than a five-fold increase. The wholesale value of these products was well over a quarter of a billion dollars. But in the plans and hopes of the industry this enormous production is only a beginning.

6 A Who's Who of pesticides is therefore of concern to us all. If we are going to live so intimately with these chemicals—eating and drinking them, taking them into the very marrow of our bones—we had better know something about their nature and their power.

Questions About "Exposition"

1. What facts does Carson present to support her statement that "synthetic pesticides . . . occur virtually everywhere" (par. 1)? Are they significant enough and sufficient in number to convince you of the truth of her judgment? Why or why not?
2. Does Carson make clear to you how "all this has come about" (par. 2)? Explain.
3. How do the statistics Carson gives in paragraph 5 serve her purpose in writing this piece?
4. Jot down, in a phrase or a short sentence, the main idea of each paragraph. Are the main ideas related one to another? Is their sequence logical? Using Carson's words as much as you please, write a one-paragraph summary of this essay. Be prepared to comment in class on whether she adequately explains to you why "we had better know something about [the] nature and [the] power" (par. 6) of pesticides.

Questions on Diction and Writing Techniques

1. Define the following words and write sentences using each of them appropriately: "synthetic" (par. 1), "pesticides" (par. 1),

"lethal" (par. 2), "ingenious" (par. 3), "inorganic" (par. 3), "leguminous" (par. 3), "enzymes" (par. 4).

2. By what means does the writer achieve coherence (see pages 29–30) in paragraph 1?
3. By what means does Carson achieve coherence elsewhere in her essay?
4. Here is an example of coordination: "They have been found in fish in remote mountain lakes, in earthworms burrowing in the soil, in the eggs of birds—and in man himself" (par. 1). Find in paragraph 4 another example of this method of expanding a sentence (see pages 64–68).
5. Is "Elixirs of Death" an appropriate title? Explain.

For Discussion, Reading, and Writing

1. Carson's conclusion in "Elixirs of Death" is (circle one):

   A. Every human being is now subjected to contact with dangerous chemicals.

   B. There has been a seemingly endless stream of synthetic insecticides.

   C. What sets the new synthetic insecticides apart is their enormous biological potency.

   D. New and more deadly chemicals are added to the list of insecticides every year.

   E. A Who's Who of insecticides is of concern to us all.

2. In 1962, when *Silent Spring*, the source of this selection, was published, Carson was criticized severely by some for being an alarmist. Does she seem so to you? Can you add other "elixirs of death" to the pesticides that prompted her concern then?
3. If your answer to the previous question is Yes, write a short essay explaining in a logical sequence of coherent paragraphs why you are concerned about one of the "elixirs of death" you listed.
4. After seeking information from newspapers, magazines, and other sources to supplement your own experiences and observations, write an expository essay on a topic such as

How to Garden Organically

How Oil Spills at Sea Affect Marine Ecology

Why Nuclear Power Plants Should (or Should Not) Be Installed in or Near Your Town or City

Where Nuclear Waste Should Be Disposed Of

What Is the Risk of Nuclear Fallout From the Sky

Why the Surgeon General's Warning on Cigarette Packs Should Be Observed

How Smoking in Public Should Be Controlled

How the Pollution of Inland Waters Can Be Avoided

What Is the Effect on One's Health of Medical X-rays

Why Nitrates and Nitrites Are Used as Food Preservatives

COTTON-PICKING TIME

Maya Angelou

Maya Angelou is a poet and also the author of three autobiographical works based on her experience as a black woman in America.

---

1 Each year I watched the field across from the Store turn caterpillar green, then gradually frosty white. I knew exactly how long it would be before the big wagons would pull into the front yard and load on the cotton pickers at daybreak to carry them to the remains of slavery's plantations.

2 During the picking season my grandmother would get out of bed at four o'clock (she never used an alarm clock) and creak down to her knees and chant in a sleep-filled voice, "Our Father, thank you for letting me see this New Day. Thank you that you didn't

allow the bed I lay on last night to be my cooling board, nor my blanket my winding sheet. Guide my feet this day along the straight and narrow, and help me to put a bridle on my tongue. Bless this house, and everybody in it. Thank you, in the name of your Son, Jesus Christ, Amen."

3 Before she had quite arisen, she called our names and issued orders, and pushed her large feet into homemade slippers and across the bare lye-washed wooden floor to light the coal-oil lamp.

4 The lamplight in the Store gave a soft make-believe feeling to our world which made me want to whisper and walk about on tiptoe. The odors of onions and oranges and kerosene had been mixing all night and wouldn't be disturbed until the wooden slat was removed from the door and the early morning air forced its way in with the bodies of people who had walked miles to reach the pickup place.

5 "Sister, I'll have two cans of sardines."

6 "I'm gonna work so fast today I'm gonna make you look like you standing still."

7 "Lemme have a hunk uh cheese and some sody crackers."

8 "Just gimme a coupla them fat peanut paddies." That would be from a picker who was taking his lunch. The greasy brown paper sack was stuck behind the bib of his overalls. He'd use the candy as a snack before the noon sun called the workers to rest.

9 In those tender mornings the Store was full of laughing, joking, boasting and bragging. One man was going to pick two hundred pounds of cotton, and another three hundred. Even the children were promising to bring home fo' bits and six bits.

10 The champion picker of the day before was the hero of the dawn. If he prophesied that the cotton in today's field was going to be sparse and stick to the bolls like glue, every listener would grunt a hearty agreement.

11 The sound of the empty cotton sacks dragging over the floor and the murmurs of waking people were sliced by the cash register as we rang up the five-cent sales.

12 If the morning sounds and smells were touched with the supernatural, the late afternoon had all the features of the normal Arkansas life. In the dying sunlight the people dragged, rather than their empty cotton sacks.

13 Brought back to the Store, the pickers would step out of the

backs of trucks and fold down, dirt-disappointed, to the ground. No matter how much they had picked, it wasn't enough. Their wages wouldn't even get them out of debt to my grandmother, not to mention the staggering bill that waited on them at the white commissary downtown.

14 The sounds of the new morning had been replaced with grumbles about cheating houses, weighted scales, snakes, skimpy cotton and dusty rows. In later years I was to confront the stereotyped picture of gay song-singing cotton pickers with such inordinate rage that I was told even by fellow Blacks that my paranoia was embarrassing. But I had seen the fingers cut by the mean little cotton bolls, and I had witnessed the backs and shoulders and arms and legs resisting any further demands.

15 Some of the workers would leave their sacks at the Store to be picked up the following morning, but a few had to take them home for repairs. I winced to picture them sewing the coarse material under a coal-oil lamp with fingers stiffening from the day's work. In too few hours they would have to walk back to Sister Henderson's Store, get vittles and load, again, onto the trucks. Then they would face another day of trying to earn enough for the whole year with the heavy knowledge that they were going to end the season as they started it. Without the money or credit necessary to sustain a family for three months. In cotton-picking time the late afternoons revealed the harshness of Black Southern life, which in the early morning had been softened by nature's blessing of grogginess, forgetfulness and the soft lamplight.

Questions About "Exposition"

1. What is Angelou's purpose in this essay?
2. Does Angelou make clear to you why "the pickers were dirt-disappointed" (par. 13)? Explain, making specific reference to the text.
3. What does description contribute to Angelou's explanation of her thesis?

Questions on Diction and Writing Techniques

1. Why does Angelou write "*caterpillar* green" and "*frosty* white" (par. 1)?
2. Why does Angelou choose to write "the remains of slavery's plantations" (par. 1)? Is the diction apt?
3. What significant details does the writer choose to portray her grandmother?
4. Contrast the second half of the sentence that constitutes paragraph 3 with this alternate: ". . . pushed her feet into slippers and across the floor to light the lamp."
5. Is the description in paragraph 4 objective or subjective?
6. Comment on the effectiveness of Angelou's use of dialogue in portraying the cotton pickers in the morning.
7. What does "like glue" contribute to the meaning of the second sentence of paragraph 10?
8. Cite examples of Angelou's use of sensory diction (see pages 205–206).

For Discussion, Reading, and Writing

1. "Cotton-picking Time" is mainly about (circle one):
   - A. cotton pickers
   - B. Angelou's grandmother's store
   - C. a day on a cotton farm
   - D. how to pick cotton
   - E. the harshness of black Southern life
2. Do you agree with Thoreau that "There is no such thing as pure objective observation"? (See the passage from his *Journal*, page 128.) Can any description be altogether objective? Support your answer with specific reference to this essay or any other in this text.
3. Incorporating description, write a paragraph or two that explains the harshness (or pleasantness) of any job you have ever had.

4. The explanation of Angelou's thesis (see pages 2–9) in this essay depends in part on a comparison between the way the farm hands felt and acted at the beginning and at the end of the day. Considering any day that was especially meaningful to you, imitate Angelou's strategy to explain that day's significance.

WHAT UNDERDEVELOPMENT MEANS

Robert Heilbroner

Robert L. Heilbroner, an eminent economist and teacher, is the author of numerous books and articles on economics and social affairs, including *The Great Ascent: The Struggle for Economic Development in Our Time* (1963), from which this selection is taken.

---

1 To begin to understand economic development we must have a picture of the problem with which it contends. We must conjure up in our mind's eye what underdevelopment means for the two billion human beings for whom it is not a statistic but a living experience of daily life. Unless we can see the Great Ascent from the vantage point of those who must make the climb, we cannot hope to understand the difficulties of the march.

2 It is not easy to make this mental jump. But let us attempt it by imagining how a typical American family, living in a small suburban house on an income of six or seven thousand dollars, could be transformed into an equally typical family of the underdeveloped world.

3 We begin by invading the house of our imaginary American family to strip it of its furniture. Everything goes: beds, chairs, tables, television set, lamps. We will leave the family with a few old

blankets, a kitchen table, a wooden chair. Along with the bureaus go the clothes. Each member of the family may keep in his "wardrobe" his oldest suit or dress, a shirt or blouse. We will permit a pair of shoes to the head of the family, but none for the wife or children.

4 We move into the kitchen. The appliances have already been taken out, so we turn to the cupboards and larder. The box of matches may stay, a small bag of flour, some sugar and salt. A few moldy potatoes, already in the garbage can, must be hastily rescued, for they will provide much of tonight's meal. We will leave a handful of onions, and a dish of dried beans. All the rest we take away: the meat, the fresh vegetables, the canned goods, the crackers, the candy.

5 Now we have stripped the house: the bathroom has been dismantled, the running water shut off, the electric wires taken out. Next we take away the house. The family can move to the toolshed. It is crowded, but much better than the situation in Hong Kong, where (a United Nations report tells us) "it is not uncommon for a family of four or more to live in a bedspace, that is, on a bunk bed and the space it occupies—sometimes in two or three tiers—their only privacy provided by curtains."

6 But we have only begun. All the other houses in the neighborhood have also been removed; our suburb has become a shantytown. Still, our family is fortunate to have a shelter; 250,000 people in Calcutta have none at all and simply live in the streets. Our family is now about on a par with the city of Cali in Colombia, where, an official of the World Bank writes, "on one hillside alone, the slum population is estimated at 40,000—without water, sanitation, or electric light. And not all the poor of Cali are as fortunate as that. Others have built their shacks near the city on land which lies beneath the flood mark. To these people the immediate environment is the open sewer of the city, a sewer which flows through their huts when the river rises."

7 And still we have not reduced our American family to the level at which life is lived in the greatest part of the globe. Communication must go next. No more newspapers, magazines, books—not that they are missed, since we must take away our family's literacy as well. Instead, in our shantytown we will allow one radio. In India the national average of radio ownership is one per 250 people,

but since the majority of radios is owned by city dwellers, our allowance is fairly generous.

8 Now government services must go. No more postman, no more fireman. There is a school, but it is three miles away and consists of two classrooms. They are not too overcrowded since only half the children in the neighborhood go to school. There are, of course, no hospitals or doctors nearby. The nearest clinic is ten miles away and is tended by a midwife. It can be reached by bicycle, provided that the family has a bicycle, which is unlikely. Or one can go by bus—not always inside, but there is usually room on top.

9 Finally, money. We will allow our family a cash hoard of five dollars. This will prevent our breadwinner from experiencing the tragedy of an Iranian peasant who went blind because he could not raise the $3.94 which he mistakenly thought he needed to secure admission to a hospital where he could have been cured.

10 Meanwhile the head of our family must earn his keep. As a peasant cultivator with three acres to tend, he may raise the equivalent of $100 to $300 worth of crops a year. If he is a tenant farmer, which is more than likely, a third or so of his crop will go to his landlord, and probably another 10 percent to the local moneylender. But there will be enough to eat. Or almost enough. The human body requires an input of at least 2,000 calories to replenish the energy consumed by its living cells. If our displaced American fares no better than an Indian peasant, he will average a replenishment of no more than 1,700–1,900 calories. His body, like any insufficiently fueled machine, will run down. That is one reason why life expectancy at birth in India today averages less than forty years.

11 But the children may help. If they are fortunate, they may find work and thus earn some cash to supplement the family's income. For example, they may be employed as are children in Hyderabad, Pakistan, sealing the ends of bangles over a small kerosene flame, a simple task which can be done at home. To be sure, the pay is small: eight annas—about ten cents—for sealing bangles. That is, eight annas per *gross* of bangles. And if they cannot find work? Well, they can scavenge, as do the children in Iran who in times of hunger search for the undigested oats in the droppings of horses.

12 And so we have brought our typical American family down to the very bottom of the human scale. It is, however, a bottom in which we can find, give or take a hundred million souls, at least a

billion people.* Of the remaining billion in the backward areas, most are slightly better off, but not much so; a few are comfortable; a handful rich.

13 Of course, this is only an impression of life in the underdeveloped lands. It is not life itself. There is still lacking the things that underdevelopment gives as well as those it takes away: the urinous smell of poverty, the display of disease, the flies, the open sewers. And there is lacking, too, a softening sense of familiarity. Even in a charnel house life has its passions and pleasures. A tableau, shocking to American eyes, is less shocking to eyes that have never known any other. But it gives one a general idea. It begins to add pictures of reality to the statistics by which underdevelopment is ordinarily measured. When we are told that half the world's population enjoys a standard of living "less than $100 a year," this is what the figures mean.

*Such an estimate is, of necessity, highly conjectural. It takes in only 300 million of India's population and 50 million of Pakistan's, a charitable figure. It includes 50 million Arabs and 100 million Africans, a large underestimate. From South and Central America's poverty it adds in but another 50 million. The remainder of the billion can be made up from mainland China alone. And we have kept as a statistical reserve the Afghans, Burmese, Indonesians, Koreans, Vietnamese—nearly 200 million in all, among whom is to be found some of the worst poverty on the face of the globe.

Questions About "Exposition"

1. What does Heilbroner try to explain to you?
2. Why does he choose the method of explanation that he does?
3. Does he make abundantly clear to you what it means to live on less than one hundred dollars a year? Explain.

Questions on Diction and Writing Techniques

1. Mark in your text those words that are new to you, but whose meaning you inferred from their context. Define them in your own words. Compare your definitions with those in your

dictionary. Look up in your dictionary any other words that are new to you. Use the words in both groups in sentences.

2. What does coherence within and between paragraphs contribute toward ease of reading? By what means does Heilbroner achieve this coherence?
3. What is Heilbroner's source(s) of material?
4. Making specific reference to the text, comment on the effect of Heilbroner's use of detailed information.

For Discussion, Reading, and Writing

1. Mark and number in your text the steps by which Heilbroner transforms a typical American family into an equally typical family of the underdeveloped world.
2. Why, according to Heilbroner, is the life expectancy at birth in India what it is?
3. Fill the blanks in this passage from memory to make it intelligible:

   To begin to _____ economic development we must have a picture of the _____ with which it contends. We must conjure up in our mind's eye what _____ means for the two billion human beings for whom it is not a _____ but a living _____ of daily life. Unless we can see the Great Ascent from the _____ point of those who must make the _____, we cannot hope to understand the _____ of the march.

   Compare your words with those in paragraph 1 of this essay.
4. Consider the probable benefits or disadvantages of your being stripped of a possession such as a car, a hi-fi, a TV set, a pocket computer, an electric hair dryer. Write a short essay on the subject, making sure to explain your ideas with sufficient detail and clarity to convince a reader of the validity of your thesis.
5. To support your ideas in a short expository essay on a subject with which you are familiar, include in it apt quotations from the writing of one or more experts.

OUSTING THE STRANGER FROM THE HOUSE

Colman McCarthy

Colman McCarthy is a journalist and freelance writer whose wide-ranging interests are evident in articles published in diverse journals.

---

1 When I turned off the television for the last time about a year ago and dumped the set for good, some friends, relatives and unasked advisers on the block predicted I would not last long without it. Few disputed the common gripe that TV is a wasteland, with irrigation offered only by the rare trickle of a quality program. Instead, they doubted that the addiction of some twenty years before the tube could be stilled by this sudden break with the past. It is true that an addiction had me, my veins eased only by a fix of 30 to 35 hours a week; my wife's dosage was similar, and our children—three boys under 7—already listened more to the television than to us.

2 Now, a year later—a family living as cultural cave men, says an anthropologist friend—the decision we made was one of the wisest of our married life. The ratings—our private Nielsens—during this year of setlessness have been high, suggesting that such common acts as talking with one's children, sharing ideas with one's wife, walking to the neighborhood library on a Saturday morning, quiet evenings of reading books and magazines aloud to each other, or eating supper as a family offer more intellectual and emotional stimulation than anything on television.

3 The severity of an addiction to TV is not that it reduces the victim to passivity while watching it but that it demands he be a compulsive activist to get in front of it. If I arrived home at 6, for example, and dinner was ready at 6:25—my wife's afternoon movie had run late, so dinner was late—I would shove down the food in five minutes. The deadline, falling like a guillotine, was at 6:30.

Chancellor came on then, Cronkite at 7; if CBS was dull, Smith and Reasoner were on ABC. If I hadn't finished dinner, I would sprint back to the table during the commercials for short-order gulps, then back to cool John, Uncle Walter or wry Harry. My wife, desperate Mav, was left at the table to control the bedlam of the kids, caused by my in-and-out sprints. The chaos I heard coming from the dining room was fitting: it was matched by the chaos in the world reported on the evening news, except the latter, in the vague "out there," was easier to handle.

4 With the set gone, these compulsions and in-turnings have gone too. We eat dinner in leisure and peace now. We stay at the playground until the children have had enough fun, not when I need to rush home to watch the 4 P.M. golf. Occasionally, my wife and I have the exotic experience of spending an evening in relaxed conversation, not the little half-stops of talk we once made in a forced march to Marital Communication. In those days, we would turn off the set in midevening and be immediately oppressed by the silence.

5 What had been happening all those years of watching television, I see now, was not only an addiction but also, on a deeper level, an adjustment. All of us had become adjusted to living with a stranger in the house. Is there any more basic definition of a television set than that? More, the stranger in the house was not there to entertain us, a notion the televisers would like to serve. The stranger was present to sell us products. The person before a set may think he is a viewer but the sponsors who pay for broadcasts know better: he is a buyer. It is a commercial arrangement, with the TV set a salesman permanently assigned to one house, and often two or three salesmen working different rooms. It is a myth that TV is free entertainment.

6 I was not only paying personally for the stranger-salesman in my house but he was often manipulating or lying to my children. I saw the effects in such places as the supermarket aisles, when the boys would loudly demand a sugared cereal, junk-snack or six pack of soda, all of these items only high-priced garbage that helps rot the teeth and keeps children from fruit and other nutritious food. My kids had been conditioned well by the sellers on TV, predatory strangers as menacing in one way as street predators are in another. But, someone told me, that's only commercial television, suggesting

that programs like "Sesame Street" and its mimics are different. They are, perhaps, but no more worthy.

7 If the televisers want to teach my children something, I suggest such subjects as obedience to parents, sharing toys with brothers and sisters, kindness to animals, respect for grandparents. These kinds of lessons were strangely missing from the "quality" childrens' shows I looked in on. It is true that these concepts must be taught by the parents but it is insufferable to note the preachings of the "Sesame"-type producers, hearing them blat about how they care for children. I see their programs as a moral hustle, conning parents into thinking it's a high educational experience to dump the kids before the tube. In the end, the yammering about letters, shapes, numbers does not liberate the child's imagination. It captures it, a quick-action lariat that ropes in the child's most precious resource, his creativity.

8 Occasionally I have feelings that I may be missing an event of special value, a feeling that the televised truth goes marching on without me. But in my straggler status I have never failed to catch up eventually with the essence of what I missed, mostly by reading the newspapers or magazines—say a Presidential press conference or the Watergate testimony.

9 The stranger is gone now. Our lives are fuller and richer. Cold turkey worked. The kids don't run to neighbors' houses to watch TV, as I had feared. As for whether we ever invite the stranger back to our house, it isn't likely unless the industry learns new manners.

10 A first sign of the kind of manners I'm thinking about would be revealed if, say, some evening this announcement was beamed into the 97 per cent of America's electrically wired homes that have TV's: "Ladies and gentlemen, until further notice we are ceasing our broadcasts. The programs we had planned are now seen to be dull, banal, pointless, not worth your time and not ours. Don't turn to another channel, because you will only be insulted there too—insulted by the programs and by the corporate advertisers who want to gull you into buying products you can live well, even better, without.

11 "Come forward and turn off your set. When the die-out dot appears, get up and take a walk to the library and get a book. Or turn to your husband and wife and surprise them with a conversation. Or call a neighbor you haven't spoken with in months. Write

a letter to a friend who has lost track of you. Turn off your set now. When we devise some worthwhile programing, we'll be back on the air. Meanwhile, you'll be missing almost nothing."

Questions About "Exposition"

1. Does McCarthy adequately explain why he defines TV the way he does? Explain, making specific reference to the text.
2. Be prepared to discuss in class whether he sufficiently explains why he banned TV.
3. Does he explain, to your satisfaction, how the quality of the life of the McCarthy family has changed since the stranger he refers to has gone?

Questions on Diction and Writing Techniques

1. Mark in your text those words that are new to you, but whose meaning you inferred from their context. Define them in your own words. Compare your definitions with those in your dictionary. Look up in your dictionary any other words that are new to you. Use the words in both groups in sentences.
2. Does McCarthy's choice of the words "wasteland" and "addiction" help to fulfill his expository purpose? Explain.
3. Rewrite sentence 2 of paragraph 2 to make all members of its series of coordinate elements of the same kind.
4. What is McCarthy's purpose in writing "for example" (par. 3)?
5. McCarthy might have written, in paragraph 3, "I would go back to the table." Why did he choose the verb he did?
6. State, in a sentence of not over twenty-five words, the main idea of this essay.
7. Summarize the essay in a paragraph of not over one hundred words.

For Discussion, Reading, and Writing

1. What, according to McCarthy, is "the severity of an addiction to TV"?

2. "It is a myth that TV is free entertainment." Do you agree? Explain.

3. Would you add to or subtract from the list of subjects that McCarthy suggests to televisers who want to teach children something? Explain.

4. Make a list of TV programs that you find beneficial and another of those you find useless. Prepare to defend your choices in class. Explain your choices in a short essay.

5. Explain in a short essay—with specific examples from your own experience—your opinion regarding any point McCarthy makes in his essay.

5

Patterns of Organization

Illustration

Organization becomes more and more clear as you understand more completely what you have in mind to say and why it is important.

—Edward M. White

THERE are a number of techniques for imposing order on and for organizing the material in expository writing. We will examine six of them – illustration, comparison and contrast, definition, division and classification, process, and causal analysis.

The simplest and most common pattern is illustration – giving examples. If you wanted to show that some doctors see their patients not merely as cases of appendicitis, measles, or athlete's foot but as whole persons, you might cite as examples humane doctors you know or have heard about. If you wanted to show that Doc Jones is considerate of his patients, you might explain what you mean with examples: He doesn't keep his patients waiting in his office; he listens attentively to their complaints; he doesn't interpose a telephone answering service between himself and them; he makes house calls. Illustration makes a generality concrete, more intelligible, and more interesting.

Illustration can be used in a sentence, a paragraph, or an essay. Consider this sentence:

> I had such wonderful toys: a real steam engine, a magic lantern, and a collection of soldiers already nearly a thousand strong [Winston Churchill, *My Early Life*].

Winston Churchill makes clear what he means by the vague generalization "I had such wonderful toys" with illustraton—by giving examples.

Here is an example of illustration in a paragraph:

> Even the most productive writers are expert dawdlers, doers of unnecessary errands, seekers of interruptions—trials to their wives or husbands, associates, and themselves. They sharpen well-pointed pencils and go out to buy more blank paper, rearrange offices, wander through libraries and bookstores, chop wood, walk, drive, make unnecessary calls, nap, daydream, and try not "consciously" to think about what they are going to write so they can think subconsciously about it [Donald M. Murray, "Write Before Writing"].

Without the examples given in the second sentence, would you know as well as you do what the writer meant by "expert dawdlers, doers of unnecessary errands, seekers of interruptions"?

Illustration is a means of explaining, with particulars, a generalization that might otherwise be obscure:

> Everybody at some time has probably felt blood pressure rise and pulse increase when loaded words have been used to diminish him. The laborer who is called "a hardhat," the poor white who is called "a redneck," the black man who is called "boy," the intellectual who is called "an egghead," the liberal who is called "a bleeding heart," the policeman who is called "a pig"—all these and many others are painfully aware how brutally the English language can be used to humiliate them [Russell Baker, "Purging Stag Words"].

Here the writer, with his examples in sentence two, supports, clarifies, and makes credible the generalization he states in sentence one.

The relationship of ideas in such a paragraph can be diagrammed:

general statement — It is a commonplace of modern technology that there is a high measure of certainty that problems have solutions before there is knowledge of how they are to be solved.

1st particular — As this is written in 1966, it is reasonably certain that a man can be landed on the moon within the next five years. However, many of the details of the procedure for doing so are not yet worked out.

2nd particular It is certain that air and water pollution can be more effectively controlled for those who, for better or worse, must remain on this planet. Uncertainty continues as to the best methods of doing so.

3rd particular It is probable that commuters can be moved in safety and some comfort into American cities. How this will be accomplished is still to be determined [John Kenneth Galbraith, *The Industrial State*].

Here is another instructive instance of the use of illustration. Its author starts a paragraph with

> There is a rule of economy in the endowments with which nature equips her creatures. For each one, there is the gift of this or that kind of competence to achieve living effectiveness; but, such competence being assured, there are not commonly given gifts beyond that necessary measure. Each possession of an endowment implies, so to speak, the sacrifice—or at any rate the lack—of others [Alan Devoe, "Snapping Turtle"].

Notice that Devoe, after making a generalization in the first sentence, gives variations of it in the second and third. Then, to explain further what he means, he adds

> It is given to a rat to be canny and quick; and a rat's body, compensatingly, is vulnerable. A porcupine is dim and slow; it has the gift of protecting armament. A hare can outrun its foes; it has not the genius of outfighting them. A mole can outburrow its enemies; it has not the gift of outthinking them. Natural economy disallows that any creature shall have at once agility, armor, fighting tools, keen senses, and shrewd wits.

The writer's four examples—a rat, a porcupine, a hare, and a mole—make plain to the reader what otherwise might not be clear about nature's "rule of economy."

To better understand what I mean when I call illustration a pattern of organization, consider the structure of Devoe's paragraph. First is the topic sentence:

> There is a rule of economy in the endowments with which nature equips her creatures.

The second and third sentences clarify, expand, restate, and make more specific the topic sentence:

> For each one, there is the gift of this or that kind of competence to achieve living effectiveness; but, such competence being assured, there are not commonly given gifts beyond that necessary measure. Each possession of an endowment implies, so to speak, the sacrifice—or at any rate the lack—of others.

Each of the next four sentences is a specific example of the generalization made in the topic sentence:

> It is given to a rat to be canny and quick; and a rat's body, compensatingly, is vulnerable. A porcupine is dim and slow; it has the gift of a protecting armament. A hare can outrun its foes; it has not the genius of outfighting them. A mole can outburrow its enemies; it has not the gift of outthinking them.

The final sentence summarizes the paragraph:

> Natural economy disallows that any creature shall have at once agility, armor, fighting tools, keen senses, and shrewd wits.

Devoe's illustration of nature's "rule of economy" not only explains his topic sentence; it also supports it—that is, it demonstrates its validity. By means of his four examples the writer makes acceptable to his readers the generalization in his topic sentence. At the same time he is also developing his paragraph. This is what I mean when I call illustration a pattern of organization.

Recall how the author of "Menial Jobs Taught Me a Lot" (pages 34–37) developed the first paragraph in the body of his essay, paragraph 2. After stating in his topic sentence the main idea of the paragraph, "jobs available to a teenager without special training do not pay well," he illustrates that idea. He gives five examples of poorly paying jobs: mowing lawns, waiting on tables, packaging groceries, tending a machine in a factory, and working as a laborer on a construction project. These examples—in explanation of his topic sentence—supply the details needed to develop the topic sentence, make out of an unsupported statement (a mere assertion) a statement with reasons, and, in addition, make the paragraph complete and its main idea convincing.

The author of "Menial Jobs Taught Me a Lot" also develops paragraph 3 with illustration, this time with two examples. The first—in support of the main idea of the paragraph, "my jobs . . . soon became boring"—is an extended example, which takes up most of the paragraph. The second, in the last two sentences of the paragraph, also in support of the paragraph's thesis, is relatively short. Paragraph 4 in the body of the essay is also developed by illustration in support of its main idea: "none of the jobs I had was fulfilling." Each of these paragraphs constitutes in itself an example of the lessons learned by the author from his menial jobs. "Menial Jobs Taught Me a Lot" is a good example of the use of illustration to develop an essay.

WRITING A LETTER

Ronald Varney

Ronald Varney's essays, profiles, and reviews have appeared in a number of contemporary journals.

1 A man who knows how to write a personal letter has at his disposal a very powerful tool. A personal letter engages in a unique way, for everyone likes to get letters, whereas some people dread getting phone calls. A letter can be enjoyed at leisure, read and

reread, reflected upon. It can set up intimate conversation between two people far apart; it can sustain a friendship with very little effort. Sometimes it is the most effective way to offer counsel or congratulations, argue a cause, remonstrate, solve a crisis, or air a grievance. In fact, a personal letter can bring out the self in a way that is not always possible in person.

2 I will give an example. A few years ago my older brother and I were not getting along. We had been close as children but had grown apart. Our meetings were awkward; our conversation was brusque and ironic; and every attempt to clear the air seemed to only deepen our misunderstandings. Then he moved to a small island in the Caribbean and we lost touch. One day he wrote me a letter. He described his island and its people, told me what he was doing, said how he felt, and encouraged me to write. Rereading the letter, I was astonished by its wit, style, intelligence, sympathy. These were all qualities I had once esteemed in my older brother but thought he no longer possessed. I had never known he could write so well. And with that one letter we became friends again.

3 It might never have occurred to my brother to write me had he not been in a place where there were no phones. For him, writing was a necessity. It also turned out to be the best way for us to get back in touch. Because we live in an age of instant communication, people often forget that they don't always have to phone. They have an option. And that is to write.

Questions About "Illustration"

1. By what means does Varney try to convince you to accept the main idea of this essay?
2. Does he amply support his thesis? Explain.

Questions on Diction and Writing Techniques

1. How does your dictionary define "engages" and "remonstrate" (par. 1), "brusque" and "wit" (par. 2), "communication" (par. 3)? Use each of these words in a sentence.

2. Is paragraph 1 coherent? Explain.
3. What is the purpose, in paragraph 1, of "in fact"?
4. What is the purpose of the first sentence of paragraph 2?
5. Comment on Varney's use of narration as an expository technique.

For Discussion, Reading, and Writing

1. In a book about AT&T, John Brooks wrote about the telephone: "Beyond doubt it has crippled if not killed the ancient art of letter writing." What do you think? For a discussion in class, compile a list of the benefits of the telephone and a list of its disabilities.
2. Personal experience is obviously Varney's main source of material in this brief selection. In an equally short essay, draw upon your own personal experience to illustrate any point whatsoever.
3. Develop a paragraph by illustrating a generalization based on your experience with any medium of communication.
4. You've been out of touch for some time with a relative or friend. Try to reestablish contact in a letter that brings him up to date with current information about yourself—your interests, priorities, life-style, or whatever. Rewrite the first draft of your letter, making sure to make clear with particulars any generalization you make.

IT'S HOW YOU ASK IT

Sydney Harris

Sydney J. Harris is an award-winning journalist and author of the widely syndicated newspaper column "Strictly Personal."

---

1 What a lot of people fail to learn, even as they grow older, is that the way you ask a question can determine the kind of answer you get. The professional pollsters are keenly aware of this and can elicit seemingly contradictory answers by asking the same question in somewhat different ways.

2 As an example, I recall the story of the two priests arguing about whether it was proper to smoke and pray at the same time. One said it was, and the other said it wasn't. To settle the matter, they agreed that both should write to the Pope for his opinion.

3 A few weeks later they met and compared notes. Each claimed that the Pope had supported his view and suspected the other of falsifying the reply he got from the Holy Office.

4 Finally, one asked, "How did you phrase your question?" The other replied, "I asked whether it was proper to smoke while one is praying, and the Pope answered, 'Certainly not, praying is a serious business and permits of no distractions.' And how did you phrase your question?"

5 "Well," said the other, "I asked if it was proper to pray while smoking, and the Pope said, 'Certainly, prayer is always in order.' "

6 Some years ago, two large auto companies made expensive public surveys at much the same time to try to find out what kind of car the American motorist might buy in the future.

7 One company's pollster asked the direct question, "What kind of car would you like to have?" The majority of auto owners replied that they wanted a car that was compact, economical, functional, and subdued in looks.

8 The other company's pollster was far shrewder and more sensitive to the self-deception most of us unconsciously practice. He asked: "What kind of car do you think your neighbor would like to have?" And there the majority replied that their neighbors coveted large, ostentatious, gimmicky models that looked more like boats or airplanes.

9 The first auto maker nearly went broke putting out sedate little cars long before the public was ready for them, while the second enjoyed a banner year with its rakish, gaudy, rear-finned models. In fact, the first company was forced to retool to meet the competition.

10 It is far harder to devise fair and "unweighted" questions than it is to find the answers. Indeed, the most significant advances in

science have come not from finding answers, but from beginning to ask the right questions in the right way. Like that simplest one of all, which no one asked until Newton, "Why do apples fall down instead of up?"

Questions About "Illustration"

1. What is the main idea of this essay?
2. Does Harris succeed in making that idea clear to you? Explain.

Questions on Diction and Writing Techniques

1. How does your dictionary define "elicit" (par. 1); "ostentatious" (par. 8); "sedate," "rakish," and "gaudy" (par. 9)? Use each of these words in a sentence.
2. Evaluate paragraph 1 as an opening paragraph and paragraph 10 as a closing paragraph.
3. Is the essay unified? Explain.

For Discussion, Reading, and Writing

1. Write a short essay on any subject, using one or two anecdotes to illustrate your main idea.
2. Find in your personal experience simple material that can be used to illustrate a meaningful generalization. Embody this information in a short essay.
3. How have your views about college changed since you first arrived on campus? Write about them in a short essay based on specific experiences.

THE ROUGHEST ROLE IN SPORTS

Bill Surface

William E. Surface is a journalist and frequent contributor of articles to a variety of American popular magazines. He writes primarily about sports.

---

1 The scene: Boston Garden, tightly packed for the fifth game in the 1976 National Basketball Association (NBA) championship series. A high-leaping Boston Celtic player swishes the ball through the basket, and the buzzer sounds to end the second overtime period —and the game. Bedlam erupts as the hometown fans cheer a Celtic victory over the Phoenix Suns.

2 But a sweat-drenched referee, Richie Powers, views the game more precisely. The timekeeper, he notices, failed to stop the clock after the goal, so Powers rules that there is one second left in the game. When the clock starts again, the score is 112–110 in favor of Boston, but in that one second the Suns tie the game and send it into a third overtime period. Now, the hometown fans feel like killing Powers. One woman throws her purse at him and screams: "You ain't even human!"

3 "In this job," Powers retorts, "that helps."

4 Indeed, it takes a special breed of man to excel at the most difficult job in all of professional basketball, baseball, football and hockey: officiating the game. Expertise is not enough. Simply no one in sports endures more pressure—and needs greater discipline—than the plucky, perceptive autocrats wearing "prison stripes" or "mortician's blue," depending on the sport.

5 Whether he's called referee, umpire or official, such a man must be superbly skilled in his job in order to instantly interpret as many as 100 pages of complex rules. And an official often needs to

outhustle the players to gain a strategic view of every frenzied battle for the ball or puck to detect player violations.

6 An official also has to be something of a detective to notice players' varied ruses to get opponents penalized for supposedly fouling them. Referees often foil these plots swiftly—as when hockey's Lloyd Gilmour simply ignored a crafty Chicago Black Hawk who pretended that he had been tripped so viciously that he somersaulted across the ice. The faker got up and fumed, "What's it take to get a penalty on that killer?" Gilmour replied: "Better acting."

7 Far different techniques are needed to detect players who conceal their violations more adroitly. Basketball players, for example, will position their bodies to keep a referee from seeing when they clutch, rather than legally touch, opponents. But referees learn through watching slow-motion films that the position of a player's arms or body tells, without fail, when he is holding an opponent.

8 All officials need superior vision. Consider the baseball umpire's task. Bent in a fatiguing crouch behind the catcher, he determines where the blurred, aspirin-sized image spinning toward him at up to 100 m.p.h. unpredictably drops, rises or curves. During 1/60 of a second, the umpire decides if the slightest part of the ball crossed the plate while traveling on a plane between the batter's armpits and knees. Even when the ball misses the strike zone, an umpire must also judge if the player—though he has drawn his bat back almost instantly—has made a swing for a strike. Likewise, an umpire needs the savvy to tell if the ball dropped suddenly because it had been illegally dampened with a pitcher's hair oil, saliva or perspiration; or because a sharpened thumbnail had cut a hole in the ball.

9 Referees must retain their composure while absorbing almost unbelievable psychological and verbal punishment. A referee, *always* working before unfriendly crowds which are apt to jeer at the first sight of him, has orders to exude poise under the most testing circumstances—no matter if pelted by ice, frankfurters, and even bottles. Tougher yet, an official must resist both teams' attempts to unnerve him and gain more favorable decisions.

10 Still, a referee cannot be too rigid. Since league authorities rarely overrule his judgment, an official must also function as the sport's supreme court and thus deliberate if he, as the district judge, might have erred. Though never swayed by how loudly a fiery coach protests, a good official will change decisions when additional evidence appears.

11 Even when a referee's instant call is correct, he's still got to face the anger that smolders long, long after a game. Sometimes that anger takes on an ominous tone, as it did in the 1975 World Series. Umpire Larry Barnett's disputed ruling that a batter did not obstruct the catcher brought him a letter warning that if he did not make up a $10,000 bet loss, the sender would "put a .38-caliber bullet in your head." Yet, as one official reasons, "An umpire's really in trouble—not in making 'bad' calls—but when his decisions bring nice mail and nice smiles."

12 A referee must be strong physically and shrug off frequent pain. Occupational hazards include torn muscles, being cut by punches and spiked shoes when breaking up fights, being stunned by frozen pucks rocketing at 120 m.p.h. Baseballs, which often travel almost as fast as hockey pucks, have snapped the steel bars of umpires' face-masks, then knocked out teeth and broken jaws. In football, even an agile referee can be knocked down by gargantuan athletes charging full speed.

13 To get into superb shape, each sport official must report to pre-season training camps at a stipulated weight. There he stretches, sprints, lifts weights, does calisthenics and other exercises needed especially for his sport. Hockey's officials, for instance, must run a mile in no more than seven minutes, do 80 sit-ups within two minutes, and skate in relay races for two hours. Then, to stretch and strengthen their leg muscles, they practice alternate squatting and standing on skates. Next comes the hand-wrestling needed to separate brawling players.

14 In an average pro-basketball game, a referee sprints some six miles on a hardwood court and loses up to ten pounds. Yet basketball's referees must satisfy a supervisor that their facial expressions show "firmness and confidence"—and that their whistle's short blast always has the requisite "sharp, crisp tone." Baseball's umpires holler "ball" and "strike" from deep in their chests to develop such a booming, authoritative voice that they seldom can ever speak in a normal tone.

15 Pre-season study sessions are equally strenuous for football officials. They plunge into a daily, 14-hour program that includes a 200-question rules examination and a concentrated film study of all the major calls made by each of the 84 officials during the previous season.

16 Referees have demonstrated their spunk long before they finally

reach a major league. Combining a fondness for sports and a need for extra income, most start officiating for as little as $2 a game in small arenas. A "take-charge" referee may be noticed by scouts as he doggedly advances to college games, to umpiring schools or league try-out camps. Even so, the grittiest ones who impress major leagues may wait for the few available jobs that, like those in pro basketball and hockey, eventually pay around $43,000 a season (plus another $8000 if selected for championship playoffs).

17 Football's weekend referees—mostly coaches, teachers and executives—wait still longer before they can hope to officiate pro football for up to $575 a game ($1500 for the Super Bowl). The National Football League (NFL) considers only men with records proving that they have officiated for at least ten years (including five years in college games) and have a lifelong dedication to the game. Nonetheless, of 150 such men found qualified to officiate, the NFL hires no more than six new ones each season.

18 Referees in all sports are evaluated by scouts, supervisors and often by wide-angle cameras focused on them. After poring over films, the supervisors rate officials and notify them of the conclusions. At season's end, usually from one to six officials in each sport who are considered unsatisfactory are quietly dismissed.

19 Even the best referees find themselves under growing scrutiny. Television's slow-motion instant replays of close decisions foster demands by angry fans that such cameras be used to overrule, or even replace, officials. But in fact TV replays pinpoint only a few dozen of pro-football officials' 41,000 split-second decisions during a season that are genuinely arguable or wrong. As a result, many athletes are *against* cameras replacing referees. Instant replay, says one, eliminates a common alibi for the mistake that cost his team a victory: "The ref missed it."

20 The members of this exclusive breed of men are proud of their oft-scorned, but indispensable, role. Such pride was perhaps best characterized in a baseball game when umpire Nestor Chylak carefully brushed home plate, then "discovered" that he needed to be resupplied with baseballs—a kindly intended ploy to enable the catcher to shake off some pain caused by a wild pitch earlier. Minutes later, the ungrateful catcher grumbled loudly and waved his arms wildly over the final call ending the game. Chylak was loudly jeered on leaving the field.

21 "Is it worth fighting off the world this way every day?" Chylak was asked later. He beamed, then said, "What other guy can walk away from a game feeling he's a winner–*every* time?"

Questions About "Illustration"

1. Surface might have written paragraph 6 as follows:

   An official also has to be something of a detective to notice players' varied ruses to get opponents penalized for supposedly fouling them. Referees often foil these plots swiftly.

   Which version do you prefer? Why?

2. Mark in your text where Surface signals his use of illustration with "for example" and with "for instance."
3. In what paragraph and by what means does Surface support his assertion: "Sometimes that anger takes on an ominous tone . . ."?
4. Mark in your text and enumerate all paragraphs in which Surface uses illustration as an expository technique.
5. Does Surface amply support his claim that the referee is "a special breed"? Explain in detail.

Questions on Diction and Writing Techniques

1. How does your dictionary define "bedlam" (par. 1), "autocrats" (par. 4), "ruses" (par. 6); "adroitly" (par. 7), "savvy" (par. 8), "ominous" (par. 11), "gargantuan" (par. 12), "scrutiny" (par. 19), "characterized" (par. 20)? Use each of these words in a sentence.
2. Point out where Surface utilizes narration as an expository technique. Show how dialogue contributes to the effectiveness of the storytelling.
3. Mark in your text the vivid verbs that Surface uses to make his writing more appealing.
4. Surface uses many transition words. Why? Mark them in your text. Explain the function of each.

5. Explain the role that each sentence in paragraph 8 plays within the paragraph.

For Discussion, Reading, and Writing

1. Attend in person or watch on TV any kind of sports event that requires a referee, umpire, or other official. To gather material for a short essay about refereeing, observe the official(s) at length, making notes as you do so about their behavior. Prewrite the essay. Repeat the process of observation as need be to assemble ample information about your subject. Write a draft of the essay. Rewrite it, making sure that it contains ample illustration to support any general statement you've made.

A RED LIGHT FOR SCOFFLAWS

Frank Trippett

Frank Trippett, a lifelong newspaperman and sometime editor of major American popular journals, is a senior writer for *Time* magazine.

---

1 Law-and-order is the longest-running and probably the best-loved political issue in U.S. history. Yet it is painfully apparent that millions of Americans who would never think of themselves as lawbreakers, let alone criminals, are taking increasing liberties with the legal codes that are designed to protect and nourish their society. Indeed, there are moments today—amid outlaw litter, tax cheating, illicit noise and motorized anarchy—when it seems as though the scofflaw represents the wave of the future. Harvard Sociologist

David Riesman suspects that a majority of Americans have blithely taken to committing supposedly minor derelictions as a matter of course. Already, Riesman says, the ethic of U.S. society is in danger of becoming this: "You're a fool if you obey the rules."

2 Nothing could be more obvious than the evidence supporting Riesman. Scofflaws abound in amazing variety. The graffiti-prone turn public surfaces into visual rubbish. Bicyclists often ride as though two-wheeled vehicles are exempt from all traffic laws. Litterbugs convert their communities into trash dumps. Widespread flurries of ordinances have failed to clear public places of high-decibel portable radios, just as earlier laws failed to wipe out the beer-soaked hooliganism that plagues many parks. Tobacco addicts remain hopelessly blind to signs that say NO SMOKING. Respectably dressed pot smokers no longer bother to duck out of public sight to pass around a joint. The flagrant use of cocaine is a festering scandal in middle- and upper-class life. And then there are (hello, Everybody!) the jaywalkers.

3 The dangers of scofflawry vary wildly. The person who illegally spits on the sidewalk remains disgusting, but clearly poses less risk to others than the company that illegally buries hazardous chemical waste in an unauthorized location. The fare beater on the subway presents less threat to life than the landlord who ignores fire safety statutes. The most immediately and measurably dangerous scofflawry, however, also happens to be the most visible. The culprit is the American driver, whose lawless activities today add up to a colossal public nuisance. The hazards range from routine double parking that jams city streets to the drunk driving that kills some 25,000 people and injures at least 650,000 others yearly. Illegal speeding on open highways? New surveys show that on some interstate highways 83% of all drivers are currently ignoring the federal 55 m.p.h. speed limit.

4 The most flagrant scofflaw of them all is the red-light runner. The flouting of stop signals has got so bad in Boston that residents tell an anecdote about a cabby who insists that red lights are "just for decoration." The power of the stoplight to control traffic seems to be waning everywhere. In Los Angeles, red-light running has become perhaps the city's most common traffic violation. In New York City, going through an intersection is like Russian roulette. Admits Police Commissioner Robert J. McGuire: "Today it's a

50-50 toss-up as to whether people will stop for a red light." Meanwhile, his own police largely ignore the lawbreaking.

5 Red-light running has always been ranked as a minor wrong, and so it may be in individual instances. When the violation becomes habitual, widespread and incessant, however, a great deal more than a traffic management problem is involved. The flouting of basic rules of the road leaves deep dents in the social mood. Innocent drivers and pedestrians pay a repetitious price in frustration, inconvenience and outrage, not to mention a justified sense of mortal peril. The significance of red-light running is magnified by its high visibility. If hypocrisy is the tribute that vice pays to virtue, then furtiveness is the true outlaw's salute to the force of law-and-order. The red-light runner, however, shows no respect whatever for the social rules, and society cannot help being harmed by any repetitions and brazen display of contempt for the fundamentals of order.

6 The scofflaw spirit is pervasive. It is not really surprising when schools find, as some do, that children frequently enter not knowing some of the basic rules of living together. For all their differences, today's scofflaws are of a piece as a symptom of elementary social demoralization—the loss by individuals of the capacity to govern their own behavior in the interest of others.

7 The prospect of the collapse of public manners is not merely a matter of etiquette. Society's first concern will remain major crime, but a foretaste of the seriousness of incivility is suggested by what has been happening in Houston. Drivers on Houston freeways have been showing an increasing tendency to replace the rules of the road with violent outbreaks. Items from the Houston police department's new statistical category—freeway traffic violence: 1) Driver flashes high-beam lights at car that cut in front of him, whose occupants then hurl a beer can at his windshield, kick out his tail lights, slug him eight stitches' worth. 2) Dump-truck driver annoyed by delay batters trunk of stalled car ahead and its driver with steel bolt. 3) Hurrying driver of 18-wheel truck deliberately rear-ends car whose driver was trying to stay within 55 m.p.h. limit. The Houston Freeway Syndrome has fortunately not spread everywhere. But the question is: Will it?

8 Americans are used to thinking that law-and-order is threatened mainly by stereotypical violent crime. When the foundations of U.S. law have actually been shaken, however, it has always been

because ordinary law-abiding citizens took to skirting the law. Major instance: Prohibition. Recalls Donald Barr Chidsey in *On and Off the Wagon:* "Lawbreaking proved to be not painful, not even uncomfortable, but, in a mild and perfectly safe way, exhilarating." People wiped out Prohibition at last not only because of the alcohol issue but because scofflawry was seriously undermining the authority and legitimacy of government. Ironically, today's scofflaw spirit, whatever its undetermined origins, is being encouraged unwittingly by government at many levels. The failure of police to enforce certain laws is only the surface of the problem: they take their mandate from the officials and constituents they serve. Worse, most state legislatures have helped subvert popular compliance with the federal 55 m.p.h. law, some of them by enacting puny fines that trivialize transgressions. On a higher level, the Administration in Washington has dramatized its wish to nullify civil rights laws simply by opposing instead of supporting certain court-ordered desegregation rulings. With considerable justification, environmental groups, in the words of *Wilderness* magazine, accuse the Administration of "destroying environmental laws by failing to enforce them, or by enforcing them in ways that deliberately encourage noncompliance." Translation: scofflawry at the top.

9 The most disquieting thing about the scofflaw spirit is its extreme infectiousness. Only a terminally foolish society would sit still and allow it to spread indefinitely.

Questions About "Illustration"

1. To better appreciate Trippett's use of illustration as a method of development, underline and enumerate the examples he gives. Making specific reference to the text, explain in detail Trippett's purpose in giving examples.

Questions on Diction and Expository Techniques

1. How does your dictionary define "illicit," "blithely," and "derelictions" (par. 1); "flouting" (par. 4); "pervasive" (par. 6); "incivility"

(par. 7); "stereotypical" and "noncompliance" (par. 8)? Use each of these words in a sentence.

2. Reexamine each paragraph. Enumerate those that contain a topic sentence. Underline each such sentence.
3. Transition words may be used to signal support, expansion, or qualification of a previous statement. What, in paragraph 3, does "however" signal? In what other paragraphs does Trippett use such words? Explain the contribution those words make to coherence within the paragraphs in which they appear.
4. Is the information in paragraph 2 sufficient to support the generalization Trippett makes in the paragraph?
5. Trippett quotes the well-known sociologist David Riesman in paragraph 1. Where else in the essay does Trippett include quotations? How does the material within quotation marks, in each instance, relate to his expository purpose?
6. Where does Trippett state his thesis? What is the advantage in his stating his main idea where he does rather than elsewhere in the essay?
7. Trippett wrote this piece for *Time* magazine. How differently might he have written it for a different audience: grammar school children, for example; or trainees at a police academy; or a society of sociologists?

For Discussion, Reading, and Writing

1. Based on information gathered from whatever source, especially from personal experience and observation, prewrite a short essay on the question raised in the quotation from David Riesman. Write a draft of such an essay one day and a final version the next.
2. Write an amply illustrated short essay about the flouting of rules in the high school you attended.
3. Are there scofflaws, in the sense Trippett uses the term, on your campus? Write a short essay about one such person.
4. Write a short essay on a particular characteristic of your classmates that you find fault with. Make your criticisms specific.

Comparison and Contrast

Easy writing makes hard reading.

—Ernest Hemingway

"I can hit a ball as far as you can."

"My brother can run as fast as your brother."

"My sister is smarter than your sister."

"I'm taller than you are."

Almost from the time that children begin to talk they compare, show similarities, and contrast, point out differences. (Since "to compare" means to examine for the purpose of noting similarities *and* differences, I will from time to time use "comparison" to denote comparison *and* contrast.)

When you bought a blue nylon long-sleeved shirt instead of a brown cotton short-sleeved one, when you decided to watch TV instead of going to a movie, when you elected to attend college A instead of college B–you used comparison. Your comparisons drew your attention to details and helped you to discover characteristics of things compared that you might not otherwise have been aware of. Your appreciation of one shirt was enhanced by comparing it with the other. Your decision to watch TV was made easier by comparing the benefits of doing so with those of attending a movie. And the virtues of college A became apparent only when you compared its facilities and opportunities with those of college B.

In your expository writing in college, you might use comparison to explain to your reader something unfamiliar by means of something familiar, as, for example, George Orwell does in "Shooting an Elephant":

> It was a serious matter to shoot a working elephant—it is comparable to destroying a large and costly piece of machinery—and obviously one ought not to do it if it can possibly be avoided.

You might want to make clear what a kibbutz is by comparing it with a commune, or what a commune is by comparing it with a family. In doing so, you are likely to give your reader a better understanding of each of the things in your comparison.

You might also use comparison to help to make evident the superiority of one thing over another. You might want to show that a white-collar job is better paying than a blue-collar job, that being a teacher is more fulfilling than being a tax collector, or that the Democrats' plan for tax reform is more helpful to wage-earners in the lower income tax brackets than is that of the Republicans.

Still another purpose might be to arrive at a general principle, idea, or theme shared by the things compared. This would be the case if you were to examine the subjects known as the humanities to see what they have in common.

Regardless of your purpose, your choice of items to compare and to contrast should comply with the following formulas. Items to be contrasted may be ones with unlike characteristics; for example, you may contrast a plant to an animal. Items to be compared should be of the same general type and in a similar area of interest. A rickshaw and an Indy 500 racing car are both vehicles, but their purposes are so different that a useful comparison could hardly be made between them. One might, however, because the comparison would be illuminating and thus useful, compare a rickshaw with a horse and buggy and an Indy 500 racing car with a stock racing car competing on a track at a county fair.

Like illustration, comparison and contrast is a helpful method of organizing exposition, as you saw in Maya Angelou's "Cotton-Picking Time" (pages 236–238). It can be used separately or together with one or more patterns of organization. In "Menial Jobs Taught Me a Lot" (pages 34–37), for example, although illustration is the predominant method of development, in the three paragraphs in the body of the essay the writer shows how his jobs were similar—"poorly paying, boring, and unfulfilling"—and is thus using comparison, along with illustration, to explain his thesis.

Observe how another writer uses contrast to develop the first half of a paragraph:

> Lenin, with whom I had a long conversation in Moscow in 1920, was, superficially, very unlike Gladstone, and yet, allowing for the difference of time and place and creed, the two men had much in common. To begin with the differences: Lenin was cruel, which Gladstone was not; Lenin had no respect for tradition, whereas Gladstone had a great deal; Lenin considered all means legitimate for securing the victory of his party, whereas for Gladstone politics was a game with certain rules that must be observed [Bertrand Russell, *Unpopular Essays*].

Notice, first of all, that Russell announces his method of paragraph development in his first, the topic, sentence. He proposes, he tells us, first to contrast: "Lenin . . . was . . . very unlike Gladstone"; then to compare: "the two men had much in common." In the second sentence, he contrasts the two men point by point, listing three points of dissimilarity: cruelty, respect for tradition, attitude toward politics. (Notice the use of "whereas" to signal one of the differences.)

Instead of contrasting point by point (sometimes called an alternating pattern), Russell might have first listed all the qualities of one man and then all the qualities of the other (sometimes called a divided or subject by subject pattern). This way of organizing the comparison requires the reader to remember or reread Lenin's qualities in order to compare them with Gladstone's:

> Lenin was cruel; he had no respect for tradition; he considered all means legitimate for securing the victory of his party. In contrast, Gladstone was not cruel; he had a great deal of respect for tradition; for him politics was a game with certain rules that must be observed.

Notice, in this version, the transitional expression "in contrast." Other expressions used to signal contrast are "on the other hand," "on the contrary," and "however." Some other transition words used to signal comparison are "likewise," "similarly," and "in a like manner."

Here is a full paragraph that is developed by use of contrast:

> As I pored over scouting reports and interviewed players and coaches from numerous NFL teams, it became clear that offensive football players like structure and discipline. They want to maintain the status quo. They tend to be conservative as people, and as football players they take comfort in repetitious practice of well-planned and well-executed plays. The defensive players, just as clearly, can't stand structure; their attitudes, their behavior, and their life-styles bear this out. They operate as though they've been put out of the tribe and are trying to show people that tribal structure is worthless anyway. Ostracism does not bother them; it serves as a source of fuel for their destructive energies. Rules or regulations put forward by anybody, anyplace, are to be challenged. Coaches find defensive players notably more difficult to control than their offensive teammates [Arnold J. Mandell, from *Saturday Review,* October 5, 1974].

Mandell first says all he has to say about offensive football players and then all he has to say about defensive players. Using this tactic, he reveals the qualities of one group by means of the qualities of the other just as Russell, using the point by point method, reveals the qualities of Lenin and Gladstone. In each case, comparison and contrast help us understand better the items the writer is trying to explain.

In this passage are two consecutive paragraphs that utilize comparison as their common pattern of organization:

> They were very different men. They had different styles of humor. They had different tastes in people. Roosevelt's closest British friend was Arthur Murray, a military attaché in Washington during the Great War, later a minor figure in the Liberal Party, whom Churchill would have scorned as an old duffer. Churchill's closest American friend was Bernard Baruch, whom Roosevelt made jokes about and regarded with distrust.
>
> Churchill worked by night, Roosevelt by day. Churchill relaxed in the company of men, Roosevelt in the company of women. Churchill painted watercolors and laid bricks; Roosevelt collected stamps. Churchill drank all the time; Roosevelt had a martini or two before dinner. Churchill believed in confrontation, order, and hierarchy; Roosevelt in evasion, competition, and improvisation.

> Churchill was a traditionalist with a grand and governing fidelity to the past and a somber sense of the tragedy of history. Roosevelt had an antiquarian's interest in the past but was an experimenter and optimist, who confidently embraced the future. They were hardly made for each other [Arthur Schlesinger, Jr., "The Supreme Partnership"].

Note, in passing, that the main idea of both paragraphs is expressed in the topic sentence, the first sentence of the first paragraph.

Here is a series of paragraphs that uses comparison *and* contrast effectively to explain the traits of two great Civil War generals:

> So Grant and Lee were in complete contrast, representing two diametrically opposed elements in American life. Grant was the modern man emerging; beyond him, ready to come on the stage, was the great age of steel and machinery, of crowded cities and a restless, burgeoning vitality. Lee might have ridden down from the old age of chivalry, lance in hand, silken banner fluttering over his head. Each man was the perfect champion of his cause, drawing both his strengths and his weaknesses from the people he led.
>
> Yet it was not all contrast, after all. Different as they were—in background, in personality, in underlying aspiration—these two great soldiers had much in common. Under everything else, they were marvelous fighters. Furthermore, their fighting qualities were really very much alike.
>
> Each man had, to begin with, the great virtue of utter tenacity and fidelity. Grant fought his way down the Mississippi Valley in spite of acute personal discouragement and profound military handicaps. Lee hung on in the trenches at Petersburg after hope itself had died. In each man there was an indomitable quality . . . the born fighter's refusal to give up as long as he can still remain on his feet and lift his two fists.
>
> Daring and resourcefulness they had, too; the ability to think faster and move faster than the enemy. These were the qualities which gave Lee the dazzling campaigns of Second Manassas and Chancellorsville and won Vicksburg for Grant.
>
> Lastly, and perhaps greatest of all, there was the ability, at the end, to turn quickly from war to peace once the fighting was over [Bruce Catton, "Grant and Lee: A Study in Contrasts"].

Like illustration and the other methods of organizing exposition to be considered farther on, comparison and contrast is a convenient way to order material in a paragraph or an essay.

THE DOG AND THE CAT

Konrad Lorenz

Konrad Z. Lorenz, Austrian zoologist, reveals in *Man Meets Dog* (1953)—the source of this excerpt—the dedication to the study of animal behavior that won him the Nobel Prize for Physiology and Medicine in 1973, as well as the ability to report his findings simply and clearly.

Only two animals have entered the human household otherwise than as prisoners and become domesticated by other means than those of enforced servitude: the dog and the cat. Two things they have in common, namely, that both belong to the order of carnivores and both serve man in their capacity of hunters. In all other characteristics, above all in the manner of their association with man, they are as different as the night from the day. There is no domestic animal which has so rapidly altered its whole way of living, indeed its whole sphere of interests, that has become domestic in so true a sense as the dog: and there is no animal that, in the course of its century-old association with man, has altered so little as the cat. There is some truth in the assertion that the cat, with the exception of a few luxury breeds, such as Angoras, Persians and Siamese, is no domestic animal but a completely wild being. Maintaining its full independence it has taken up its abode in the houses and outhouses of man, for the simple reason that there are more mice there than elsewhere. The whole charm of the dog lies in the depth of the friendship and the strength of the spiritual ties with which he has bound himself to man, but the appeal of the cat lies in the very fact that she has formed no close bond with him, that she has the uncompromising independence of a tiger or a leopard while she is hunting in his stables and barns; that she still remains mysterious and remote when she is rubbing herself gently against the legs of her mistress or purring contentedly in front of the fire. The purring cat is, for me, a symbol of the hearthside and the hidden security which it stands for. I should no more like to be without a cat in my home than to be without the dog that trots behind me in field or street. Since my earliest youth I have always had dogs and cats about me, and it is about them that I shall talk in this book. Business-like friends have advised me to write a dog-book and a cat-book separately, because dog-lovers often dislike cats and cat-lovers frequently abhor dogs. But I consider it the finest test of genuine love and understanding of animals if a person has sympathies for both these creatures, and can appreciate in each its own special virtues.

Questions About "Comparison and Contrast"

1. How, according to Lorenz, are the dog and the cat alike?
2. How, according to Lorenz, do dogs and cats differ?
3. Do comparison and contrast help Lorenz to explain to you each animal's features? If so, how?

Questions on Diction and Writing Techniques

1. Lorenz might have written his first sentence like this: "Only two animals, the dog and the cat, have entered the human household otherwise than as prisoners and become domesticated by other means than those of enforced servitude." Why did he write the sentence as he did?
2. What does "namely" signal?
3. How does your dictionary define "carnivores"?

4. In the sentence beginning "The whole charm of the dog," what is the function of "but"?
5. What is the connotation (see page 84) of "hearthside" to Lorenz?
6. Lorenz might have used "characteristics" in lieu of "virtues." How do the words differ in meaning? Use each in a sentence.

For Discussion, Reading, and Writing

1. Fill the blanks in this passage from memory to make it intelligible:

   Only two animals have entered the human household otherwise than as _____ and become _____ by other means than those of enforced _____: the dog and the cat. Two things they have in common, namely, that both belong to the order of carnivores and both _____ man in their capacity of _____.

   Compare your words with those in Lorenz's paragraph.
2. Use comparison and contrast in a paragraph to explain the characteristics of any two animals or plants that you are familiar with.
3. Write a paragraph or two comparing and contrasting things such as two

cars	TV shows
musical instruments	beverages
athletes	rock groups

A GLIMPSE OF WHAT IT WAS

Charles Kuralt

Charles Kuralt is an award-winning CBS News reporter and author of its *On the Road* and *Dateline America* series.

---

1 That irrepressible old tourist, Mark Twain, walked up the mountain from Carson City carrying an ax and a couple of blankets to take a look at Lake Tahoe and found it worth the climb.

2 "As it lay there," he wrote, "with the shadows of the mountains brilliantly photographed upon its still surface, I thought it must surely be the fairest picture the whole earth affords."

3 That was 115 years ago. Today there is smog about the lake.

4 "So singularly clear was the water," Mark Twain wrote, "that even where it was 80 feet deep, the bottom was perfectly distinct. . . . The water was not merely transparent, but dazzlingly, brilliantly so."

5 Today brown smudges muddy the water hundreds of yards out into the lake, the runoff from the towns on shore.

6 "Three miles away," Mark Twain wrote, "was a sawmill and some workmen, but there were not 15 other human beings throughout the wide circumference of the lake. . . . We did not see a human being but ourselves."

7 This afternoon fifteen people can be found at any crap table at Lake Tahoe. There is no such thing as solitude here, and never again will there be.

8 "We liked the appearance of the place," Mark Twain wrote, "and so we claimed some three hundred acres of it and stuck our notices on a tree. We were landowners now."

9 Here is an ad from this week's *San Francisco Chronicle:* "3.7 acres on Lake Tahoe, 4-bedroom house, 2-car garage, 200 feet lake frontage, $525,000."

10 Looking at what Lake Tahoe has become makes you want to turn back to Mark Twain for a glimpse of what it was.

11 "Lake Tahoe," he wrote, "would restore an Egyptian mummy to his pristine vigor and give him an appetite like an alligator. I do not mean the oldest and driest mummies, of course, but the fresher ones. The air up there in the clouds is very pure and fine, bracing and delicious. And why shouldn't it be?—it is the same the angels breathe."

12 Ah, Mark, the angels have moved. The condominium salesmen have taken their place.

Questions About "Comparison and Contrast"

1. Where, in this essay, does Kuralt first make clear to you what his main pattern of organization will be?
2. Show how Kuralt's choice of comparison and contrast relates to his expository purpose. What other patterns of organization does he use?
3. Does Kuralt succeed in his purpose? Explain, making specific reference to the text.

Questions on Diction and Writing Techniques

1. Explain whether paragraph 12 is a fitting conclusion to this essay.
2. State in your own words, in a sentence of not over twenty-five words, the point that Kuralt is trying to get across to you.

For Discussion, Reading, and Writing

1. For the benefit of a friend, contrast, in a short essay, the best place and the worst place to vacation you know of.
2. Compare and contrast, in a short essay, a walk in a place such as a large city with a walk in a place such as a state or national park.

TRAVELLING IN WHITE MAN'S STYLE

Farley Mowat

Farley Mowat, Canadian author, has written many books about the lands, seas, and peoples of the Far North. *People of the Deer* (1952), the source of this passage, tells of his experiences with and observation of the Ihalmiut, a nearly extinct group of Eskimos.

---

1 Summer, which follows spring so closely that the two are almost one, was upon us before it was possible to travel to the shores of Ootek's Lake and meet the People. I had arranged with Franz to take me there while Hans and the children were to remain at Windy Bay to feed the dogs we left behind, and to care for the camp.

2 As Franz and I prepared for the journey north, I was excited and at the same time depressed. Much as I wished to meet the Ihalmiut in their own land, the fragmentary glimpses of their lives that I had from Franz had left me with a strong feeling of unease at the prospect of meeting them face to face. I wondered if they would have any conception as to how much of their tragedy they owed to men of my color, and I wondered if, like the northern Indians, they would be a morose and sullen lot, resentful of my presence, suspicious and uncommunicative.

3 Even if they welcomed me into their homes, I was still afraid of my own reactions. The prospect of seeing and living with a people who knew starvation as intimately as I knew plenty, the idea of seeing with my own eyes this disintegrating remnant of a dying race, left me with a sensation closely akin to fear.

4 We could not make the journey northward by canoe, for the raging streams which had cut across the Barrens only a few weeks before were now reduced to tiny creeks whose courses were interrupted by jumbled barriers of rock. No major rivers flowed the way we wished to go, and so the water routes were useless to us. Since the only alternative was a trek overland, we prepared to go on foot, as the Ihalmiut do.

5 But there was a difference. The Ihalmiut travel light, and a man of the People crossing the open plains in summer carries little more than his knife, a pipe, and perhaps a spare pair of skin boots called *kamik*. He eats when he finds something to eat. There are usually suckers in the shrunken streams, and these can sometimes be caught with the hands. Or if the suckers are too hard to find, the traveller can take a length of rawhide line and snare the orange-colored ground squirrels on the sandy esker slopes. In early summer there are always eggs, or flightless birds, and if the eggs are nearly at the hatching point, so much the better.

6 Franz and I, on the other hand, travelled in white man's style. We were accompanied by five dogs and to each dog we fastened a miniature Indian travois—two long thin poles that stretched behind

to support a foot-square platform on which we could load nearly thirty pounds of gear that included bedrolls, ammunition, cooking tools, and presents of flour and tobacco for the Eskimos. With this equipment we were also able to carry a little tent, and food for the dogs and ourselves: deer meat for them, and flour, tea, and baking powder for us. We had more than the bare essentials, but we had to pay a stiff price for them.

7 Equipped with pack dogs, it took us better than a week to cover the same sixty miles that the Ihalmiut cross in two days and a night. I shall not soon forget the tortures of that march. While the sun shone, the heat was as intense as it is in the tropics, for the clarity of the Arctic air does nothing to soften the sun's rays. Yet we were forced to wear sweaters and even caribou skin jackets. The flies did that to us. They rose from the lichens at our feet until they hung like a malevolent mist about us and took on the appearance of a low-lying cloud. *Milugia* (black flies) and *kiktoriak* (mosquitoes) came in such numbers that their presence actually gave me a feeling of physical terror. There was simply no evading them. The bleak Barrens stretched into emptiness on every side, and offered no escape and no surcease. To stop for food was torture and to continue the march in the overwhelming summer heat was worse. At times a kind of insanity would seize us and we would drop everything and run wildly in any direction until we were exhausted. But the pursuing hordes stayed with us and we got nothing from our frantic efforts except a wave of sweat that seemed to attract even more mosquitoes.

8 From behind our ears, from beneath our chins, a steady dribble of blood matted into our clothing and trapped the insatiable flies until we both wore black collars composed of their struggling bodies. The flies worked down under our shirts until our belts stopped them. Then they fed about our waists until the clothing stuck to us with drying blood.

9 The land we were passing over offered no easy routes to compensate for the agonies the flies inflicted upon us. It was rolling country, and across our path ran a succession of mounding hills whose sides and crests were strewn with angular rocks and with broken fragments filling the interstices between the bigger boulders. On these our boots were cut and split and our feet bruised until it was agony to walk at all. But at that the hills were better walking than the broad wet valleys which lay in between.

10 Each valley had its own stream flowing down its center. Though those streams were often less than five feet in width, they seemed to be never less than five feet in depth. The valley floors were one continuous mattress of wet moss into which we sank up to our knees until our feet found the perpetual ice that lay underneath. Wading and stumbling through the icy waters of the muskegs, floundering across streams or around the countless ponds (all of whose banks were undercut and offered no gradual descent), we would become numbed from the waist down, while our upper bodies were bathed in sweat. If, as happened for three solid days, it rained, then we lived a sodden nightmare as we crossed those endless bogs.

11 I am not detailing the conditions of summer travel in order to emphasize my own discomforts but to illustrate the perfectly amazing capacity of the Ihalmiut as travellers. Over sixty miles of such country, the People could move with ease, yes, and with comfort, bridging the distance in less than two days of actual walking. And they, mind you, wore only paper-thin boots of caribou skin on their feet. It is not that they are naturally impervious to discomfort, but simply that they have adjusted their physical reactions to meet the conditions they must face. They have bridged the barriers of their land not by levelling them, as we would try to do, but by conforming to them. It is like the difference between a sailing vessel and one under power, when you compare an Ihalmio and a white traveller, in the Barrens. The white man, driven by his machine instincts, always lives at odds with his environment; like a motor vessel he bucks the winds and the seas and he is successful only while the intricate apparatus built about him functions perfectly. But the Barrens People are an integral part of *their* environment. Like sailing ships, they learn to move with wind and water; to mold themselves to the rhythm of the elements and so accomplish gently and without strain the things that must be done.

Questions About "Comparison and Contrast"

1. What is Mowat's purpose in "detailing the conditions of summer travel" in the Far North?

2. By what means does he signal to you that he intends to contrast the style of travel of a man of the People with that of the white man?
3. What phrase in paragraph 6 does Mowat use to signal a contrast?
4. How does Mowat's contrast of a sailing vessel with one under power (par. 11) relate to his purpose?
5. Does Mowat convince you of the adaptability of the Barrens People to their environment? Explain.

Questions on Diction and Writing Techniques

1. Underline in your text those words that are new to you, but whose meaning you inferred from their context. Define them in your own words. Compare your definitions with those in your dictionary. Look up in your dictionary any other words that are new to you. Use the words in both groups in sentences.
2. Why does Mowat tell you the meaning of "travois" (par. 6)?
3. What is Mowat's purpose in writing the five-word sentence in paragraph 5? What effect does it have on you?

For Discussion, Reading, and Writing

1. Which of the following, according to Mowat, are true (T), which false (F)?
   A. ______ As he prepared for the journey he was excited and at the same time depressed.
   B. ______ Mowat and Franz couldn't make the journey northward by canoe because the major rivers were reduced to tiny creeks.
   C. ______ It took the white men three or four times as long as it did the Ihalmiut to cover the same sixty miles.
   D. ______ The Barrens People are an integral part of their environment.
   E. ______ The People are naturally impervious to discomfort.
2. Compare and contrast, in a short essay, any two modes of traveling that you are familiar with.

TWO LYNDON B. JOHNSONS

Robert Caro

Robert A. Caro, formerly a Nieman Fellow at Harvard and for seven years an investigative reporter for *Newsday*, won the 1975 Pulitzer Prize for his first biography, *The Power Broker*.

1 There was one glaring difference between Lyndon Johnson's 1941 campaign and his 1937 campaign—the candidate himself.

2 The candidate of 1941 bore little resemblance to the skinny, gawky, nervous youth of four years before. When he took off his suit jacket, it became apparent that the only part of Lyndon Johnson that was still thin was his shoulders, conspicuously narrow in proportion to the middle of his body which had become quite wide. His belt sagged a little around the beginning of a paunch, and his rear end was now quite large. The jacket was seldom doffed, but not through concern over his bulk. His speeches, he instructed his speechwriters, were to be "senatorial"—statesmanlike and dignified—and he wanted his appearance to match, as the handkerchief painstakingly arranged in his breast pocket matched his necktie. His suits, most of them with a vest, were of good materials, mostly dark blue. There was often a carnation in his lapel, and his white shirt was starched and stiff; gold cufflinks gleamed on the sleeves. Bare-headed in 1937, now he often wore a hat, not a Stetson but a fedora, which he would wave to the crowds, and there was frequently a briefcase under his arm from which he would remove the text of his speech as ostentatiously as if it had been papers of state; to read the speech he would fussily put on a pair of eyeglasses. The gaunt face of 1937 was a broad, heavy face now: flesh had filled in the lines and filled out the cheeks; there was a full-fledged double chin, and the big jaw jutted now out of heavy jowls. The candidate of 1937 had looked so young; the candidate of 1941 was not young at all; he looked at least a decade older than his thirty-two years.

3 The difference was accentuated by his bearing. In 1937, he had been as ineffective reading a prepared speech as he was persuasive speaking extemporaneously. Now he almost never gave an extemporaneous talk, and he was, if possible, even worse now at reading prepared speeches—but in a very different way. In 1937, he had given the impression of being afraid to look at his audience lest he lose his place in the text. He still did not look at his audience nearly as much as his mother, the elocution teacher, would have liked, but fear was no part of the impression he made now. On a stage, he was a dominant, powerful figure, tall, long-armed; the spotlight glittered on his gold-rimmed eyeglasses, glistened off the waves of his black, carefully pomaded, shiny black hair and highlighted the pale whiteness of his skin, the blackness of the heavy eyebrows that the glasses did little to conceal, and the sheen of beard that was present on the jutting jaw no matter how closely he shaved. A powerful figure, but not a pleasant one. The modest tone in the text of most of his speeches (Charles Marsh, who wrote many of them, was constantly urging upon the candidate at least a public humility) was belied by the domineering tone in which they were delivered. Johnson shouted his speeches in a harsh voice almost without inflection except when he was especially determined to emphasize a point, when his voice would rise into a bellow; the tone was the tone of a lecturer uninterested in any opinion but his own: dogmatic, pontifical, the tone of a leader demanding rather than soliciting support. Reinforcing the tone were the gestures, as awkward as ever but now authoritarian to the point of arrogance. He spoke with his big head thrust aggressively forward at his listeners, and sometimes it would thrust forward even more and he would raise his hand and repeatedly jab a finger down at them. Sometimes he spoke with one hand on a hip, with his big head thrown back a little, shouting over their heads. His attitude went beyond mere inability to learn public speaking. His rare smiles were so mechanical that they seemed calculated to let the audience know they were mechanical, as if he wanted to let them know that he didn't need them, that he was the leader and they the followers. Early in the campaign, the ability of his advance men, the skill with which they were organized, and the waves of radio and newspaper ads which preceded each speech ensured large crowds at his rallies, and, spurred on by introductions from the best local orators (only

the best were hired) and by the cheers of the Johnson campaign workers and federal and Brown & Root employees with which it was liberally seeded, the audience would welcome him with enthusiasm. As he spoke, though, the enthusiasm would steadily diminish; all too often, by the end of a speech the only cheers would be the cheers of his claque. His speeches were invariably long—too long, not infrequently an hour or more; the audience would begin to drift away relatively soon, and by the end of a speech it would often be embarrassingly smaller than it had been at the beginning. Word about Johnson's lack of speaking ability began to get around: despite the unprecedented publicity, crowds at Johnson's rallies began growing smaller than expected.

4 The difference was as noticeable after the speech as during it. During the 1937 campaign, a handshake from Lyndon Johnson had been an exercise in instant empathy; circulating among an audience with a face glowing with friendliness, he would keep a voter's hand in his for long minutes while he asked him for his help and told him that he too was a farmer, and wanted to help farmers; he had established rapport with the rapidity of a man who had a "very unusual ability to meet and greet the public." Now, in 1941, that ability was not often in evidence, for Johnson did not often choose to use it. In part, of course, this was because there were so many more voters to meet and greet now, but the difference went beyond that circumstance. When, after a speech, Johnson shook hands with voters lined up to meet him, he did so in a manner so mechanical that a friend from Washington commented on it—Justice Douglas happened to be in Big Spring to make a speech on the night Johnson spoke there. "As LBJ came to the close of his speech, he shouted, 'I want all you good folks of Big Spring to line up and shake the hand of the next Senator from Texas, Lyndon B. Johnson.' " And Douglas noticed that "Lyndon gave each of them two pumps with the arm and one slap on the back before greeting the next comer." The two-pump, one-slap technique was, in fact, one that Johnson had rehearsed; he boasted that, using it, he could, with his aides prodding the voters past him in a fast-moving single line, shake forty-two hands per minute. The method was efficient, but not effective. Far from establishing rapport with voters, he only managed to emphasize the feeling that he was not one of them, and that, while he might be asking for their help, he didn't really need it. And he

would not allow a voter more than a hurried word or two, if that; Bill Deason says, "He never missed anybody on the street. . . . He shook hands with every one of them, but he never let them involve him in an argument. He moved fast. . . ." In fact, he seldom let them involve him in a conversation; the candidate moved through crowds in a cordon of officious aides who pushed people aside, none too gently, hurrying him along as he flashed mechanical smiles to left and right. And his aides were around him, and hurrying him along, because he had ordered them to. He wasn't always so coldly mechanical, of course. With "important people"—some local politician he recognized on the line of voters—his face would light up, and his greeting would be warm and unhurried, his handshake again as good as a hug. On some nights, his greeting of the public would also be warm, reminiscent of the campaigning of 1937, but such nights did not occur frequently during the first six weeks of the 1941 campaign. In 1941, his campaigning was as strikingly cold and mechanical as it had been strikingly warm and individual four years before; indeed at times his manner was almost contemptuous, making it clear that the individual to whom he was speaking simply didn't matter.

There was another difference between the two campaigns. Johnson was campaigning hard in 1941, was still putting in long days on the campaign trail, but there was a marked drop in his energy level. The desperation, the frantic, driving work was gone. He wasn't, in fact, even the hardest-working candidate. Gerald Mann in 1941 displayed the willingness Johnson had displayed in 1937: the willingness to do everything—to work day and night, without regard to hours—in order to win. The Attorney General was determined to go everywhere, to shake the hand of every voter who wanted to shake his. Mann had done it twice before, and in 1941, he was doing it again. Johnson's speeches were, thanks to money, reaching more voters, through being broadcast, but Mann was determined to overcome that difference with sheer physical effort. Johnson was making far fewer speeches, visiting far fewer towns. He concentrated largely on the big cities, where, of course, the votes were concentrated, and in the big cities he concentrated on the big men. Arriving, he would huddle, generally in a suite in the hotel in which he was staying, with the city's political and business bosses—in Texas, often the same men. Then he would make telephone calls or rest until the evening's rally. The pace was still grueling—the travel between cities made any campaign in Texas grueling—but it was much slower than the 1937 pace. It was the pace of a man confident of victory. Implicit in Johnson's delivery of speeches, and in his manner of greeting voters, was the feeling that with the mighty President behind him, he couldn't lose.

6 And, indeed, for the first six weeks of the campaign, the President's support, combined with Johnson's money and organization, suggested that Johnson's confidence was well founded. Although the May 12 Belden Poll showed Mann still far in front of Johnson, 28 percent to 9 percent, both his advisors and Johnson's—and the state's veteran political observers—felt that the poll was not accurately measuring the rapid shift toward Johnson, an opinion that would be confirmed by the May 26 poll, which found that Johnson had narrowed the gap from nineteen points to eight—19 percent for Johnson to 27 percent for Mann. Out on the campaign trail, Mann realized that the shift was continuing—and accelerating. He knew—and Austin knew—that Johnson was going to win.

Questions About "Comparison and Contrast"

1. Where does Caro tell you what will be his pattern of organization?
2. Explain, with specific references to paragraphs 2, 3, and 4, the method of comparison Caro uses in each.
3. To what significant details of appearance, bearing, and behavior is your attention drawn by Caro's comparison between the Johnson of 1941 and the Johnson of 1937?

Questions on Diction and Writing Techniques

1. How does your dictionary define "Stetson," "fedora," and "ostentatiously" (par. 1); "extemporaneously" (par. 2); "empathy," "rapport," and "officious" (par. 3); "implicit" (par. 4)? Use each of these words in a sentence.
2. Evaluate paragraph 1 as an opening paragraph.

3. Would any benefit result from dividing one or more of Caro's paragraphs into shorter paragraphs? Where might one properly make the break(s)? Explain.
4. Why is it useful for your understanding of at least a portion of paragraph 2 for Caro to tell you what Johnson meant by "senatorial"?
5. Show what description contributes to exposition in this essay.
6. Underline in your text the words by means of which Caro helps achieve coherence among paragraphs 2–5. To what idea in paragraph 5 is "Johnson's confidence was well founded" (par. 6) related?

For Discussion, Reading, and Writing

1. In what ways did Johnson, in 1941, not resemble the skinny, gawky, nervous youth of four years before?
2. How was the difference between 1941 and 1937 accentuated?
3. What specific differences between 1941 and 1937 were noticeable during Johnson's speeches?
4. What difference was noticeable after the speeches?
5. What was Johnson's "two-pump, one-slap technique"?
6. What is the final difference between the Johnson of 1941 and the Johnson of 1937 that Caro points out?
7. Write a paragraph of not over a hundred words in which you summarize details of Johnson, the candidate of 1937. Write a second paragraph of similar length describing him as a candidate in 1941. Using the point-by-point pattern, combine the information in these paragraphs in a short essay.
8. Utilizing reading as your main source of material, write a short essay in which you use comparison and contrast as your main pattern of organization to reveal Ronald Reagan as a candidate for the presidency in 1980 and in 1984 or to show him as president during his first and second terms in office.

Definition

The writer's best friend is the wastebasket.

—Isaac Bashevis Singer

TO communicate with a reader, a writer must choose language that clearly conveys what he or she is trying to say. To use words that are vague and words that are ambiguous is to risk putting meaning in doubt. When a word might mean one thing to the writer and another to the reader, it is useful for the writer to explain what he or she means.

To avoid misunderstanding between you and your readers, you may find it necessary to explain what you mean by words you use. "Liberal" and "conservative" have no commonly accepted definition because different people use the terms to convey different ideas. Thus if you were to write an essay on the topic "Is Ronald Reagan a liberal or a conservative?" you would do well to make sure that you explain to your readers what you mean by "liberal" and "conservative." You would want to define these terms early in your essay, and clearly.

Such an essay might be organized in this way:

1. *Opening paragraph:* A statement of your purpose—to determine whether the president might properly be termed "liberal" or "conservative."
2. *Paragraph 2:* A definition of "liberal," using as many methods as seem necessary to make your meaning clear.
3. *Paragraph 3:* A definition of "conservative."

4. *Paragraphs 4 and 5:* Examples of Mr. Reagan's acts that convince you that one or the other of the two terms would more appropriately be applicable to him.
5. *Concluding paragraph:* Summary and conclusion. Thesis: "The president is a liberal"; or "The president is a conservative."

Defining "liberal" and "conservative" and classifying the president's acts in those categories would be the focus of your writing effort. The words would dictate the pattern of your studies and the area and extent of your research. They would lead you to a discovery of your thesis. They would also indicate a likely manner of arranging your information to best achieve your ultimate purpose: a clear explanation of the main idea.

One obvious advantage of explaining vague words, words that cannot be understood in a clear and specific way, and ambiguous words, words that can be understood in more than one sense, is to facilitate communication. There is another benefit. You may not be fully aware that your understanding of a term is fuzzy, even though it is. In the process of defining it for your readers' sake, you will make it clear to yourself as well.

You know from your studies with what precision terms in mathematics and the sciences are defined:

Triangle: a closed plane figure having three sides and three angles.

Test tube: a hollow cylinder of thin glass with one end closed, used in chemical and biological laboratories.

Other words can be defined precisely, in the same way:

Aquatics: sports practiced on or in water.

Wax: a solid, yellowish substance secreted by bees.

Blue jeans: a garment made of stout twilled cotton fabric.

These are known as *formal definitions.* In each instance the term defined was put in a general class and then differentiated from other members of the class, as in these illustrations:

TERM	CLASS	DIFFERENTIATION
Dime	is a silver coin	of the U.S., the 10th part of a dollar, equal to 10 cents.
Dike	is an embankment	for controlling the waters of the sea or a river.
House	is a building	in which people live.

When, to clarify the meaning of a term you use in your writing, you find it useful to give a formal definition, you should follow the procedure in the examples of formal definition just given.

Sometimes a writer may assume that readers have some knowledge of a term and thus may define the term by naming *examples* of it that they may be expected to be familiar with:

Contact sports such as ice hockey and football . . .

A felony, for example, burglary . . .

A Gothic novel like Ann Radcliffe's *The Mysteries of Udolfo* . . .

Another way to define a term is by the use of a *synonym,* a word having the same or nearly the same meaning:

Pal: a companion, a chum

Film: a motion picture, a movie

Lexicon: a word book, a dictionary

Another way still to define a term is by giving its *etymology,* or derivation, which is found in a dictionary, as in this instance where the writer had an appropriate occasion and audience for using this method:

> I believe a liberal education is an education in the root meaning of "liberal"–"liber"–"free"–the liberty of the mind free to explore itself, to draw itself out, to connect with other minds and spirits in the quest for truth. Its goal is to train the whole person to be at once intellectually discerning and humanly flexible, tough-minded and open-hearted; to be responsive to the new and responsible for

values that make us civilized. It is to teach us to meet what is new and different with reasoned judgment and humanity. A liberal education is an education for freedom, the freedom to assert the liberty of the mind to make itself new for the others it cherishes.

The audience was the incoming class of freshmen, Yale '85; the writer, A. Bartlett Giamatti, then president of Yale University.

Extended definition, whose essential characteristic is its relative elaborateness, is an important means of developing a paragraph or an entire essay. It is especially useful in explaining an uncommon term—whether newly coined or not—or an abstract term. Gail Sheehy uses extended definition to make clear what she means by the expression "jailbreak marriage" (pages 162–163).

John Kenneth Galbraith, in this example of a relatively short extended definition, explains the meaning of a phrase he coined, which has since come into widespread use:

Because familiarity is such an important test of acceptability, the acceptable ideas have great stability. They are highly predictable. It will be convenient to have a name for the ideas which are esteemed at any time for their acceptability. I shall refer to these ideas henceforth as *the conventional wisdom* [John Kenneth Galbraith, *The Affluent Society*].

Having explained what he meant by the term, Galbraith was free to and in fact did use "the conventional wisdom" often in his book without confusing his readers.

Here is an example of the use of extended definition to explain an abstract term, "erotic love":

Brotherly love is love among equals; motherly love is love for the helpless. Different as they are from each other, they have in common that they are by their very nature not restricted to one person. If I love my brother, I love all my brothers; if I love my child, I love all my children; no, beyond that, I love all children, all that are in need of my help. In contrast to both types of love is *erotic love;* it is the craving for complete fusion, for union with one other person. It is by its very nature exclusive and not universal; it is also perhaps the most deceptive form of love there is [Erich Fromm, *The Art of Loving*].

The writer first explains what erotic love is by *differentiation*, showing what it is *not*; it is, he says, *different* from brotherly love and motherly love. In the next-to-last sentence, he gives a formal definition of his term. In the concluding sentence, Fromm elaborates on the definition and on the rest of the paragraph.

The kinds of words that you are most likely to find in need of definition are:

General words: democracy, freedom, human rights

Newly coined terms: black power, common market, hardhat

Words that imply an opinion: free society, happy marriage, beautiful people

Language peculiar to a particular trade, profession, or group: binary fission, differential gear, write-off, meltdown

Metaphorical phrases: bamboo curtain, spring fever

Even terms whose meanings we assume are clear to ourselves and our readers may usefully be explained, as in the first paragraph of the first chapter of *This Fascinating Animal World* by Alan Devoe:

> Perhaps the easiest way to put it, in a rough nontechnical fashion, is to say that animals are all of earth's living creatures that are not plants. An animal is a being able to make locomotor movements and perform actions that appear to be what we call voluntary. It shows a certain quickness and "aliveness" in its responses to stimulation. It ingests and digests foods consisting of other animals or plants, and it doesn't contain chlorophyll or perform photosynthesis. Not every animal need meet every one of the requirements; but in a general way this is the stuff of the definition.

In the first sentence Devoe gives a formal definition; he puts the term to be defined ("animals") into a class ("earth's living creatures") and then differentiates ("that are not plants"). In the rest of the paragraph, to further clarify his meaning, he amplifies how animals differ from plants.

In the second paragraph, Devoe extends his definition further:

> Where the higher animals are concerned—a deer, say, or a raccoon or a squirrel—an animals' animality of course seems abundantly obvious, and a need for definition may appear a little absurd. But the kingdom of the animals runs right down to the roots of things. There are animals that consist of only a single cell. There are animals in which there is scarcely discoverable any distinct nervous system; and there are plant forms that look, at least to casual observation, a good deal livelier than these developed animals. Down in the very lowest life levels, in the elementary ooze, so to speak, of the creation, animals and plants are so almost indistinguishably alike that it seems hardly possible that the one line leads to oaks and redwoods and the other one to rabbits and foxes.

Here Devoe adds to his clarification of the meaning of "animal" by adding to his formal definition examples of the term as well as by comparing and contrasting "animal" with "plant."

Each of the methods of defining may be combined with one or more other methods. Recall the definition of "inference" on page 128. Now read it in the context of the passage as originally written by Hayakawa in *Language in Thought and Action:*

> An inference, as we shall use the term, *is a statement about the unknown made on the basis of the known.* We may *infer* from the material and cut of a woman's clothes her wealth or social position; we may *infer* from the character of the ruins the origin of the fire that destroyed the building; we may *infer* from a man's calloused hands the nature of his occupation; we may *infer* from a senator's vote on an armaments bill his attitude toward Russia; we may *infer* from the structure of the land the path of a prehistoric glacier; we may *infer* from a halo on an unexposed photographic plate its past proximity to radioactive materials; we may *infer* from the sound of an engine the condition of its connecting rods. Inferences may be carefully or carelessly made. They may be made on the basis of a broad background of previous experience with the subject matter or with no experience at all. For example, the inferences a good mechanic can make about the internal condition of a motor by listening to it are often startlingly accurate, while the inferences made by an amateur (if he tries to make any) may be entirely wrong. But the common characteristic of inferences is

that they are statements about matters which are not directly known, made on the basis of what has been observed.

Hayakawa uses formal definition and examples to make the meaning of "inference" abundantly clear.

HOW INTELLIGENT IS ROVER?

Felicia Ames

Felicia Ames is the pseudonym of Jean Burden, author, editor, award-winning poet, and lecturer on poetry at numerous universities.

---

1 Mr. and Mrs. Isenberg will never forget that day in Scarsdale, New York, and the intelligence of their three-year-old beagle, Snooper. They had gone shopping and had locked the dog in the car. Returning from the store, all heaven broke loose on them and they found themselves at the mercy of a torrential rain. It was then that they discovered they had locked more than Snooper in the car; they had no keys. The dog went to work and, with very little coaxing from the drenched pair, lifted the door lock with his teeth.

2 "How intelligent are dogs?" is a frequent question. Many owners believe absolutely that Rover or Fido or Schroeder has to be the smartest animal this side of a primate and there are some who won't stop there. On the other hand, quite a number of authorities feel that what passes for intelligence in canines is nothing more than cleverness, an ability to learn by rote or imitation.

3 We have to agree that cleverness is a better word for dogs who can stand on one leg or bow-wow to ninety. We are oversaturated with pictures of dogs swimming, diving, climbing trees and catching anything from fly balls to frisbees. Clever are those pets, too, who pose with cigar in mouth, nautical hat atop head and spectacles

over eyes. And, of course, all those dogs who can roll over, play dead or jump through a flaming hoop.

4 Something other than cleverness, though, must account for dogs who have been known to find their way across strange and rugged miles, back to a house whence they roamed or were removed, often long before. This trait—not all dogs reveal it—is mostly labeled the homing instinct or built-in radar, but no one has ever been able to explain it.

5 There is also the dog who, finding himself lost, determines to stay by a bit of his owner's clothing, often for days, apparently knowing that there is a chance of the owner's return.

6 Judgment reflects intelligence and many dogs are capable of making decisions. For example, consider any seeing-eye dog. If he stopped when the light turned red and moved on green, it might be possible to assume, first that he was trained to react to light changes and, secondly, that he wasn't color blind. But we have yet to observe any of these dogs who allow the light to be their only cue for action. Invariably, the dog will watch the traffic, in all directions, as well as any pedestrians nearby, before determining whether to wait or lead his master across the intersection.

7 A story involving an English seeing-eye dog and his master really does much to prove that dogs possess keen intelligence. The dog, named Kim, was taken suddenly ill while walking with his master in the city. Deliberately disobeying his master's pressures on the lead—the man was en route to an appointment—the dog went, instead, to a veterinarian whom he knew to have an office nearby. After the doctor had treated him for a severe stomach distress, he went on to help his master keep the appointment.

8 Another story we like involved another English guide dog. Simba was her name and she was a three-year-old Alsatian. Every day, in her house in Kent, she led Minky downstairs and then opened the door to let her outside. Minky was a seven-year-old spaniel. The owner of the two dogs, Esme Bidlake, said: "As soon as Minky went blind, Simba seemed to sense it and, with no training from me, started guiding the little spaniel about the house. She even leads Minky to her feeding bowl and sits beside her while she has her meal." When the dogs went out for a walk, Simba held onto Minky's ear, waited for traffic to pass, then gently escorted her across the road, still holding her ear.

9 Dogs have long been respected for their ability to hear and smell. But it also required some intelligence for a dog named Schmutz to rescue a man buried under an avalanche in the Swiss Alps. The man reported later that he could hear his would-be rescuers digging with their shovels. He screamed to them to keep digging, but they didn't hear him. The dog did hear him and went on digging after the men had abandoned the search. Fourteen others were eventually rescued from the same avalanche, thanks to the hearing of a dog and his intelligence to sense danger.

10 Another dog with a sense of danger and the intelligence to act was Spooky, a two-year-old pit bull terrier. The dog observed an injured sea gull struggling about a hundred yards offshore of Hutchinson Island, Florida. The dog's owner watched as the dog climbed down a bridge construction site, swam the distance, grabbed the gull in his mouth and brought it to shore without ruffling a feather. The owner freed a fishing lure that had been hooked from the beak of the bird to its wing, and the gull was able to fly away.

11 For clinching arguments, though, there are Prince, a four-year-old Cockapoo in Los Angeles and a moonshine dog in McNairy County, West Tennessee. The owner of the latter used to operate a still and was in the habit of hiding his product. Since he was either drunk when he hid the stuff or drunk when he went to find it, the poor man never knew quite where to go. But the dog did. Confronted with a sale, the moonshiner would indicate with his fingers how many pint bottles the transaction required and the dog would do the rest. There was one problem. The man would become very ugly and offensive with too much to drink. When this happened, the dog would leave home and stay away until his boss was sober. This never lasted too long, of course, because the boss could never remember where he stashed the hootch. We never did find out if the dog took a drink, but we presume he was too smart for that.

12 As for Prince, the Los Angeles cocker and poodle cross, his thing is cigarettes. He hates them with such abandon that his owner wonders whether he might be of some use to the American Cancer Society. We're not sure how many people have given up smoking because of Prince, but we know that there isn't one smoker who dares practice his habit in the dog's presence. Ever since he was a pup, says his owner, Margaret Eiden, he's been curling his lip whenever he sees a cigarette being lit. If the lighter of the weed persists

and takes a drag, Prince emits a low, horrifying snarl. If the dragger drags on, the dog goes into a crouch that can only spell kill. No one, needless to say, pushes at that point for another puff.

13 A dog with a cause, and more intelligent than many of us, it seems.

Questions About "Definition"

1. Why is it necessary for Ames to explain what she means by intelligence in dogs?
2. What purpose is served by Ames' explanation of what she means by cleverness in dogs? What method(s) does she use to define the term?
3. What method(s) of definition does she use to make clear to you what she means by intelligence in dogs?
4. Does Ames fulfill her purpose in writing this essay? Explain.

Questions on Diction and Writing Techniques

1. Match each item in Column A with the word closest in meaning to it in Column B:

Column A	*Column B*
torrential	soaked
by rote	rumpling
saturated	from memory
avalanche	violent
ruffling	snowslide

Use in a sentence each word or term in Column A.

2. How useful to Ames' purpose is paragraph 1?
3. What does "on the other hand" (par. 2) signal? Find two or more other examples of Ames' use of transition words. Explain in each instance her reason for using the word(s).

4. As an alternative to paragraph 13, write your own concluding paragraph for this essay.

For Discussion, Reading, and Writing

1. Which of these statements, according to Ames, are true (T), which false (F)?

   A. ______ Snooper is clever.

   B. ______ Quite a number of authorities feel that what passes for cleverness in canines is nothing more than intelligence.

   C. ______ An example of intelligence in dogs is the ability to catch frisbees.

   D. ______ No one has been able to explain dogs' homing instinct or built-in radar.

   E. ______ Judgment reflects intelligence.

   F. ______ Kim, taken ill suddenly, disobeyed his master's pressures on the lead but, nonetheless, after going to a veterinarian for treatment, went on to help his master keep an appointment.

   G. ______ A dog named Schmutz dug out a man buried in an avalanche in the Swiss Alps.

   H. ______ Spooky brought a gull to shore without a feather.

   I. ______ Prince's thing is cigarettes.

   J. ______ The moonshine dog would leave home and stay away until his boss was sober.

2. Find a term that best fits a characteristic of any animals, including persons, you are familiar with—for example, the curiosity of cats. Write a short essay in which you make clear to your reader the appropriateness of applying the term to them.

GETTING PERSONAL: *AD HOMINEM*

Stuart Chase

Stuart Chase has written on a variety of subjects, most frequently on economics and matters relating to it. He is the author of *The Tyranny of Words* (1938), chiefly concerned with the misuse of language, and *Guides to Straight Thinking* (1956), the source of this excerpt.

---

1 The classic example of this fallacy is a scene in a British court of law. As the attorney for the defense takes the floor, his partner hands him a note: "No case. Abuse the plaintiff's attorney."

2 If you can't shake the argument, abuse the person who advances it, and so discredit it through the back door. Go from facing the issue, which jurists call *ad rem*, to the man, *ad hominem*.

3 A story is told about Lincoln as a young lawyer. In one of his first jury cases, he showed his political shrewdness by an adroit and quite non-malicious use of *ad hominem*. His opponent was an experienced trial lawyer, who also had most of the fine legal points on his side. The day was warm and Lincoln slumped in his chair as the case went against him. When the orator took off his coat and vest, however, Lincoln sat up with a gleam in his eye. His opponent was wearing one of the new city-slicker shirts of the 1840's, which buttoned up the back.

4 Lincoln knew the reaction of frontiersmen, who made up the jury. When his turn came, his plea was brief: "Gentlemen of the jury, because I have justice on my side, I am sure you will not be influenced by this gentleman's pretended knowledge of the law. Why, he doesn't even know which side of his shirt ought to be in front!"

5 Lincoln's *ad hominem* is said to have won the case.

6 This fallacy, like over-generalizing, has been around for a long

time. The Sophists must have used it freely, and I suspect it goes back to the dawn of the race.

7 *First cave man:* "Heard the latest on old man Fist Ax? He's putting feathers on his arrows. Says they go straighter."

8 *Second cave man:* "Forget it. Nobody who's such a wife-stealer could come up with a decent idea."

9 Not every personal attack, however, can be classed as faulty logic. When the scandal of Grover Cleveland's illegitimate son was used against him in the presidential campaign, the argument had some point. Did Americans want a President of such a character? (The sovereign voters decided that his virtues overrode his defects.) If, however, Cleveland's enemies had introduced the natural son as an argument against his tariff policy, then a true *ad hominem* would appear. In the first case, Cleveland himself was the issue; in the second the tariff was the issue. When a man is running for office, or being chosen for any position in government or elsewhere, his personal behavior is always relevant. A corporation would naturally hesitate to hire as treasurer a man who had been convicted of embezzlement.

10 The health of President Eisenhower was an important consideration in the nominations of 1956. Was he well enough to serve out another four years in the toughest job in the world? Similarly with Franklin Roosevelt in 1944. But when the enemies of Roosevelt charged that a given government policy was wrong because it originated with "that cripple in the White House," they were practicing a particularly vicious kind of *ad hominem.*

Questions About "Definition"

1. How does your dictionary define "*ad hominem*" (par. 2)? What is the derivation of the term?
2. Which methods of defining does Chase use?
3. What does Chase's extended definition add to the dictionary definition?
4. After reading this selection, do you have a clear idea of what "*ad hominem*" means? Explain.

Questions on Diction and Writing Techniques

1. Does paragraph 1 fulfill the requirements of an opening paragraph? (See page 33.) Explain.
2. What methods of definition does your dictionary use to define "city-slicker" (par. 3)?
3. Define "Sophists" (par. 6). List two or three words derived from "sophist."
4. What is Chase's purpose in writing paragraphs 7 and 8?
5. Why does Chase choose to use "however" in paragraph 9?

For Discussion, Reading, and Writing

1. Chase says that Lincoln's tactic was "non-malicious" (par. 3). Do you agree? In view of the result, does it matter whether the tactic was malicious or not? What risk did Lincoln take by using *ad hominem*? If you had been an opposing lawyer, how might you have countered Lincoln's move?
2. Using a combination of two or more methods, define in a paragraph one of these terms:

   anchorman
   lonesome end
   back-seat driver
   feminist
   male chauvinist
3. In a short essay, write an extended definition of one of these terms:

   hypocrisy
   romantic love
   ideal marriage
   population explosion
   maternal overprotection

APPETITE

Laurie Lee

Laurie Lee, British author, has written books of poetry, travel, and autobiography. This selection is from *I Can't Stay Long* (1976), a collection of essays.

1 One of the major pleasures in life is appetite, and one of our major duties should be to preserve it. Appetite is the keenness of living; it is one of the senses that tells you that you are still curious to exist, that you still have an edge on your longings and want to bite into the world and taste its multitudinous flavours and juices.

2 By appetite, of course, I don't mean just the lust for food, but any condition of unsatisfied desire, any burning in the blood that proves you want more than you've got, and that you haven't yet used up your life. Wilde said he felt sorry for those who never got their heart's desire, but sorrier still for those who did. I got mine once only, and it nearly killed me, and I've always preferred wanting to having since.

3 For appetite, to me, is this state of wanting, which keeps one's expectations alive. I remember learning this lesson long ago as a child, when treats and orgies were few, and when I discovered that the greatest pitch of happiness was not in actually eating a toffee but in gazing at it beforehand. True, the first bite was delicious, but once the toffee was gone one was left with nothing, neither toffee nor lust. Besides, the whole toffeeness of toffees was imperceptibly diminished by the gross act of having eaten it. No, the best was in wanting it, in sitting and looking at it, when one tasted an inexhaustible treasure-house of flavours.

4 So, for me, one of the keenest pleasures of appetite remains in the wanting, not the satisfaction. In wanting a peach, or a whisky,

or a particular texture or sound, or to be with a particular friend. For in this condition, of course, I know that the object of desire is always at its most flawlessly perfect. Which is why I would carry the preservation of appetite to the extent of deliberate fasting, simply because I think that appetite is too good to lose, too precious to be bludgeoned into insensibility by satiation and over-doing it.

5 For that matter, I don't really want three square meals a day—I want one huge, delicious, orgiastic, table-groaning blow-out, say every four days, and then not be too sure where the next one is coming from. A day of fasting is not for me just a puritanical device for denying oneself a pleasure, but rather a way of anticipating a rare moment of supreme indulgence.

6 Fasting is an act of homage to the majesty of appetite. So I think we should arrange to give up our pleasures regularly—our food, our friends, our lovers—in order to preserve their intensity, and the moment of coming back to them. For this is the moment that renews and refreshes both oneself and the thing one loves. Sailors and travellers enjoyed this once, and so did hunters, I suppose. Part of the weariness of modern life may be that we live too much on top of each other, and are entertained and fed too regularly. Once we were separated by hunger both from our food and families, and then we learned to value both. The men went off hunting, and the dogs went with them; the women and children waved goodbye. The cave was empty of men for days on end; nobody ate, or knew what to do. The women crouched by the fire, the wet smoke in their eyes; the children wailed; everybody was hungry. Then one night there were shouts and the barking of dogs from the hills, and the men came back loaded with meat. This was the great reunion, and everybody gorged themselves silly, and appetite came into its own; the long-awaited meal became a feast to remember and an almost sacred celebration of life. Now we go off to the office and come home in the evenings to cheap chicken and frozen peas. Very nice, but too much of it, too easy and regular, served up without effort or wanting. We eat, we are lucky, our faces are shining with fat, but we don't know the pleasure of being hungry any more.

7 Too much of anything—too much music, entertainment, happy snacks, or time spent with one's friends—creates a kind of impotence of living by which one can no longer hear, or taste, or see, or

love, or remember. Life is short and precious, and appetite is one of its guardians, and loss of appetite is a sort of death. So if we are to enjoy this short life we should respect the divinity of appetite, and keep it eager and not too much blunted.

8 It is a long time now since I knew that acute moment of bliss that comes from putting parched lips to a cup of cold water. The springs are still there to be enjoyed—all one needs is the original thirst.

Questions About "Definition"

1. How does Lee's definition agree with or differ from your dictionary's definition of "appetite"?
2. Making specific reference to the text, say what methods Lee uses to define "appetite."
3. What is Lee's thesis (see pages 6–9)? Comment on whether he could have explained it intelligibly without making clear to you the sense in which he used "appetite."

Questions on Diction and Writing Techniques

1. Why does Lee choose to write, "bite into the world and taste its multitudinous flavours and juices" (par. 1)? What does this diction contribute to your understanding of his definition?
2. Is "lust" (par. 2) an apt word? What other words might the writer have used? In the context of this essay, which word do you prefer?
3. Does Lee use personal experience to good effect? Explain.
4. Which paragraph does Lee develop by means of comparison and contrast (see pages 271–276)? What does this pattern of organization contribute to the clarification of the paragraph's main idea?

For Discussion, Reading, and Writing

1. Laurie Lee's conclusion in "Appetite" is (circle one):

   A. Appetite is the keenness of living.

B. Appetite is the lust for food.

C. One of the major pleasures in life is appetite.

D. One of the keenest pleasures of appetite is in the wanting, not the satisfaction.

E. Nowadays we don't know the pleasure of being hungry.

2. According to Lee, "One of the keenest pleasures of appetite remains in the wanting, not the satisfaction" (par. 4). Do you agree? Cite examples from your own experience to support your view.

3. Explaining the terms you use with definitions, write a paragraph or two of comment on the statement just quoted.

4. Giving specific examples from your personal experience and observations of others, write a paragraph defining one of these terms:

   boredom
   gamesmanship
   generation gap
   happiness
   guilt

5. Write an extended definition of one of these terms:

   ripoff
   cool cat
   gravy train
   weirdo
   no sweat
   vibes
   spaced out

THE ASCENT OF MAN

Jacob Bronowski

Jacob Bronowski (1908–1974) was a senior fellow and trustee of Salk Institute for Biological Studies in San Diego and the author of a dozen books, including *The Ascent of Man* (1973).

1 Man is a singular creature. He has a set of gifts which make him unique among the animals: so that, unlike them, he is not a figure in the landscape—he is a shaper of the landscape. In body and in mind he is the explorer of nature, the ubiquitous animal, who did not find but has made his home in every continent.

2 It is reported that when the Spaniards arrived overland at the Pacific Ocean in 1769 the California Indians used to say that at full moon the fish came and danced on these beaches. And it is true that there is a local variety of fish, the grunion, that comes up out of the water and lays its eggs above the normal high-tide mark. The females bury themselves tail first in the sand and the males gyrate round them and fertilise the eggs as they are being laid. The full moon is important, because it gives the time needed for the eggs to incubate undisturbed in the sand, nine or ten days, between these very high tides and the next ones that will wash the hatched fish out to sea again.

3 Every landscape in the world is full of these exact and beautiful adaptations, by which an animal fits into its environment like one cog-wheel into another. The sleeping hedgehog waits for the spring to burst its metabolism into life. The humming-bird beats the air and dips its needle-fine beak into hanging blossoms. Butterflies mimic leaves and even noxious creatures to deceive their predators. The mole plods through the ground as if he had been designed as a mechanical shuttle.

4 So millions of years of evolution have shaped the grunion to fit and sit exactly with the tides. But nature—that is, biological evolution—has not fitted man to any specific environment. On the contrary, by comparison with the grunion he has a rather crude survival kit; and yet—this is the paradox of the human condition—one that fits him to all environments. Among the multitude of animals which scamper, fly, burrow and swim around us, man is the only one who is not locked into his environment. His imagination, his reason, his emotional subtlety and toughness, make it possible for him not to accept the environment but to change it. And that series of inventions, by which man from age to age has remade his environment, is a different kind of evolution—not biological, but cultural evolution. I call that brilliant sequence of cultural peaks *The Ascent of Man.*

Questions About "Definition"

1. What is the phrase Bronowski coined to describe humanity's "series of inventions"?
2. Using his words or your own, write a formal definition of the phrase.
3. Making specific reference to the text, point out how Bronowski makes the meaning of that phrase clear to you.

Questions on Diction and Writing Techniques

1. How does your dictionary define "singular" and "ubiquitous" (par. 1), "gyrate" (par. 2), "metabolism" and "predators" (par. 3); "paradox" and "cultural" (par. 4)? Use each of these words in a sentence.
2. Why, in paragraph 1, did Bronowski choose "gifts," instead of, for example, "attributes" or "characteristics"?
3. In what sense can it properly be said that paragraphs 2 and 3 are a unit? How are they and the ideas they express related? Do they have a common topic sentence? Explain.

4. Mark in your text examples of patterns of organization *other* than definition that Bronowski chooses to explain one or another idea in this essay. He uses "like" to signal an example of one of them. What word or phrase does he choose to introduce another example of that pattern of organization?

5. Show how Bronowski utilizes a conjunction to emphasize the relationship of the idea in one sentence of paragraph 4 and that in the sentence immediately following.

6. Explain whether the ideas in paragraph 1 and those in the second half of paragraph 4 are similar and whether those in the rest of the essay are properly related to them. Does Bronowski make clear to you what he means by "Man is a singular creature"? Is his essay unified? Explain.

For Discussion, Reading, and Writing

1. Write a paragraph that explains, as simply as possible, the meaning of "biological evolution," and another paragraph that explains "cultural evolution." (You may find it useful to refer to texts you studied in high school or a course you are taking now in a physical or social science.) To clarify further those terms, write a paragraph in which you compare and contrast them. Rewrite your material in a short essay.

2. In what ways that you are familiar with from personal experience or observation are humans like or unlike other animals? Ponder this question, make notes, jot down ideas, and then write a draft of a short essay on the subject, making sure to define the terms you use. Write the essay.

3. What do "shaper of the landscape" and "explorer of nature" signify to you? Be prepared to discuss in class your ideas about what Bronowski means by these phrases.

Division and Classification

. . . of late years I have tried to write less picturesquely and more exactly.

—George Orwell

IMAGINE, if you will, that the manager of a supermarket were to leave about pell-mell, as they arrived from warehouses, the numerous items his store offers for sale. Contemplation of the confusion that would result may help you to appreciate how useful is the purposeful arrangement of retail stores' goods, which we take for granted, in creating order out of what otherwise would be disarray.

A supermarket divides its commodities into groups: meat, delicatessen, frozen foods, and so forth. Within a major group it arranges goods in lesser categories: meat, for example, in sections of beef, veal, lamb, and chicken. Conversely, the store groups preparations of the curd of milk under the heading of cheese and classifies cheese, milk, cream, and butter as dairy products. These methods of arrangement are called division and classification.

Division and classification are a means of establishing order among things having some common characteristic. Division is the separation of something into groups or of a group into subgroups. Examples of this process are the separation of all living creatures into plants and animals and the further separation of animals into mammals, fish, birds, and so forth. Classification is the placement of units in a group or of groups in a more inclusive category. Examples of this process are the grouping of the whale, the cow, and the chimpanzee in the class of mammals; the grouping of the trout, the salmon, and the herring in the class of fish; and the further grouping of mammals and fish in the category of animal.

Division and classification are a filing system of a kind whose objective is to explain relationships and to make information comprehensible, handy, and easy to communicate. They have in common that they relate general classes and subclasses. They are so closely associated—being, in a sense, opposite sides of the same coin—that they are often considered together under the single heading of classification.

A system of filing will depend on the classifier. A politician might classify constituents as liberal and conservative to discover how to gear an election campaign. A police chief might classify the areas in a town or city as law-abiding and law-breaking to find out how best to patrol them. A school administrator might classify the population of a district as preschool or school age in order to prepare a school budget. Whatever the purpose, the categories used must have different and mutually exclusive characteristics, as in this amusing passage from *Essays of Elia* by Charles Lamb:

> The human species, according to the best theory I can form of it, is composed of two distinct races, *the men who borrow,* and *the men who lend.* To these original diversities may be reduced all those impertinent classifications of Gothic and Celtic tribes, white men, black men, red men. All the dwellers upon earth, "Parthians, and Medes, and Elamites," flock hither, and do naturally fall in with one or another of these primary distinctions.

In the paragraph that follows, the writer, having defined his term, groups clichés in significant classes to make a semblance of order of their diversity and to show how varied in kind they are:

> There are many varieties of clichés. Some are foreign phrases (*coup de grâce; et tu, Brute*). Some are homely sayings or are based on proverbs ("You can't make an omelet without breaking eggs," *blissful ignorance*). Some are quotations ("To be or not to be, etc."; "Unwepted, unhonored, and unsung"). Some are allusions to myth or history (*Gordian knot, Achilles' heel*). Some are alliterative or

rhyming phrases (*first and foremost, high and dry*). Some are paradoxes (*in less than no time, conspicuous by its absence*). Some are legalisms (*null and void, each and every*). Some are playful euphemisms (*a fate worse than death, better half*). Some are figurative phrases (*leave no stone unturned, hit the nail on the head*). And some are meaningless small change (*in the last analysis, by the same token*) [Theodore M. Bernstein, *The Careful Writer*].

Classification resembles comparison and contrast insofar as it makes an implicit or, as in this paragraph, an explicit comparison between entities:

There are three kinds of book owners. The first has all the standard sets and best sellers—unread, untouched. (This deluded individual owns woodpulp and ink, not books.) The second has a great many books—a few of them read through, most of them dipped into, but all of them as clean and shiny as the day they were bought. (This person would probably like to make books his own, but is restrained by a false respect for their physical appearance.) The third has a few books or many—every one of them dog-eared and dilapidated, shaken and loosened by continual use, marked and scribbled in from front to back. (This man owns books.) [Mortimer J. Adler, "How to Mark a Book"].

Classification is a kind of analysis that facilitates explanation by permitting the discussion, in turn, of each part (subclass) of the whole (major class), as the writer of this introductory paragraph promises to do in the body of his essay:

We all listen to music according to our separate capacities. But for the sake of analysis, the whole listening process may become clearer if we break it up into its component parts, so to speak. For lack of a better terminology, one might name these: (1) the sensuous plane, (2) the expressive plane, (3) the sheerly musical plane. The only advantage to be gained from mechanically splitting up the listening process into these hypothetical planes is the clearer view to be had of the way in which we listen [Aaron Copland, *What to Listen for in Music*].

How classification can be utilized as a pattern of organization may be seen from its use by Vance Bourjaily in two essays on the same subject. In "You Can Tell a Hunter by What He Hunts," his purpose is to explain "that the term *hunter* covers a considerable variety of men, seeking a considerable variety of values." To do this he arranges hunters into groups—duck hunters, quail hunters, deer hunters, and so on—that include the variety of people who hunt and that demonstrate the varying pleasures hunters derive from the sport.

In "In Defense of Hunting," Bourjaily's purpose is to respond to those who advocate laws designed to restrict hunting. In that essay, he uses classification to help him fit responses to the various kinds of detractors of hunting:

> I can distinguish three kinds of attacker, and each deserves a different answer. There are the moralists, who must be answered with an invitation to examine themselves. There are the sentimentalists, who must be answered with straightforward information. The third are simply the politicians, who may be answered with contempt.

Here Bourjaily orders his material and announces to the reader the plan of organization of what is to follow.

DISCIPLINING CHILDREN

John Holt

John Holt (1923–1985), formerly a teacher, first achieved recognition as an innovator in education with *How Children Fail* (1964).

---

1 A child, in growing up, may meet and learn from three different kinds of disciplines. The first and most important is what we

might call the Discipline of Nature or of Reality. When he is trying to do something real, if he does the wrong thing or doesn't do the right one, he doesn't get the result he wants. If he doesn't pile one block right on top of another, or tries to build on a slanting surface, his tower falls down. If he hits the wrong key, he hears the wrong note. If he doesn't hit the nail squarely on the head, it bends, and he has to pull it out and start with another. If he doesn't measure properly what he is trying to build, it won't open, close, fit, stand up, fly, float, whistle, or do whatever he wants it to do. If he closes his eyes when he swings, he doesn't hit the ball. A child meets this kind of discipline every time he tries to *do* something, which is why it is so important in school to give children more chances to do things, instead of just reading or listening to someone talk (or pretending to). This discipline is a great teacher. The learner never has to wait long for his answer; it usually comes quickly, often instantly. Also it is clear, and very often points toward the needed correction; from what happened he can not only see that what he did was wrong, but also why, and what he needs to do instead. Finally, and most important, the giver of the answer, call it Nature, is impersonal, impartial, and indifferent. She does not give opinions, or make judgments; she cannot be wheedled, bullied, or fooled; she does not get angry or disappointed; she does not praise or blame; she does not remember past failures or hold grudges; with her one always gets a fresh start, this time is the one that counts.

2 The next discipline we might call the Discipline of Culture, of Society, of What People Really Do. Man is a social, a cultural animal. Children sense around them this culture, this network of agreements, customs, habits, and rules binding the adults together. They want to understand it and be a part of it. They watch very carefully what people around them are doing and want to do the same. They want to do right, unless they become convinced they can't do right. Thus children rarely misbehave seriously in church, but sit as quietly as they can. The example of all those grownups is contagious. Some mysterious ritual is going on, and children, who like rituals, want to be part of it. In the same way, the little children that I see at concerts or operas, though they may fidget a little, or perhaps take a nap now and then, rarely make any disturbance. With all those grownups sitting there, neither moving nor talking, it is the most natural thing in the world to imitate them. Children

who live among adults who are habitually courteous to each other, and to them, will soon learn to be courteous. Children who live surrounded by people who speak a certain way will speak that way, however much we may try to tell them that speaking that way is bad or wrong.

3 The third discipline is the one most people mean when they speak of discipline—the Discipline of Superior Force, of sergeant to private, of "you do what I tell you or I'll make you wish you had." There is bound to be some of this in a child's life. Living as we do surrounded by things that can hurt children, or that children can hurt, we cannot avoid it. We can't afford to let a small child find out from experience the danger of playing in a busy street, or of fooling with the pots on the top of a stove, or of eating up the pills in the medicine cabinet. So, along with other precautions, we say to him, "Don't play in the street, or touch things on the stove, or go into the medicine cabinet, or I'll punish you." Between him and the danger too great for him to imagine we put a lesser danger, but one he can imagine and maybe therefore want to avoid. He can have no idea of what it would be like to be hit by a car, but he can imagine being shouted at, or spanked, or sent to his room. He avoids these substitutes for the greater danger until he can understand it and avoid it for its own sake. But we ought to use this discipline only when it is necessary to protect the life, health, safety, or well-being of people or other living creatures, or to prevent destruction of things that people care about. We ought not to assume too long, as we usually do, that a child cannot understand the real nature of the danger from which we want to protect him. The sooner he avoids the danger, not to escape our punishment, but as a matter of good sense, the better. He can learn that faster than we think. In Mexico, for example, where people drive their cars with a good deal of spirit, I saw many children no older than five or four walking unattended on the streets. They understood about cars, they knew what to do. A child whose life is full of the threat and fear of punishment is locked into babyhood. There is no way for him to grow up, to learn to take responsibility for his life and acts. Most important of all, we should not assume that having to yield to the threat of our superior force is good for the child's character. It is never good for *anyone's* character. To bow to superior force makes us feel impotent and cowardly for not having had the strength or courage to resist.

Worse, it makes us resentful and vengeful. We can hardly wait to make someone pay for our humiliation, yield to us as we were once made to yield. No, if we cannot always avoid using the Discipline of Superior Force, we should at least use it as seldom as we can.

Questions About "Division and Classification"

1. Before you read this essay what did discipline mean to you?
2. Where does Holt announce his pattern of organization for this essay?
3. What does Holt's classification contribute to your understanding of discipline?

Questions on Diction and Writing Techniques

1. Mark in your text those words that are new to you, but whose meaning you inferred from their context. Define them in your own words. Compare your definitions with those in your dictionary. Look up in your dictionary any other words that are new to you. Use the words in both groups in sentences.
2. What is Holt's purpose in writing "also" and "finally" (par. 1); "thus" and "in the same way" (par. 2); "therefore" "but," and "for example" (par. 3)?
3. To what, in paragraph 2, does "they" refer?
4. Find in paragraph 1 two instances of Holt's making a generalization supported by examples.
5. What is Holt's purpose in paragraph 1 in writing a short, six-word sentence? Find another instance in this essay of his use of a short sentence for a similar reason.

For Discussion, Reading, and Writing

1. What, according to Holt, is the most important kind of discipline for a child? Why?

2. Why is Nature important as "the giver of the answer"?
3. Write a short essay in which you use classification to help you to organize any collection of related experiences, for example, people you know, places you've been to, teachers you've had.

THREE TYPES OF PRESIDENTS

Louis Koenig

Louis W. Koenig, a professor of government at New York University, has held important posts with federal agencies in Washington, D.C.

---

1 Without undue violence to history, it is possible to divide the Presidents the United States has had into three recurrent types with a view to assessing their suitability as models for the contemporary chief executive in all his rugged circumstances.

2 The most numerous type is one that might be styled a "literalist" President. James Madison, James Buchanan, Taft, and, to a degree, Eisenhower are of this school. The mark of the "literalist" President, as his title suggests, is close obedience to the word and letter of the Constitution. Taft, who with Buchanan is the most literal of the Presidents, formulated its operative belief:

> The true view of the Executive function is . . . that the President can exercise no power which cannot be fairly and reasonably traced to some specific grant of power or justly implied and included within such express grant as proper and necessary to its exercise. Such specific grant must be either in the Federal Constitution or in an act of Congress passed in pursuance thereof. There is no

undefined residuum of power which he can exercise because it seems to him to be in the public interest.

3 The Taft-like President tends also to live by the Whig assumption that the legislative power is popular and the executive monarchical. He is respectful, even deferential, to Congress. "My duty," James Buchanan was prone to say, "is to execute the laws . . . and not my individual opinions." When Congress did nothing in the face of gathering rebellion, Buchanan too did nothing. In a later day, President Eisenhower is reported sometimes to have remarked privately to his aides that he felt called upon to "restore" to Congress powers that Franklin Roosevelt had "usurped." In public pronouncement and personal act, Eisenhower was respectful of Congressional prerogative and the doctrine of separation of powers. "Our very form of Government," he declared to the Convention of the National Young Republican Organization in 1953, "is in peril unless each branch willingly accepts and discharges its own clear responsibilities—and respects the rights and responsibilities of the others."

4 The Taft-like President makes little use of his independent powers or prerogative (his powers, for example, as commander-in-chief and as implied in the executive power clause). He exerts political pressure sparingly. Symptomatic of his approach is James Bryce's observation that the typical nineteenth-century President's communications to Congress were so perfunctory that "the expression of his wishes . . . in messages has not necessarily any more effect on Congress than an article in a prominent party newspaper."

5 The Taft-like President has little taste for innovation in social policy. He is nostalgic for the past and urges it be used as a blueprint for the future. He feels, as Taft did, that the bane of government is "ill-digested legislation" and that "real progress in government must be by slow stages." It is a view that Theodore Roosevelt found upheld in society by "most able lawyers who are past middle age" and "large numbers of well-meaning, respectable citizens."

6 The Presidency in the manner of Taft and Buchanan is, on its face, inadequate for the necessities of the contemporary Presidency. The past, which it venerates, can be only a partial and imperfect guide to the present and future. It excessively neglects the President's independent powers, which again and again have been a mighty sword in times of crisis and change. Its neglect of politics

abdicates action to passivity and, as the experience of several nineteenth-century Presidents proves, can thoroughly reduce the President from leader to clerk. The best proof of the inadequacy of the "literalist" model is the abandonment of its key concepts by Presidents who once had taken them up. Cleveland at first proposed to be a "literalist" President, spurning to use patronage and pressure upon Congress and declaring, "I did not come here to legislate." But when Congress blocked the bills he was driven to sponsor, his attitude changed, and he went furiously to work to win votes by promising jobs. Dwight Eisenhower, for all his professed deference to Congress and distaste for politics, in time did push his legislative program, and his campaigning in the 1954 Congressional elections was on a scale comparable to Franklin Roosevelt's.

7 At the opposite end of the spectrum from the "literalist" President is the "strong" President, typified by Lincoln, Washington, Jackson, Wilson, and the Roosevelts. He generally, although not exclusively, flourishes in times of crisis—during a war or a depression—and when political movements such as liberalism or social progressivism are at their crest. He interprets his powers with maximum liberality; he is a precedent-maker and -breaker to the point where the legality of his acts is questioned and attacked. His legal bible is the "stewardship theory" of Theodore Roosevelt, who felt that it was the President's "duty to do anything that the needs of the nation demanded unless such action was forbidden by the Constitution or by the laws." "I acted for the public welfare," Roosevelt said, "I acted for the common well-being of all our people."

8 The strong President provides leadership, in Franklin Roosevelt's words, "alert and sensitive to change," which in the Jefferson-Jackson tradition means that the government must act positively in promoting a good life, and in the Wilson tradition means that the nation cannot shun or escape its obligations of world leadership. The strong President is, on the historical record, assertive and masterful in times of crisis and change. His orientation is less to the past than to the future, which he approaches with hope and plan. He is skillful politically and is concerned more with substance than with form. When necessary, he resorts to bold action, whether economic, social, or military, which he does not shun for the sake of lowering the national debt. He accepts and abides a strong Congress, but purposefully uses the lawmaking process. He has the gift

of inspiring and rallying the people with messages that mix practicality and prophecy. In his view, the President as a person must dominate the Presidency as an institution. He, a fleeting political figure, must bend, divert, and lead the cumbrous bureaucratic executive branch according to his purpose.

9 Between the "strong" and "literalist" Presidents is a middle ground which many chief executives have occupied; it unites elements of both extremes. This middle ground need not now detain us. The urgencies of the 1960's and beyond make emphatically clear that only one of the three available Presidential types is suitable for the future. The United States's world responsibilities and domestic urgencies require a Presidency that is continuously strong. The great, if not the foremost, task of American politics is to convert the strong Presidency, which has appeared only intermittently, into an assured and constant feature of our government. To be sure, particular actions of past strong Presidents have to a degree been institutionalized over the years. Theodore Roosevelt's "stewardship" in the 1902 coal strike is regularized in the Taft-Hartley Act; Wilson's and Franklin Roosevelt's venturings into world affairs set precedents for our many routine commitments to alliances and especially to the United Nations. But, as John Kennedy's experience as chief executive testifies, many pieces in the mosaic of the strong President lack a coating of permanence. The President is weak rather than strong as party chief, legislative leader, and general manager of the executive branch. His weaknesses there spawn further weaknesses in his capacities as chief diplomat, commander-in-chief, and decision-maker. Charles de Gaulle, beholding the American Presidential system in 1963, concluded that it was functioning in a limping way. Our task is to see where weakness eats upon strength, to discover what combination of arrangements will satisfy our most urgent governmental need: a Presidency that has continuous strength in all its parts.

Questions About "Division and Classification"

1. Koenig might have chosen other categories into which to group Presidents of the United States: Republicans and Democrats;

conservatives and liberals; one-term presidents and two-term presidents. Name at least three other pairs of categories.

2. Show how Koenig's stated purpose determines the system of division of classification he chose in this essay.
3. What does Koenig's pattern of organization in this essay tell you about the presidency that you did not know before? Is it a useful means of explaining the Presidency, for example, of Jimmy Carter? Of Ronald Reagan? Be specific.

Questions on Diction and Writing Techniques

1. How does your dictionary define "recurrent" (par. 1); "operative" (par. 2); "Whig," "monarchical," and "prerogative" (par. 3); "symptomatic" (par. 4); "nostalgic" (par. 5); "spectrum" and "progressivism" (par. 7); "cumbrous" (par. 8); "mosaic" (par. 9)? Use each of these words in a sentence.
2. Aside from division and classification, what other pattern of organization does Koenig use? Mark examples of it in your text. Show how they help Koenig communicate his ideas.
3. Mark in your text all instances of Koenig's use of quotations. Comment on the effectiveness of their use in developing paragraphs and in making Koenig credible.
4. What are the topic sentences of paragraphs 3, 4, and 5? What is the advantage of placing those sentences where Koenig does?
5. Write a summary of this essay in a paragraph of not over a hundred words.

For Discussion, Reading, and Writing

1. Be prepared with specific information to place President Reagan in one of the categories Koenig chooses in this essay. Prepare also to discuss in class whether his type of presidency is suitable for these times.
2. Use the ideas generated in your discussion in class of President Reagan as part of your prewriting for a short essay about his

presidency. Add to your information by reading in your college library: newspaper reports, magazine articles, whatever. Write the essay.

3. Use division and classification as a pattern of organization for a short essay on the kinds of information to be found in your favorite newspaper or magazine.
4. How might you classify your teachers, classmates, friends, relatives? Write, in a short essay, about the characteristics of one of these groups.

MALE-FEMALE LIAISONS

Vance Packard

Vance Packard is well known as an observer and critic of American life. His ninth and most recent book is *Our Endangered Children: Growing Up in a Changing World* (1983).

---

1 Most of the rules regulating marriages and their dissolution were made in eras when the bride and groom could look forward to fewer than half the number of years together that the couples marrying in the next few years can anticipate. For that reason alone, entering into wedlock calls for a new high level of prudence. There is now obviously a greater chance the partners will outgrow each other, lose interest, or become restless. In the past quarter-century, instead of greater prudence, however, we have seen a considerable increase in imprudent embarkations upon marriage.

2 Wives in the future surely will spend an increasing proportion of their married life as equal partners of the husband free of the "motherhood-service" role, and so will have more options for the

From *The Sexual Wilderness* by Vance Packard. Reprinted by permission of the author.

outlet of their surplus energy. They can no longer view marriage as a haven where they will be looked after by a husband in return for traditional services rendered.

3 Instead, more than ever before, women will have not only the opportunity but the expectation to push out for themselves and function as autonomous individuals who happen to have marriage partners. Marriages will apparently continue to be brittle for some time. Families in the immediate future will be expected to be highly mobile, and ever smaller in size.

4 While, as noted, the traditional economic functions of marriage have shrunk, there are 2 particularly compelling reasons looming why people will be marrying in the coming decade despite the relatively free availability of unmarried sexual partners:

5 • The warm, all-embracing companionship that in marriage can endure through the confusion, mobility, and rapid social change of our times.

6 • The opportunity to obtain immortality and personal growth for married individuals who perpetuate themselves through reproduction as they help mold personalities of their children and proudly induct them into the larger community.

7 This opportunity is so profoundly desired by most adult humans who are capable of reproduction that childlessness by choice would seem to be almost as difficult to popularize on any large scale as singleness by choice. Both would probably require intensive, prolonged social conditioning.

8 The institution of marriage is obviously in need of modifications to fit the modern needs. Author Jerome Weidman made an important point in his book *Your Daughter Iris* when he wrote of today's marriages: "Human beings do not obtain permanent possession of each other when they marry. All they obtain is the right to work at the job of holding on to each other." In pressing for modification of marriage as an institution we should seek above all to assure that the 2 functions of marriage just stated be fulfilled.

9 A variety of predictions and proposals are being heard today as to how the male-female liaison will or should evolve in the next few decades to meet the changing conditions of modern life. Here, for example, are 8 possible patterns of marriage or near-marriage that are being discussed:

10 1. *Serial mating.* Sometimes it is called serial monogamy,

sometimes serial polygamy, sometimes consecutive polygamy. But the basic idea is pretty much the same for all. It would assume a turnover of partners over the 50-odd years that a man and a woman can expect to live after they first consider marriage. Swedish sociologist Joachim Israel suggested that 4 or 5 marriages might be about par for a lifetime. The mood behind such proposals was summed up by a New York model when she said, "Why lie to yourself? We know we're not going to love one man all our lives." Among others, a psychologist-social worker in California, Virginia Satir, has advocated the adoption of renewable marriage contracts. She suggests the contract lapse unless renewed every 5 years.

11 2. *Unstructured cohabitation.* These are the prolonged affairs without any assumption of permanence or responsibility. Such so-called unstructured liaisons—long popular in the lower classes—have been springing up in many of the larger universities in the off-campus housing. A psychiatrist at the University of California in Berkeley has suggested these liaisons may be the shape of the future. He said, "Stable, open nonmarital relationships are pushing the border of what society is going to face in 10 years."

12 A man's magazine in the mid-1960s presented some unconventional views of a woman who had been involved in a national controversy. During the presentation, she was asked, "How many lovers have you had, if you don't mind our asking?"

13 She responded, "You've got a helluva nerve, but I really don't mind. I've had five, if you count my marriage as an affair . . . five affairs, all of them really wing-dings."

14 3. *Mutual polygamy.* At a conference of marriage specialists in 1966 one expert from a Midwestern university speculated, "If we are moving into a new pattern where we are not claiming that marriage can do all the things that have been assumed, we may be moving into a kind of situation where there will be more than one partner. A compartmentalizing." Each partner in any particular marriage might have several mates, each chosen for a special purpose—for example, economic, recreational, procreational. A more informal variant of this would be "flexible monogamy," which in the view of Phyllis and Eberhard Kronhausen would frankly allow "for variety, friendships, and even sexual experiences with other individuals, if these are desired."

15 4. *Single-parent marriages by intent.* These, on the Swedish

model, would be the females—and occasional males—who yearn for parenthood without the burdens of wedlock.

16 5. *Specialists in parenthood.* Anthropologist Margaret Mead, in looking a few decades ahead, suggests the time may come when pressures to keep the birth rate low will produce a social style "in which parenthood would be limited to a smaller number of families whose principal function would be child-rearing; the rest of the population would be free to function—for the first time in history—as individuals."

17 6. *Communal living.* In such a situation, several adult females and several adult males might live together in the same large dwelling and consider themselves an enlarged communal family, much as the hippies and other unconventional family groups have already been doing for some time.

18 7. *Legalized polygamy for senior citizens.* This is a form of polygamy that enables a man to have several wives at the same time. It has been advanced as a way to ease the demographic problem created by the fact that after the age of 60 there are increasingly more females than males in the population. One such proposal was advanced in the magazine *Geriatrics* by Dr. Victor Kassel, of Salt Lake City (the Mormon capital). The idea was taken seriously enough to be debated and unofficially turned down by the National Council on the Aging. A widow in South Carolina gave one feminine viewpoint when she said, "I am lonesome—but not that lonesome!"

19 8. *A variety of liaison patterns functioning in society simultaneously.* David Mace suggests we are moving toward a 3-layer cake type of society as far as male-female liaisons are concerned. He speculated that there may be a coexistence of several patterns. One pattern, as he sees it, will be that a proportion of the people will settle for sex freedom. They will not marry, but will drift into liaisons of long and short terms. There will be no attempt to punish or suppress such persons. He suggested that the second layer of this cake would involve somewhat more structuring, with a number of people choosing to go in and out of marriage and probably having several marriages in a lifetime, as in the common Hollywood pattern. Probably in this second layer there will be an attitude of freedom regarding extramarital sex while the couples are married. He suggested that in the third layer of the cake will be those who accept the concept of exclusive monogamy, preceded in at least some cases by premarital chastity.

[20] Moral standards aside, one complication of most of the 8 possible patterns cited above is that they do not allow sufficiently for the intense desire that most women have for a secure arrangement —or at least women have had this intense desire until very recent times. They have had greater difficulty accepting fluid arrangements, especially after they pass the age of 30, than males.

[21] An even bigger complication is that while most of these arrangements might seem attractive in terms of providing the companionship so important to male-female partnerships today, they do not come to terms with the second crucial ingredient of modern marriages: a partnership where there is a sound environment for reaching for immortality through the rearing of children. Thus most should be rejected from serious consideration as socially unfeasible —at least for people interested in having children (and we suspect that those who don't will remain a small minority). Some of these patterns, of course, might seem more attractive after the child-rearing phase has passed.

[22] But whatever hope we have for the future lies in the quality—not the quantity—of the children our homes produce. The highest-quality children, we now know, are *wanted* children who have both mothers and fathers as visible models, two parents who offer them affection, a sense of security, stability, and family unity. In the future we should settle for nothing less. It is the one-parent homes, the broken homes, parental abdication, and inadequate parental models that account for much of our social distress today: delinquency, deviance, dope, and divorce.

Questions About "Division and Classification"

1. What is the main idea of the essay?
2. What does Packard's use of division and classification contribute to your understanding of that idea?
3. What systems, other than the one he chose, might Packard have used for his division of male–female liaisons?
4. Show why the system he chose is appropriate for this essay.

Questions on Diction and Writing Techniques

1. How does your dictionary define "haven" (par. 2), "autonomous" (par. 3), "monogamy" and "polygamy" (par. 10), "cohabitation" (par. 11), "wing-dings" (par. 13), "variant" (par. 14)? Use each of these words in a sentence.
2. What does "however" signal about the relationship of ideas within paragraph 1?
3. How are the ideas in paragraph 2 related to those in paragraph 1?
4. How are the ideas in paragraph 3 related to those in paragraph 2? How does Packard signal this relationship?
5. Underline in your text all instances of Packard's use of quotations. Explain the purpose and effect of each quotation.
6. Explain whether there is explicit or implicit comparison and contrast between entities of Packard's division and classification.
7. Find examples of Packard's use of causal analysis (see pages 347–370) to help him explain ideas in this essay.
8. What words does Packard utilize to signal illustration? Mark them in your text.

For Discussion, Reading, and Writing

1. Why, according to Packard, does "entering into wedlock call for a new high level of prudence"?
2. Why, according to him, will wives in the future have more options for using their surplus energy?
3. Why, despite the relatively free availability of unmarried sexual partners, will people be marrying in the coming decade?
4. What is the basic idea of serial mating?
5. What does Packard mean by "single-parent marriages by intent"?
6. What are the complications of the male–female liaisons he enumerates?

7. Using division and classification as your main pattern of organization, write about the TV ads that please (bore) you most.
8. In a short essay, classify in some meaningful way your most embarrassing (distressful, satisfying, disastrous) teenage experiences.
9. Use division and classification to explain in a short essay the kinds of sexual encounters you have had.

Process

There may be inspired writers for whom the first draft is just right. But anyone who is not certifiably a Milton had better assume that the first draft is a very primitive thing. The reason is simple: Writing is difficult work.

—John Kenneth Galbraith

A process is a sequence of actions or operations. Process, the pattern of organization, is a method of exposition whose function is to analyze such a sequence and to convey a clear understanding of it to the reader.

There are two kinds of process analysis. One is an explanation that tells *how to do something*—how to bake a cake, how to change a tire, how to plant corn, how to fish for trout. The paragraph on page 230 telling how to use a handsaw is an example of this kind. The writer's purpose is instructive: to make the consecutive steps so clear that the reader will know how to use the tool. The second is an explanation of *how something is (or was) done*—how you selected your college, how an electric motor works, how General Grant took Richmond, how you dissected a frog. They are alike insofar as both kinds explain the successive and interdependent steps that lead to an end. To make clear to the reader how that end is reached is the purpose of the writer who uses process as a pattern of organization.

The writer of "Menial Jobs Taught Me a Lot" (analyzed on pages 34–37) uses process in his third paragraph (italics added):

> . . . *The first thing each morning,* I had to drive a truck to a supply depot to pick up odds and ends of building materials. *Then,* having

> driven back to the construction site, I had to unload them where they were needed. *After that,* I had to haul materials from one or another location on the site to others. *That done, and for most of the rest of the day,* I had to unload by hand from trailers and to stack in orderly piles tons and tons of bulky materials such as rough lumber, roofing shingles, and kegs of nails. *At the end of the day,* I was obliged to clean up rubbish from the outside and inside of buildings under construction, load it on my truck and *then* unload it at a refuse dump on the site.

In using this method of exposition he has two purposes: (1) to explain how something was done—how he did the work of a laborer on a construction project, and (2) to make clear, through this example, why his jobs "soon become boring." In his essay, process is one of three patterns of organization. The others are illustration (see pages 252–270) and comparison and contrast (see pages 271–290). All are used for the common purpose of clarifying the thesis and supporting its generalization.

Here are some things to keep in mind when you write a process analysis:

1. *Process must not be confused with narration.* Process relates a sequence of events, so it is in a way like narration (see pages 176–204). But narration generally is concerned with the story itself; whereas the purpose of process analysis is expository: to set forth information and ideas.
2. *Be sure you know your subject well.* To obtain the information you need for your explanation, draw on as many of the writer's sources of material (discussed in Part Three) as your topic requires.
3. *Organize your material systematically.* The safest procedure by far is to present its parts in sequence, making sure that no part of a series needed for clarity is omitted.
4. *Explain each step simply and in sufficient detail.* How much detail is needed will depend on who your readers are. You should be aware of how much information they already have about your subject. You run the risk of boring a knowledgeable reader if you say too much, of leaving confused an

ignorant one if you say too little. The general rule is to tell your readers whatever they may reasonably want to know in order to understand clearly how to do something or how something is or was done.

5. *Use appropriate language.* Define terms that may require special knowledge or whose meaning your readers may not get from the context. Your writing should not be obscure or confusing. Your audience is entitled to an explanation that is easy to understand.

6. *Be sure the time sequence is clear.* To achieve clarity and coherence in process analysis it is often helpful to stress the time sequence. Use temporal diction: *first,* do this; *then,* do that; *finally,* do thus and so. Notice with what care, in the italicized words in the paragraph quoted on pages 331–332, the writer emphasizes the sequence of action.

The use of these suggestions is demonstrated in this exemplary passage from Vilhjalmur Stefansson's *My Life With the Eskimo:*

> The whole principle of successfully stalking a seal is just in realizing from the first that he is bound to see you and that your only hope is in pretending that you also are a seal. If you act and look so as to convince him from the first that you are a brother seal, he will regard you with unconcern. To simulate a seal well enough to deceive a seal is not difficult, for, to begin with, we know from experience that his eye-sight is poor. You can walk up without taking any special precautions until, under ordinary conditions of light, you are within two hundred and fifty or three hundred yards. Then you have to begin to be more careful. You move ahead while he is asleep, and when he wakes up you stop motionless. You can safely proceed on all fours until within something less than two hundred yards, but after that you will have to play seal more faithfully. Your method of locomotion will then have to be that of the seal, which does not differ very materially from that of a snake, and which therefore has its disadvantages at a season of

the year when the surface of the ice is covered with puddles of water anywhere from an inch to twenty inches in depth, as it is in spring and early summer. You must not only crawl ahead, seal-fashion, but you must be careful to always present a side view of your body to the seal, for a man coming head-on does not look particularly like a seal.

Until you are within a hundred yards or so the seal is not likely to notice you, but somewhere between the hundred yard and the seventy-five yard mark his attention will suddenly be attracted to you, and instead of going to sleep at the end of his ordinary short period of wakefulness, he will remain awake and stare at you steadily. The seal knows, exactly as well as the seal hunter knows, that no seal in this world will sleep continuously for as much as four minutes at a time. If you lie still that long, he will know you are no seal, and up will go his tail and down he will slide into the water in the twinkling of an eye. When the seal, therefore, has been watching you carefully for twenty or thirty seconds, you must raise your head twelve or fifteen inches above the ice, look around seal-fashion, so that your eyes will sweep the whole circle of the horizon, and drop your head again upon the ice. By the time he has seen you repeat this process two or three times in the space of five or six minutes he will be convinced that you are a seal, and all his worries will be gone. From then on you can proceed more rapidly, crawling ahead while he sleeps and stopping while he remains awake, never doing anything unbecoming a seal. In this way you can crawl within five or ten yards of him if you like, and as a matter of fact I have known of expert seal hunters who under emergencies would go after a seal without any ordinary weapon and crawl so near him that they could seize him by a flipper, pull him away from his hole, and club or stab him. My Eskimo companions generally used to crawl within about fifteen or twenty yards; but I have found under ordinary circumstances that fifty yards is close enough for a man with a rifle. The animal lies on a slippery incline beside his hole, so that the shot that kills him must kill him instantly. It must shatter the brain or break the spinal cord of the neck; the slightest quiver of a muscle will send him sliding into the water and all your work will have been to no purpose.

THE JEANING OF AMERICA—AND THE WORLD

Carin Quinn

Carin C. Quinn, a freelance writer, did graduate work in immigration and folklore.

[1] This is the story of a sturdy American symbol which has now spread throughout most of the world. The symbol is not the dollar. It is not even Coca-Cola. It is a simple pair of pants called blue jeans, and what the pants symbolize is what Alexis de Tocqueville called "a manly and legitimate passion for equality. . . ." Blue jeans are favored equally by bureaucrats and cowboys; bankers and deadbeats; fashion designers and beer drinkers. They draw no distinctions and recognize no classes; they are merely American. Yet they are sought after almost everywhere in the world—including Russia, where authorities recently broke up a teen-aged gang that was selling them on the black market for two hundred dollars a pair. They have been around for a long time, and it seems likely that they will outlive even the necktie.

[2] This ubiquitous American symbol was the invention of a Bavarian-born Jew. His name was Levi Strauss.

[3] He was born in Bad Ocheim, Germany, in 1829, and during the European political turmoil of 1848 decided to take his chances in New York, to which his two brothers already had emigrated. Upon arrival, Levi soon found that his two brothers had exaggerated their tales of an easy life in the land of the main chance. They were landowners, they had told him; instead, he found them pushing needles, thread, pots, pans, ribbons, yarn, scissors, and buttons

From *American Heritage*, April–May 1978, pp. 16–18.

to housewives. For two years he was a lowly peddler, hauling some 180 pounds of sundries door-to-door to eke out a marginal living. When a married sister in San Francisco offered to pay his way West in 1850, he jumped at the opportunity, taking with him bolts of canvas he hoped to sell for a living.

4 It was the wrong kind of canvas for that purpose, but while talking with a miner down from the mother lode, he learned that pants—sturdy pants that would stand up to the rigors of the diggings—were almost impossible to find. Opportunity beckoned. On the spot, Strauss measured the man's girth and inseam with a piece of string and, for six dollars in gold dust, had them tailored into a pair of stiff but rugged pants. The miner was delighted with the result, word got around about "those pants of Levi's," and Strauss was in business. The company has been in business ever since.

5 When Strauss ran out of canvas, he wrote his two brothers to send more. He received instead a tough, brown cotton cloth made in Nimes, France—called *serge de Nimes* and swiftly shortened to "denim" (the word "jeans" derives from *Gênes,* the French word for Genoa, where a similar cloth was produced). Almost from the first, Strauss had his cloth dyed the distinctive indigo that gave blue jeans their name, but it was not until the 1870s that he added the copper rivets which have long since become a company trademark. The rivets were the idea of a Virginia City, Nevada, tailor, Jacob W. Davis, who added them to pacify a mean-tempered miner called Alkali Ike. Alkali, the story goes, complained that the pockets of his jeans always tore when he stuffed them with ore samples and demanded that Davis do something about it. As a kind of joke, Davis took the pants to a blacksmith and had the pockets riveted; once again, the idea worked so well that word got around; in 1873 Strauss appropriated and patented the gimmick—and hired Davis as a regional manager.

6 By this time, Strauss had taken both his brothers and two brothers-in-law into the company and was ready for his third San Francisco store. Over the ensuing years the company prospered locally, and by the time of his death in 1902, Strauss had become a man of prominence in California. For three decades thereafter the business remained profitable though small, with sales largely confined to the working people of the West—cowboys, lumberjacks, railroad workers, and the like. Levi's jeans were first introduced to

the East, apparently, during the dude-ranch craze of the 1930s, when vacationing Easterners returned and spread the word about the wonderful pants with rivets. Another boost came in World War II, when blue jeans were declared an essential commodity and were sold only to people engaged in defense work. From a company with fifteen salespeople, two plants, and almost no business east of the Mississippi in 1946, the organization grew in thirty years to include a sales force of more than twenty-two thousand, with fifty plants and offices in thirty-five countries. Each year, more than 250,000,000 items of Levi's clothing are sold—including more than 83,000,000 pairs of riveted blue jeans. They have become, through marketing, word of mouth, and demonstrable reliability, the common pants of America. They can be purchased pre-washed, pre-faded, and pre-shrunk for the suitably proletarian look. They adapt themselves to any sort of idiosyncratic use; women slit them at the inseams and convert them into long skirts, men chop them off above the knees and turn them into something to be worn while challenging the surf. Decorations and ornamentations abound.

7 The pants have become a tradition, and along the way have acquired a history of their own—so much so that the company has opened a museum in San Francisco. There was, for example, the turn-of-the-century trainman who replaced a faulty coupling with a pair of jeans; the Wyoming man who used his jeans as a towrope to haul his car out of a ditch; the Californian who found several pairs in an abandoned mine, wore them, then discovered they were sixty-three years old and still as good as new and turned them over to the Smithsonian as a tribute to their toughness. And then there is the particularly terrifying story of the careless construction worker who dangled fifty-two stories above the street until rescued, his sole support the Levi's belt loop through which his rope was hooked.

Questions About "Process"

1. Does Quinn explain clearly the steps by which Levi's invention became "the common pants of America" (par. 6)? Explain, making specific reference to the text.

2. To what extent does this essay increase your knowledge of how blue jeans came to be popular?
3. Does Quinn appear to know her subject well? What is her major source of material?

Questions on Diction and Writing Techniques

1. Quinn uses "it" in sentences 3 and 4 of paragraph 1 to help achieve coherence in the paragraph. Find another example of her use of a pronoun for the same reason in that paragraph and elsewhere in the essay (see page 37).
2. Define the following words and write sentences using each of them appropriately: "ubiquitous" (par. 2), "sundries" (par. 3), "mother lode" (par. 4), "gimmick" (par. 5), "idiosyncratic" (par. 6).
3. What is Quinn's purpose in writing the short sentence, "Opportunity beckoned" (par. 4)?
4. By what means does the writer try to convince you that blue jeans "adapt themselves to any sort of idiosyncratic use" (par. 6)?
5. What is the writer's purpose in using "for example" in paragraph 7?
6. Explain the organization of this essay by stating the function of single paragraphs or groups of paragraphs.

For Discussion, Reading, and Writing

1. "The Jeaning of America—and the World" is mainly about:
   - A. how a simple pair of pants called blue jeans became a sturdy American symbol which has spread throughout most of the world.
   - B. the ingenuity of Levi Strauss.
   - C. the adaptability of blue jeans to any sort of idiosyncratic use.
   - D. the phenomenal success of the company that Levi Strauss founded.
   - E. the future of blue jeans in America—and the world.

2. Why, according to Quinn, is "a simple pair of pants called blue jeans" (par. 1) a symbol of America? Why a symbol of equality? Do you agree with her judgment? Why or why not?
3. Write a paragraph explaining how to wash, repair, patch, or cut off the legs of blue jeans.

FREEWRITING

Peter Elbow

Peter Elbow has taught at a number of colleges and has directed writing programs in universities and community groups. In this excerpt from *Writing Without Teachers* (1973), he explains a technique he recommends to improve one's ability to write.

---

1 The most effective way I know to improve your writing is to do freewriting exercises regularly. At least three times a week. They are sometimes called "automatic writing," "babbling," or "jabbering" exercises. The idea is simply to write for ten minutes (later on, perhaps fifteen or twenty). Don't stop for anything. Go quickly without rushing. Never stop to look back, to cross something out, to wonder how to spell something, to wonder what word or thought to use, or to think about what you are doing. If you can't think of a word or a spelling, just use a squiggle or else write, "I can't think of it." Just put down something. The easiest thing is just to put down whatever is in your mind. If you get stuck it's fine to write "I can't think what to say, I can't think what to say" as many times as you want; or repeat the last word you wrote over and over again; or anything else. The only requirement is that you *never* stop.

2 What happens to a freewriting exercise is important. It must be a piece of writing which, even if someone reads it, doesn't send

any ripples back to you. It is like writing something and putting it in a bottle in the sea. The teacherless class helps your writing by providing maximum feedback. Freewritings help you by providing no feedback at all. When I assign one, I invite the writer to let me read it. But also tell him to keep it if he prefers. I read it quickly and make no comments at all and I do not speak with him about it. The main thing is that a freewriting must never be evaluated in any way; in fact there must be no discussion or comment at all.

3 Here is an example of a fairly coherent exercise (sometimes they are incoherent, which is fine):

> I think I'll write what's on my mind, but the only thing on my mind right now is what to write for ten minutes. I've never done this before and I'm not prepared in any way—the sky is cloudy today, how's that? now I'm afraid I won't be able to think of what to write when I get to the end of the sentence—well, here I am at the end of the sentence—here I am again, again, again, again, at least I'm still writing—Now I ask is there some reason to be happy that I'm still writing—ah yes! Here comes the question again—What am I getting out of this? What point is there in it? It's almost obscene to always ask it but I seem to question everything that way and I was gonna say something else pertaining to that but I got so busy writing down the first part that I forgot what I was leading into. This is kind of fun oh don't stop writing—cars and trucks speeding by somewhere out the window, pens clittering across peoples' papers. The sky is still cloudy—is it symbolic that I should be mentioning it? Huh? I dunno. Maybe I should try colors, blue, red, dirty words—wait a minute—no can't do that, orange, yellow, arm tired, green pink, violet magenta lavendar red brown black green—now that I can't think of any more colors—just about done—relief? maybe.

Questions About "Process"

1. What is Elbow's purpose in writing this piece?
2. Does Elbow use any technical terms that you might not be expected to understand?

3. What does "They are sometimes called 'automatic writing,' 'babbling,' or 'jabbering' exercises" (par. 1) contribute to your understanding of the meaning of "freewriting exercise"?
4. Would you have difficulty following Elbow's instructions? Why or why not?
5. Does the inclusion of an example of freewriting help Elbow achieve his purpose? Explain.

Questions on Diction and Writing Techniques

1. Is Elbow's use of commands—"don't stop," "go quickly"—appropriate? Explain.
2. What is Elbow's purpose in writing the last sentence of paragraph 1?
3. Is this diction meaningful to you: "doesn't send any ripples back to you. It is like writing something and putting it in a bottle in the sea" (par. 2)? Why or why not?
4. How much of the success of Elbow's explanation can you attribute to its being based on personal experience?
5. What is Elbow's thesis (see pages 6–9)? Does his essay convince you to accept it as valid? Explain.

For Discussion, Reading, and Writing

1. Which of these statements, according to Elbow, are true (T), which false (F)?

   A. ______ The most effective way to improve your writing is to do freewriting exercises once in a while.

   B. ______ The point of freewriting is to rush through it as quickly as possible.

   C. ______ If you can't think of a word, just use a squiggle.

   D. ______ The only requirement of freewriting is that you never stop.

   E. ______ Lack of coherence in freewriting is fine.

2. Follow Elbow's instructions. Freewrite for ten minutes. Be prepared to comment in class about your experience.
3. Write a short essay, based on your personal experience, about how to

   buy a used car

   plan a party

   apply for a summer job

   prepare a meal

   make a laboratory experiment

MISSILES

Robert Jastrow

The founder of NASA's Institute for Space Studies and Professor of Earth Studies at Dartmouth College, Robert Jastrow has been prominent in the space program since its beginning.

---

1 A missile is a tank of fuel with an engine at one end and a bomb at the other. When fuel burns in the engine, hot gases jet out of the exhaust. As the gases leave, they push back on the missile and propel it upward. The strength of the backward push is enormous. In a matter of minutes, it accelerates the rocket to speeds as high as 15,000 miles an hour and altitudes as great as 700 miles.

2 The working principle of a rocket engine is simpler than that of any other engine. Suppose a chamber or rocket casing is filled with a hot gas and tightly sealed. The gas consists of molecules which continually bombard the walls of the chamber. They move in every direction, and through the impact of these molecules a

pressure is exerted on the walls of the chamber. The gas is distributed uniformly through the chamber and therefore the gas molecules hit each wall at the same rate and with the same speed. Accordingly they exert the same forces up and down; and also to the left and to the right. The forces balance, and the casing remains at rest.

3 Now consider the consequence of removing the bottom wall. The upper force is no longer balanced by the lower one. There is a net force upward, and the rocket takes off.

4 A continuing supply of hot gas, and a continuing force upward are maintained by burning fuel drawn from the rocket's tank. Large rockets have a rapacious appetite for fuel; the Saturn rocket used for the landings on the moon burned ten tons of fuel each *second.*

5 The jet engines on a commercial airliner like the 707 work in the same way. Fuel burns in the jet engine, and the hot gases rush out of the engine exhaust and push back on the aircraft, propelling it forward. In fact, commercial airliners and missiles can use the same fuel—kerosene. The main difference between a jet airplane and a rocket is that in the case of the jet, the oxygen needed for burning the fuel comes from the atmosphere where it is present in a rather dilute, gaseous form; whereas a rocket carries its oxygen along with it in a liquid and highly condensed form. Liquid oxygen is about a thousand times denser than the oxygen in the atmosphere. As a consequence of the concentrated supply of oxygen available to the rocket, its fuel burns with ferocious intensity, and generates more energy per pound than the explosion of nitroglycerine. The extraordinarily intense burning creates the enormous forces that boost the rocket to a very high speed in a short time.

6 The idea of using liquid oxygen in a rocket came from Robert Goddard, an American physics professor. Dr. Goddard tested the first liquid-fueled rocket in 1926 on his "Aunt" Effie's farm in Massachusetts. It rose to a height of 41 feet, traveled 184 feet before it hit the ground, and reached a top speed of 60 miles per hour. Dr. Goddard predicted that man could reach the moon with this invention but very few people believed him. A New York Times editorial rebuked the physics professor for failing to grasp basic principles of science that were "ladled out daily in high schools." After all, said the editorial writer, everyone knew that you couldn't push against a vacuum. But of course Dr. Goddard's science was quite sound, and the *Times* editorial writer was confused.

7 At any rate, Professor Goddard persisted in his experiments. One day the phone rang, and Charles Lindbergh came on the line. Lindbergh wanted to drive up to Massachusetts to talk to Goddard about his rocket. That evening Professor Goddard told his wife that Lindbergh, the famous aviator had called for an appointment, and she said, "Yes, and I had tea with Marie, Queen of Rumania."

8 Lindbergh was impressed by what he saw. He obtained money for Goddard from the Guggenheim Foundation, and the experiments continued. One rocket rose to a height of 1-½ miles, and another reached a top speed of 500 miles an hour, probably the fastest any man-made device had ever gone up to that time.

9 The U.S. War Department, informed by Dr. Goddard of his progress, had no quarrel with his basic physics, but found his rockets to be militarily uninteresting. In 1940, with the shadow of war looming over America, Goddard came to Washington to describe his experiments. The officer presiding at the briefing had also heard of work just getting started on the newfangled atom bomb. Getting up at the end of the briefing, he managed to dismiss two of the most significant military inventions in the history of warfare when he said that what we needed in this war was not fancy bombs and rockets, but a better trench mortar.

10 But in Germany a band of rocket enthusiasts, following along the same path as Dr. Goddard, was received with greater interest by the military leaders of the re-arming German nation. In 1936, the German Army and Air Force jointly kicked in enough money to set up Wernher von Braun and a group of rocket scientists and engineers near the village of Pennemunde. From Pennemunde, a straight line of development led to the V-2 and the bombardment of London in 1945. In all, more than a thousand V-2s were launched against England each carrying a 1500-pound bomb. The V-2s were a terrifying weapon that crossed the Channel in five minutes and descended on their target without noise or other warning. No defense existed against them. However, the Allies overran their launch sites, and the war ended before the V-2 could exact a heavier toll.

11 The Soviets captured the plans and production facilities for the V-2 and an even larger rocket with twice the range, and scaled them upward to a mammoth rocket designed to carry an A-bomb across intercontinental distances. Then the H-bomb was invented. The H-bomb was considerably smaller and lighter than the A-bomb

and did not require a rocket as massive as the scaled-up V-2 the Soviets had built. But a Soviet scientist pointed out that this oversized rocket was powerful enough to put a satellite into orbit. That is how the Russians came to launch the first Sputnik.

12 Meanwhile, Von Braun and his team had surrendered to the American forces, which brought them to the United States and installed them in the Army arsenal at Huntsville, Alabama. There, Von Braun resumed the line of development that led eventually to the Saturn rocket, project Apollo, and the landing of men on the moon.

Questions About "Process"

1. Making specific reference to the text, show how missiles originated and were developed.

2. Jastrow is noted for his ability to make clear to the average person complex scientific processes. Is that ability evidenced in this essay? Be specific in your answer.

Questions on Diction and Writing Techniques

1. How does your dictionary define "rapacious" (par. 4), "dilute" and "gaseous" (par. 5), "liquid oxygen" (par. 6), "newfangled" (par. 9)? Use each of these words or phrases in a sentence.

2. Show why scientific jargon is inevitable in an essay such as this but how, nonetheless, Jastrow manages to make his subject comprehensible to you.

3. Show how and in which paragraphs Jastrow uses definition, comparison and contrast, and causal analysis (see pages 347–370) as patterns of organization.

4. Mark in your text all transitional words. Show the function of each and how Jastrow uses them to relate ideas between sentences and between paragraphs.

For Discussion, Reading, and Writing

1. In a short essay, explain the working of combustion engines, electric motors, or of any other device you are familiar with.
2. Using the resources of your college library, gather information about any inventor who interests you—Alexander Graham Bell or Thomas Edison, for example—and write a short essay about him and one of his inventions, using process as your main pattern of organization.

Causal Analysis

There are those . . . who think that the man who works with imagination should allow himself to wait till—inspiration moves him. . . . To me it would not be more absurd if the shoemaker were to wait for inspiration, or the tallow-chandler for the divine moment of melting.

—Anthony Trollope

WHEN your car doesn't start on a cold morning, you wonder why, reasoning from the fact of its failure to start to a possible cause or causes: empty gas tank, frozen fuel line, run-down battery, or defective coil. You might also consider possible effects of your car's failure: being late for an appointment, missing a class, losing your job. In both instances, you would be making a causal analysis—establishing and explaining the relationship between cause and effect and between effect and cause.

We use this method of reasoning daily to get answers to everyday questions:

Why didn't Mary phone yesterday?

Why is John late?

Why does my head ache this morning?

Why is the price of food so high?

Why must I study today?

We use it to answer weightier questions:

What makes tides?

What caused World War II?

Why is logic a useful discipline?

Why did Columbus sail the Atlantic?

Why is there an energy crisis?

There are three kinds of cause: necessary, contributory, and sufficient.

A *necessary* cause *must be present* for the effect to occur but by itself cannot produce the effect. Oxygen, for example, is necessary to produce fire but by itself cannot produce fire. Other factors are needed: combustible material and ignition.

A *contributory* cause *may lead* to an effect but cannot produce it by itself. For instance: Jogging contributes to Maria's good health, but a balanced diet, daily calisthenics, and eight hours' sleep a night are also important. As long as she continues to exercise regularly and eat and sleep well, Maria might give up jogging yet maintain her good health. Another example:

> In its effect on family relationships, in its facilitation of parental withdrawal from an active role in the socialization of their children, and its replacement of family rituals and special events, television has played an important role in the disintegration of the American family. But of course it has not been the only contributing factor, perhaps not even the most important one. The steadily rising divorce rate, the increase in the number of working mothers, the decline of the extended family, the breakdown of neighborhoods and communities, the growing isolation of the nuclear family—all have seriously affected the family [Marie Winn, *The Plug-In Drug: TV and the American Family*].

A *sufficient* cause *by itself* can produce an effect. A speeding bullet is sufficient to kill a deer. A bullet is not a necessary cause of a deer's death; the animal might die from other causes such as old age or starvation. Here is another example of a sufficient cause:

> Malaria was for centuries a baffling plague. It was observed that persons who went out at night often developed the malady. So, on the best *post hoc* reasoning, night air was assumed to be the cause of malaria, and elaborate precautions were taken to shut it out of sleeping quarters. Some scientists, however, were skeptical of this theory. A long series of experiments eventually proved that malaria was caused by the bite of the *anopheles* mosquito. Night air entered the picture only because mosquitoes prefer to attack in the dark [Stuart Chase, *Guides to Straight Thinking*].

Since the bite of the anopheles mosquito, unlike night air, can by itself produce malaria, it is a sufficient cause.

An example of a common error that beginning writers make in causal analysis is a statement such as this:

> Crime in America is caused by poverty.

Although poverty may be a contributory cause, it is not a sufficient cause. Contrast that oversimplified assertion with the more cautious

> One of the causes of crime in America is poverty.

and with this judicious statement:

> Most crime in America is born in environments saturated in poverty and its consequences: illness, ignorance, idleness, ugly surroundings, hopelessness. Crime incubates in places where thousands have no jobs, and those who do have the poorest jobs; where houses are old, dirty and dangerous; where people have no rights [Ramsey Clark, *Crime in America*].

Clark, in his causal analysis, is careful to qualify "crime" by saying "*most* crime" and to claim that crime is the effect not of poverty alone but of "poverty *and its consequences*." He then specifies what these consequences are. He also makes clear that poverty is a *remote* cause, one that is distant from an effect; and that "illness, ignorance, idleness, ugly surroundings, hopelessness" are a *proximate* cause, one that is close to the effect. The following diagram shows this relationship.

REMOTE CAUSE
Poverty
↓
PROXIMATE CAUSE
Illness, ignorance,
idleness, ugly surroundings,
hopelessness
↓
EFFECT
Crime

When you use causal analysis, you must avoid oversimplification and keep in mind that an effect may be the consequence of two or more causes or a chain of causes, as in this example:

> The chain of events which brought the children into the hospital began in the 1950s when the AEC started a long series of nuclear explosions at its Nevada test site in the conviction that ". . . these explosives created no immediate or long-range hazard to human health outside the proving ground." But among the radioactive particles of the fallout clouds that occasionally escaped into the surrounding territory was the isotope iodine-131. As these clouds passed over the Utah pastures, iodine-131 was deposited on the grass; being widely spread, it caused no alarming readings on outdoor radiation meters. But dairy cows grazed these fields. As a result, iodine-131, generated in the mushroom cloud, drifted to Utah farms, was foraged by cows, passed to children in milk, and was gathered in high concentration in the children's thyroid glands. Here in a period of a few weeks the iodine-131 released its radiation. If sufficiently intense, such radiation passing through the thyroid cells may set off subtle changes which, though quiescent and hidden for years, eventually give rise to disease [Barry Commoner, *Science and Survival*].

Observe that a writer may use causal analysis both as a means of explaining and as a way of imposing order on material—that is, as a pattern of organization. You can see this function of causal analysis in part of a paragraph from Will Durant's *Caesar and Christ.* First comes the topic sentence:

> The political causes of decay were rooted in one fact—that increasing despotism destroyed the citizen's civic sense and dried up statesmanship at the source.

Then comes the development:

> Powerless to express his political will except by violence, the Roman lost interest in government and became absorbed in his business, his amusements, his legion, or his individual salvation. Patriotism and the pagan religion had been bound together, and now decayed. The Senate, losing ever more of its power and prestige after Pertinax, relapsed into indolence, subservience, or venality; and the last barrier fell that might have saved the state from militarism and anarchy. Local governments . . . no longer attracted first-rate men.

We might diagram the organization of this paragraph thus:

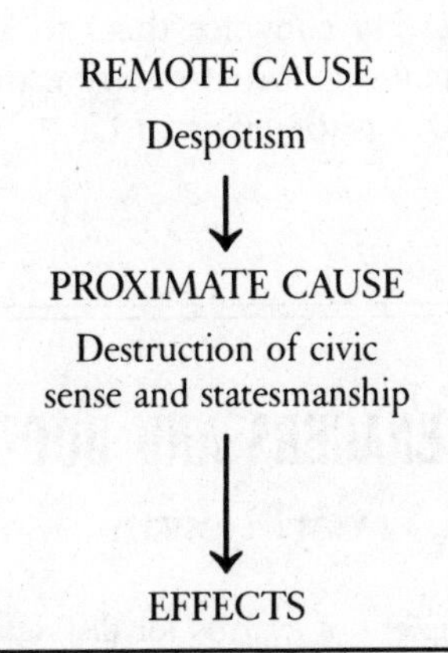

1. The Romans lost interest in government.
2. Patriotism decayed.
3. The Senate weakened.
4. Local governments no longer attracted first-rate men.

Here are some points to keep in mind when you use causal analysis:

1. *Consider the available data and supporting evidence.* Like a detective seeking to solve a crime, the writer looking for causal relationships must decide on lines of inquiry and kinds of useful information. All material gathered should be analyzed with care before you assign causes.
2. *Re-examine your material for possible alternative causes and effects.* Don't let your preconceptions divert you from this task, which is necessary for success in causal analysis. Even in the case of the relationship between cigarette smoking and lung cancer, where preponderant evidence points to a correlation between the two, other causes may be contributory or sufficient causes—gypsum particles, coal dust, radiation, polluted air, carcinogens still unknown.
3. *Offer evidence to support what might otherwise be merely an assertion of a causal relationship.* Where appropriate, use facts and figures to convince your readers of the validity of your causal analysis. Statistics and the testimony of experts will often more readily convince them to accept your analysis than will your unsupported assertion that A was the cause of B or that D was the effect of C.

TEENAGERS AND BOOZE

Carl Rowan

Carl T. Rowan, recipient of awards for distinguished journalism, is a well-known newspaperman and commentator on the American scene.

---

1 America's young people have found a potent, sometimes addictive, and legal drug. It's called alcohol.

2 Drinking is nothing new for teen-agers. In fact, it's a kind of ritual of youth. In recent years, however, a great many youngsters from all walks of life have turned to drugs like marijuana, heroin and barbiturates. Reports coming in now from schools and national studies tell us that there's a change occurring. The newest way for kids to turn on is an old way—with alcohol.

3 Listen to these words of a high school senior in Brooklyn, as told to a reporter from *Newsweek* magazine: "A lot of us used to smoke pot, but we gave that up a year or two ago. Now my friends and I drink a lot . . . and in my book, a high is a high."

4 Why are youngsters rediscovering booze? One reason is pressure from other kids to be one of the gang. Another is the ever-present urge to act grown-up. For some, it eases the burden of problems at home or at school. And it's cheaper. You can buy a couple of six-packs of beer for the price of three joints of pot.

5 Perhaps the main reason is that parents don't seem to mind. They tolerate drinking—sometimes almost seem to encourage it. In part this may be due to the fact that parents themselves drink; in part it's because they're relieved to find that their children are "*only*" drinking, and are not involved with pot, LSD or other drugs.

6 What these parents may not realize is that alcohol is also a drug, and a potentially dangerous one. Furthermore, few are aware just how young the drinkers are these days. The National Council on Alcoholism reports that in 1972 the age of the youngest alcoholics brought to its attention dropped from fourteen to twelve. Other studies have found that three fourths of senior-high students have used alcohol—an increase of 90 per cent in three years. And 56 per cent of junior-high students have tried alcohol.

7 The Medical Council on Alcoholism warns: The potential teen-age drinking problem should give far more cause for alarm than drug addiction. Many schools have reacted to teen-age drinking. They've started alcohol-education programs. But a lot of experts feel that teen-agers are not going to stop drinking until adults do.

Questions About "Causal Analysis"

1. Where does Rowan announce the subject of his causal analysis?
2. Does Rowan amply analyze the teenage drinking problem? Explain. Can you think of a cause that he fails to mention?
3. Which of the causes that Rowan enumerates is itself an effect?
4. How does Rowan support his statement about "how young the drinkers are these days" (par. 6)?

Questions on Diction and Writing Techniques

1. What is Rowan's purpose in writing the short sentence, "It's called alcohol" (par. 1)? Find another instance in this essay of his using a short sentence for the same reason.
2. Why does Rowan choose to write "in fact" in paragraph 2?
3. What purpose is served by "however" in paragraph 2? What do "furthermore" (par. 6) and "but" (par. 7) contribute to the paragraphs in which they appear?
4. Rowan might have written the last sentence of paragraph 2 like this: "The newest way for kids to turn on, with alcohol, is an old way." Why did he write the sentence as he did?
5. Why does Rowan quote from the interview of the high school senior from Brooklyn?
6. There is a circumlocution – a roundabout expression – in the first part of the last sentence of paragraph 5. Revise that portion of the sentence to eliminate unnecessary words.

For Discussion, Reading, and Writing

1. Drinking, according to Rowan, is "a kind of ritual of youth" (par. 2). Do you agree? Why or why not?
2. Using causal analysis as your main pattern of organization, explain in a short essay why you do or do not drink alcoholic beverages.

3. Using interviews as one of your sources of material, write a short essay in which you explain why some of the people you know drink.
4. In a short essay, show by causal analysis how any person you know well has affected some aspect of your life for better or worse.

STRAIGHT-A ILLITERACY

James Degnan

James P. Degnan, professor of English at the University of Santa Clara in California, uses personal experience and observation as his sources of material for this essay about a widespread kind of illiteracy.

---

1 Despite all the current fuss and bother about the extraordinary number of ordinary illiterates who overpopulate our schools, small attention has been given to another kind of illiterate, an illiterate whose plight is, in many ways, more important, because he is more influential. This illiterate may, as often as not, be a university president, but he is typically a Ph.D., a successful professor and textbook author. The person to whom I refer is the straight-A illiterate, and the following is written in an attempt to give him equal time with his widely publicized counterpart.

2 The scene is my office, and I am at work, doing what must be done if one is to assist in the cure of a disease that, over the years, I have come to call straight-A illiteracy. I am interrogating, I am cross-examining, I am prying and probing for the meaning of a student's paper. The student is a college senior with a straight-A average, an extremely bright, highly articulate student who has just been awarded a coveted fellowship to one of the nation's outstanding

From *Harper's* magazine, September 1976, pp. 37–38. Reprinted by permission of the author.

graduate schools. He and I have been at this, have been going over his paper sentence by sentence, word by word, for an hour. "The choice of exogenous variables in relation to multi-colinearity," I hear myself reading from his paper, "is contingent upon the derivations of certain multiple correlation coefficients." I pause to catch my breath. "Now that statement," I address the student–whom I shall call, allegorically, Mr. Bright–"that statement, Mr. Bright, what on earth does it mean?" Mr. Bright, his brow furrowed, tries mightily. Finally, with both of us combining our linguistic and imaginative resources, finally, after what seems another hour, we decode it. We decide exactly what it is that Mr. Bright is trying to say, what he really *wants* to say, which is: "Supply determines demand."

3 Over the past decade or so, I have known many students like him, many college seniors suffering from Bright's disease. It attacks the best minds, and gradually destroys the critical faculties, making it impossible for the sufferer to detect gibberish in his own writing or in that of others. During the years of higher education it grows worse, reaching its terminal stage, typically, when its victim receives his Ph.D. Obviously, the victim of Bright's disease is no ordinary illiterate. He would never turn in a paper with misspellings or errors in punctuation; he would never use a double negative or the word "irregardless." Nevertheless, he is illiterate, in the worst way: he is incapable of saying, in writing, simply and clearly, what he means. The ordinary illiterate–perhaps providentially protected from college and graduate school–might say: "Them people down at the shop better stock up on what our customers need, or we ain't gonna be in business long." Not our man. Taking his cue from years of higher education, years of reading the textbooks and professional journals that are the major sources of his affliction, he writes: "The focus of concentration must rest upon objectives centered around the knowledge of customer areas so that a sophisticated awareness of those areas can serve as an entrepreneurial filter to screen what is relevant from what is irrelevant to future commitments." For writing such gibberish he is awarded straight As on his papers (both samples quoted above were taken from papers that received As), and the opportunity to move, inexorably, toward his fellowship and eventual Ph.D.

4 As I have suggested, the major cause of such illiteracy is the stuff–the textbooks and professional journals–the straight-A illiterate

is forced to read during his years of higher education. He learns to write gibberish by reading it, and by being taught to admire it as profundity. If he is majoring in sociology, he must grapple with such journals as the *American Sociological Review,* journals bulging with barbarous jargon, such as "ego-integrative action orientation" and "orientation toward improvement of the gratificational-deprivation balance of the actor" (the latter of which monstrous phrases represents, to quote Malcolm Cowley, the sociologist's way of saying "the pleasure principle"). In such journals, Mr. Cowley reminds us, two things are never described as being "alike." They are "homologous" or "isomorphic." Nor are things simply "different." They are "allotropic." In such journals writers never "divide anything." They "dichotomize" or "bifurcate" things.

Questions About "Causal Analysis"

1. What is Degnan's purpose in this essay?
2. What, according to Degnan, is the major cause of straight-A illiteracy?
3. Does Degnan convince you of a clear-cut relationship between cause and effect?
4. Does he fulfill his announced purpose? Explain.
5. Explain how the organization of the material helps accomplish Degnan's causal analysis.

Questions on Diction and Writing Techniques

1. Why is it necessary for the writer to define the "straight-A illiterate" (par. 1)?
2. What methods does he use in his definition? (See pages 291–297.)
3. Write in a sentence how Degnan defines the "straight-A illiterate."
4. Define the following words and write sentences using each of them appropriately: "allegorically" (par. 2), "gibberish" (par. 3), "providentially" (par. 3), "inexorably" (par. 3).

5. Why, according to Degnan, is "the victim of Bright's disease . . . no ordinary illiterate" (par. 3)? How does he explain this idea?
6. What is the function of "Not our man" (par. 3)?
7. How does Degnan explain what he means by "barbarous jargon" (par. 4)?
8. Does Degnan's choice of "stuff" (par. 4) reveal his attitude toward his subjects? Explain.

For Discussion, Reading, and Writing

1. Contrast the first paragraph with the second paragraph. Which do you prefer? Why?

   I returned, and saw under the sun, that the race is not to the swift, nor the battle to the strong, neither yet bread to the wise, nor yet riches to men of understanding, nor yet favor to men of skill; but time and chance happeneth to them all [Ecclesiastes 9:11].

   Objective consideration of contemporary phenomena compels the conclusion that success or failure in competitive activities exhibits no tendency to be commensurate with innate capacity, but that a considerable element of the unpredictable must invariably be taken into account [George Orwell, "Politics and the English Language"].

2. According to Degnan, the straight-A illiterate "may, as often as not, be a . . . textbook author" (par. 1). Bring to class an example or two of straight-A illiteracy that you have encountered in your textbooks.
3. Find a paragraph exemplifying "straight-A illiteracy" in a journal such as *American Sociological Review* or elsewhere. What is the effect on you of such writing? Rewrite the paragraph in acceptable language.
4. Making sure to clearly establish connections between causes and effects and to distinguish between necessary, contributory, and sufficient causes, write a short essay on a subject, properly restricted, such as

Inflation
Violence on TV
Poverty and Crime
What Makes Airplanes Fly
What College Has Done for Me

FROM UNHAPPY PATIENT TO ANGRY LITIGANT

Louise Lander

Louise Lander, an attorney with extensive experience with health and the law, is the author of *Defective Medicine: Risk, Anger, and the Malpractice Crisis*.

---

1 The medical press was triumphant; on June 1, 1976, after over a year of nothing but disaster to report on the malpractice front, a victory had finally been scored on the side of the medical profession. A doctor sued for malpractice had had the guts to sue his patient back, and a jury in Chicago had found the patient, her husband, and her lawyers liable for "willful and wanton involvement in litigation without reasonable cause" and the lawyers also liable for legal malpractice.

2 One of the exuberant articles recording that landmark event was written by the doctor-plaintiff himself, a radiologist named Dr. Leonard Berlin, who took to the pages of the magazine *Medical Economics* to tell his story to his fellow physicians. That story does vindicate Dr. Berlin in the sense of making his medical and legal innocence convincing. But, more to the point, his story inadvertently

reveals what motivates patients to take the extraordinary step of hauling their doctors into court.

3 Mrs. Harriet Nathan injured the little finger of her right hand while playing tennis and went to the emergency room of a suburban Chicago hospital, where Dr. Berlin had an office in the radiology department. He supervised the taking of a series of X rays, diagnosed the injury as a dislocated joint, and sent her on to see an orthopedic surgeon named Dr. William Meltzer. Dr. Meltzer's treatment, which apparently followed generally accepted orthopedic procedures, nonetheless failed to completely relieve the pain and deformity of the injured finger.

4 Five months after the injury, Dr. Berlin relates in his article, he was telephoned by Mrs. Nathan's husband, Gilbert, who told him that "his wife's finger was deformed and still painful, and that they were both angry at Dr. Meltzer. The orthopedist, Gilbert said, had not taken Harriet's injury seriously, and had been rude and abrupt. Gilbert intimated that they might bring a malpractice suit against Meltzer, and that if they did, they'd 'have to involve' me, too."

5 What Mr. Nathan said over the telephone reflects precisely those elements of a doctor-patient encounter that are indispensable to a patient's decision to bring a malpractice suit. Actual medical malpractice—professional performance that demonstrably falls below professional standards—is not indispensable. Some sort of injury or unhappy outcome *is* indispensable; here no one disputed that Mrs. Nathan's hand was permanently deformed, and we may assume that it gave her pain and made certain activities difficult or impossible. But the injury, the objective sign that something went wrong, is not sufficient; injury by itself does not translate into the intense hostility that a lawsuit expresses. That objective sign must be joined with the subjective state of being angry—here, the Nathans' natural reaction to their perception that Dr. Meltzer "had not taken Harriet's injury seriously, and had been rude and abrupt."

6 The anger is usually provoked by a doctor, although increasingly hospitals are finding themselves defending lawsuits that reflect anger at their employees. And the rules of the legal game may dictate a lawyer's tactical decision to sue others beyond the original object of the patient's anger, as Dr. Berlin discovered when he was drawn into the net cast by the Nathans' anger at his colleague.

7 We should therefore grant what many doctors, for their own purposes, loudly insist on: that there is a difference between actual

malpractice and a malpractice suit or claim. The injured patient, as he attempts to cope with pain, disappointment, and economic loss, rarely has the means of knowing at the outset whether negligence, fluke, or some unalterable body process is responsible for his misery. Conversely, there can be malpractice in the sense of medical negligence without its causing injury. A doctor, for example, may stupidly make an erroneous diagnosis, but the treatment he prescribes for what he thinks is wrong may turn out to be substantially the same as the treatment for what is really wrong.

8 While malpractice as a legal concept declares both injury and negligence to be equally indispensable, malpractice claims as a social disruption declare the supremacy of injury. There are, moreover, a few statistical indications that the number of injuries is enormously larger than the number of malpractice claims, a disproportion that confirms the notion that although a medical injury is necessary to a malpractice claim, it is not by itself sufficient to trigger one.

9 A federally sponsored interview study conducted in 1972, for example, found that over 40 percent of the sample had had some "negative medical care experience"; of those, over 85 percent believed that some kind of medical failure had been involved, but only 8 percent had even considered seeking legal advice.

10 Another statistical tidbit implies that what a medical or hospital observer perceives as an injury differs from what a patient perceives as an injury worth filing a claim about. A risk-management program of an unnamed hospital association generated about 700,000 reports of unusual incidents (such as equipment failures, anesthesia deaths, slips and falls) over a 20-year period. During the same period, only 15,000 malpractice claims were filed, and 85 percent of these involved incidents that were *not* reported.

11 What distinguishes injuries that do not become malpractice claims from injuries that do, and what even colors the patient's perception of what constitutes an injury, is the subjective element of patient anger; without anger, an act as hostile as a lawsuit, particularly against as well-established an authority figure as a physician, is impossible to contemplate. Thus, while for legal purposes medical malpractice represents the intersection of patient injury and physician negligence, for social purposes a malpractice claim represents the intersection of patient injury and patient anger.

Questions About "Causal Analysis"

1. According to Lander, is "actual malpractice" a necessary cause for a patient to sue a doctor for malpractice? Explain.
2. Is injury of some sort a sufficient cause for a suit for medical malpractice? Explain.
3. Is the anger of a patient provoked by a doctor a necessary, contributory, or sufficient cause for malpractice? Explain.
4. In the chain of causality that ends with a malpractice suit, what is the proximate cause, what the remote cause?

Questions on Diction and Writing Techniques

1. Mark in your text those words that are new to you, but whose meaning you inferred from their context. Define them in your own words. Compare your definitions with those in your dictionary. Look up in your dictionary any other words that are new to you. Use the words in both groups in sentences.
2. Match each italicized word in Column A with its synonym in Column B.

Column A	***Column B***
had the *guts*	unreserved
wanton involvement	suggested
exuberant articles	understanding
Gilbert *intimated*	unjustifiable
the patient's *perception*	courage

3. What is the function of "But" in paragraph 2? Find another paragraph in this essay where that word serves the same purpose. Find two or more other examples of Lander's use of transition words.
4. Instead of the second sentence of paragraph 3, Lander might have written: "He supervised the taking of a series of X rays. He diagnosed the injury as a dislocated joint. He sent her to see an orthopedic surgeon named William Meltzer." Which version do you prefer? Why?

For Discussion, Reading, and Writing

1. Which of these statements, according to Lander, are true (T), which false (F):

   A. ______ The medical press was triumphant because a radiologist, Dr. Leonard Berlin, had the guts to sue his own patient.

   B. ______ Dr. Berlin claimed in his lawsuit that the patient, Mrs. Nathan, had a deformed and painful finger because she had not followed his advice.

   C. ______ Mr. and Mrs. Nathan were angry because Dr. Meltzer, to whom Dr. Berlin referred her, had not taken her injury seriously.

   D. ______ Actual medical malpractice is not indispensable to a patient's decision to bring a malpractice suit.

   E. ______ Injury by itself can translate into the intense hostility that a lawsuit expresses.

   F. ______ The anger of patients that is translated into malpractice suits is usually provoked by overcrowded hospitals.

   G. ______ A malpractice claim represents the intersection of patient injury and patient anger.

2. In the book from which this piece is taken, Lander writes, "The surgeon is concerned with thingness–to the state of the wound, not the state of the person." Do you agree? If the statement is in accord with your judgment of medical doctors, write a paragraph or two of causal analysis explaining why, in your view, the statement is valid.

3. Explain in a short essay the effect on you of any person you now know or once knew well.

DISCOVERY OF A FATHER

Sherwood Anderson

Sherwood Anderson (1876–1941) was an American novelist and short-story writer.

---

1 You hear it said that fathers want their sons to be what they feel they cannot themselves be, but I tell you it also works the other way. A boy wants something very special from his father. I know that as a small boy I wanted my father to be a certain thing he was not. I wanted him to be a proud, silent, dignified father. When I was with other boys and he passed along the street, I wanted to feel a flow of pride: "There he is. That is my father."

2 But he wasn't such a one. He couldn't be. It seemed to me then that he was always showing off. Let's say someone in our town had got up a show. They were always doing it. The druggist would be in it, the shoe-store clerk, the horse doctor, and a lot of women and girls. My father would manage to get the chief comedy part. It was, let's say, a Civil War play and he was a comic Irish soldier. He had to do the most absurd things. They thought he was funny, but I didn't.

3 I thought he was terrible. I didn't see how mother could stand it. She even laughed with the others. Maybe I would have laughed if it hadn't been my father.

4 Or there was a parade, the Fourth of July or Decoration Day. He'd be in that, too, right at the front of it, as Grand Marshal or something, on a white horse hired from a livery stable.

5 He couldn't ride for shucks. He fell off the horse and everyone hooted with laughter, but he didn't care. He even seemed to like it. I remember once when he had done something ridiculous, and right out on Main Street, too. I was with some other boys and they

were laughing and shouting at him and he was shouting back and having as good a time as they were. I ran down an alley back of some stores and there in the Presbyterian Church sheds I had a good long cry.

6 Or I would be in bed at night and father would come home a little lit up and bring some men with him. He was a man who was never alone. Before he went broke, running a harness shop, there were always a lot of men loafing in the shop. He went broke, of course, because he gave too much credit. He couldn't refuse it and I thought he was a fool. I had got to hating him.

7 There'd be men I didn't think would want to be fooling around with him. There might even be the superintendent of our schools and a quiet man who ran the hardware store. Once I remember there was a white-haired man who was a cashier of the bank. It was a wonder to me they'd want to be seen with such a windbag. That's what I thought he was. I know now what it was that attracted them. It was because life in our town, as in all small towns, was at times pretty dull and he livened it up. He made them laugh. He could tell stories. He'd even get them to singing.

8 If they didn't come to our house they'd go off, say at night, to where there was a grassy place by a creek. They'd cook food there and drink beer and sit about listening to his stories.

9 He was always telling stories about himself. He'd say this or that wonderful thing had happened to him. It might be something that made him look like a fool. He didn't care.

10 If an Irishman came to our house, right away father would say he was Irish. He'd tell what county in Ireland he was born in. He'd tell things that happened there when he was a boy. He'd make it seem so real that, if I hadn't known he was born in southern Ohio, I'd have believed him myself.

11 If it was a Scotchman the same thing happened. He'd get a burr into his speech. Or he was a German or a Swede. He'd be anything the other man was. I think they all knew he was lying, but they seemed to like him just the same. As a boy that was what I couldn't understand.

12 And there was mother. How could she stand it? I wanted to ask but never did. She was not the kind you asked such questions.

13 I'd be upstairs in my bed, in my room above the porch, and father would be telling some of his tales. A lot of father's stories

were about the Civil War. To hear him tell it he'd been in about every battle. He'd known Grant, Sherman, Sheridan and I don't know how many others. He'd been particularly intimate with General Grant so that when Grant went East, to take charge of all the armies, he took father along.

14 "I was an orderly at headquarters and Sim Grant said to me, 'Irve,' he said, 'I'm going to take you along with me.' "

15 It seems he and Grant used to slip off sometimes and have a quiet drink together. That's what my father said. He'd tell about the day Lee surrendered and how, when the great moment came, they couldn't find Grant.

16 "You know," my father said, "about General Grant's book, his memoirs. You've read of how he said he had a headache and how, when he got word that Lee was ready to call it quits, he was suddenly and miraculously cured.

17 "Huh," said father. "He was in the woods with me.

18 "I was in there with my back against a tree. I was pretty well corned. I had got hold of a bottle of pretty good stuff.

19 "They were looking for Grant. He had got off his horse and come into the woods. He found me. He was covered with mud.

20 "I had the bottle in my hand. What'd I care? The war was over. I knew we had them licked."

21 My father said that he was the one who told Grant about Lee. An orderly riding by had told him, because the orderly knew how thick he was with Grant. Grant was embarrassed.

22 "But, Irve, look at me. I'm all covered with mud," he said to father.

23 And then, my father said, he and Grant decided to have a drink together. They took a couple of shots and then, because he didn't want Grant to show up potted before the immaculate Lee, he smashed the bottle against the tree.

24 "Sim Grant's dead now and I wouldn't want it to get out on him," my father said.

25 That's just one of the kind of things he'd tell. Of course the men knew he was lying, but they seemed to like it just the same.

26 When we got broke, down and out, do you think he ever brought anything home? Not he. If there wasn't anything to eat in the house, he'd go off visiting around at farmhouses. They all wanted him. Sometimes he'd stay away for weeks, mother working to keep

us fed, and then home he'd come bringing, let's say, a ham. He'd got it from some farmer friend. He'd slap it on the table in the kitchen. "You bet I'm going to see that my kids have something to eat," he'd say, and mother would just stand smiling at him. She'd never say a word about all the weeks and months he'd been away, not leaving us a cent for food. Once I heard her speaking to a woman in our street. Maybe the woman had dared to sympathize with her. "Oh," she said, "it's all right. He isn't ever dull like most of the men in this street. Life is never dull when my man is about."

27 But often I was filled with bitterness, and sometimes I wished he wasn't my father. I'd even invent another man as my father. To protect my mother I'd make up stories of a secret marriage that for some strange reason never got known. As though some man, say the president of a railroad company or maybe a Congressman, had married my mother, thinking his wife was dead and then it turned out she wasn't.

28 So they had to hush it up but I got born just the same. I wasn't really the son of my father. Somewhere in the world there was a very dignified, quite wonderful man who was really my father. I even made myself half believe these fancies.

29 And then there came a certain night. He'd been off somewhere for two or three weeks. He found me alone in the house, reading by the kitchen table.

30 It had been raining and he was very wet. He sat and looked at me for a long time, not saying a word. I was startled, for there was on his face the saddest look I had ever seen. He sat for a time, his clothes dripping. Then he got up.

31 "Come on with me," he said.

32 I got up and went with him out of the house. I was filled with wonder but I wasn't afraid. We went along a dirt road that led down into a valley, about a mile out of town, where there was a pond. We walked in silence. The man who was always talking had stopped his talking.

33 I didn't know what was up and had the queer feeling that I was with a stranger. I don't know whether my father intended it so. I don't think he did.

34 The pond was quite large. It was still raining hard and there were flashes of lightning followed by thunder. We were on a grassy bank at the pond's edge when my father spoke, and in the darkness and rain his voice sounded strange.

35 "Take off your clothes," he said. Still filled with wonder, I began to undress. There was a flash of lightning and I saw that he was already naked.

36 Naked, we went into the pond. Taking my hand he pulled me in. It may be that I was too frightened, too full of a feeling of strangeness, to speak. Before that night my father had never seemed to pay any attention to me.

37 "And what is he up to now?" I kept asking myself. I did not swim very well, but he put my hand on his shoulder and struck out into the darkness.

38 He was a man with big shoulders, a powerful swimmer. In the darkness I could feel the movement of his muscles. We swam to the far edge of the pond and then back to where we had left our clothes. The rain continued and the wind blew. Sometimes my father swam on his back and when he did he took my hand in his large powerful one and moved it over so that it rested always on his shoulder. Sometimes there would be a flash of lightning and I could see his face quite clearly.

39 It was as it was earlier, in the kitchen, a face filled with sadness. There would be the momentary glimpse of his face and then again the darkness, the wind and the rain. In me there was a feeling I had never known before.

40 It was a feeling of closeness. It was something strange. It was as though there were only we two in the world. It was as though I had been jerked suddenly out of myself, out of my world of the schoolboy, out of a world in which I was ashamed of my father.

41 He had become blood of my blood; he the strong swimmer and I the boy clinging to him in the darkness. We swam in silence and in silence we dressed in our wet clothes, and went home.

42 There was a lamp lighted in the kitchen and when we came in, the water dripping from us, there was my mother. She smiled at us. I remember that she called us "boys."

43 "What have you boys been up to?" she asked, but my father did not answer. As he had begun the evening's experience with me in silence, so he ended it. He turned and looked at me. Then he went, I thought, with a new and strange dignity out of the room.

44 I climbed the stairs to my own room, undressed in the darkness and got into bed. I couldn't sleep and did not want to sleep. For the first time I knew that I was the son of my father. He was a

story teller as I was to be. It may be that I even laughed a little softly there in the darkness. If I did, I laughed knowing that I would never again be wanting another father.

Questions About "Causal Analysis"

1. Does Anderson's causal analysis make clear to you why his father was not the kind of person he wanted him to be? Explain, making specific reference to the text.
2. Anderson says that he often was filled with bitterness. Is this an effect, or cause, or both? Explain.
3. Explain in detail the cause of Anderson's ultimate feeling of closeness to his father.

Questions on Diction and Writing Techniques

1. Mark in your text those words that are new to you, but whose meaning you inferred from their context. Define them in your own words. Compare your definitions with those in your dictionary. Look up in your dictionary any other words that are new to you. Use the words in both groups in sentences.
2. Anderson uses words like "shucks." Find four or five more examples of colloquial words and slang. Are such words appropriate? Why or why not? Among these words is "windbag." What does Anderson's choice of this and similar words tell you about his attitude toward his father in the first two thirds of the essay?
3. What is the point of view in this essay? Is it that of Anderson as a small boy, as a grownup, or as a combination of both? Support your answer with specific reference to the text.
4. What does "But" (par. 2) signal to you? Find another example of Anderson's use of the word for a similar reason.
5. Anderson organizes his material in two main groups. Which are the paragraphs in each? How does he signal to you that a change in his description of his father is coming?

6. Anderson uses patterns of organization other than cause and effect. Name them and point out examples of each.

7. Making ample reference to the text, comment on Anderson's use of narration and description to achieve his expository purpose.

For Discussion, Reading, and Writing

1. Does Anderson, in this essay, seem close to you or distant? Why?

2. Did you at any point have difficulty in reading or understanding Anderson's writing? If so, why?

3. In a paragraph of not over one hundred words, write a summary of this essay.

4. Does any statement that Anderson makes about his father, or any incident he reports, parallel your experience with a parent or guardian? If so, write a paragraph or two on the subject, using causal analysis to explain any generalization you make about him or her.

5. Write a letter (one that you might want to mail) to a parent, teacher, friend, lover, or anyone else, in which you explain what effect his or her behavior has had on you.

Argumentation

In many ways writing is the act of saying I, *of imposing oneself on other people, of saying* listen to me, see it my way, change your mind.

—Joan Didion

ARGUMENTATION, as the term is generally used, is that type of composition in which writers seek to convince others to agree with their point of view or to agree and to take a recommended action. It uses the expository techniques we have been considering and thus is somewhat like exposition. The purpose of argumentation, however, differs from that of exposition. The purpose of exposition is to explain merely. The purpose of argumentation is to explain in order to assure agreement, or to effect a change in point of view, or to influence an action.

You probably know more about argumentation than you realize. If you have ever written to a parent or guardian asking for an increase in your allowance, to a police department urging it to cancel a parking ticket, to the admissions officer of a school requesting the speedy acceptance of your application for admission, to the personnel office of a business applying for a job, or to a lover hoping to patch up a quarrel–you have written argumentation. In other words, you proposed, giving reasons based on relevant facts and ideas, that someone accept your views on a given subject. Such a proposal, in argumentation, is termed a proposition–a statement for or against something that can be shown to be true or false.

Among the meanings of the term "argument" is disagreement, as in "The short-tempered Jack Jones had a violent argument with his landlord." However, the word is used here in another sense: the expression of opinions for or against some point, as in "Attorney Mary Smith presented a convincing argument in favor of the dismissal of the charges against her client."

An argument cannot be about a fact—a statement about what is known and can be verified. That Abe Lincoln was the sixteenth president of the United States; that the headquarters of the United Nations is in New York City; that the chemical composition of water is H_2O; that sailboats are propelled by wind; that bronze is an alloy consisting essentially of copper and tin—these are certifiable statements about what is known. They leave nothing to argue about.

Nor can an argument be about matters of taste. Your preference for strawberry rather than vanilla ice cream; for chino trousers rather than blue jeans; for hiking rather than mountain climbing—these, insofar as they indicate merely what you happen to like, do not permit the presentation of reasons for or against them.

Here are a few suggestions to help you write a convincing argumentative essay:

1. *Get your facts.* If your readers are to believe what you say, you must know what you're writing about. Study your subject and marshal all the information about it that you can. Except when you rely heavily on personal experience and observation, cite established facts wherever possible and when appropriate introduce the testimony of recognized authorities to support your propositions. Your college library, with its general and specialized books of reference, probably has all the data you need. Among the many other useful sources of information are agencies of the U.S. government and the U.S. Government Printing Office, various departments of state and city governments, chambers of commerce, and innumerable business and professional associations.

2. *Formulate your position.* After you have assembled your material, restrict your subject to what you can argue strongly with the information on hand and within the limits of the length of your essay. Then decide what your position, pro or con, on your proposition will be. (See Part One, pages 2–5, for a discussion of restricting broad subjects.)

3. *State your proposition clearly.* The proposition "General Grant was a greater man than General Lee" is vague because it sets up no criteria for measuring greatness. "Grant was a greater general than Lee" would be an improvement because there are standards by which skills as the commander of a large military force may be measured. Better still would be "Grant was a greater strategist than Lee" because it sets up military strategy as a criterion and also thereby limits the proposition. Unless you define your terms carefully (see "Definition," pages 291–297), you cannot arrange the evidence needed to prove the truth of your proposition.

4. *Be aware of your audience.* Ask yourself: Who am I trying to convince? What are their views, their biases, their likely responses?

5. *Write the introduction.* In a short introductory paragraph, announce your subject and the position you are taking on it, as in this example:

   Today's inflation cannot be controlled by voluntary means. The only way to curb it is with wage and price controls.

   Notice that this introductory paragraph sets up the organization of the rest of the essay. The first part of the body of the essay might show why voluntary controls are ineffective; the second part might tell why wage and price controls would be effective. Announcing the division of a subject in an introductory paragraph is a sound tactic and helps the writer to organize the parts of the argument.

6. *Build an argument.* Argue your position on a proposition by advancing individual points in support of it—that is, by presenting the reasons for your judgment. These should be stated as minor propositions to which the rule of clarity applies. Let's consider possible minor propositions in support of this proposition: Final grades in college should be abolished:

   (a) Final grades encourage students to learn by rote.
   (b) Grades lead to harmful competition among students.
   (c) Low grades discourage some students.

(d) There are adequate substitutes for final grades: (1) pass-fail system of grading; and (2) teachers' written comments on students' performance.

Each minor proposition would have to be supported with proof consisting of sound, relevant evidence.

7. *Test your argument.* The simplest way to test your position on a proposition is to evaluate its opposite. It is thus useful, while planning the first draft of your essay, to list points in opposition to the minor propositions you intend to advance, matching them point by point. In the case of the minor propositions just listed, this is how you might arrange your material.

Pro	***Con***
(a) Final grades encourage students to learn by rote.	Many students need prodding. Final exams serve this purpose.
(b) Grades lead to harmful competition among students.	In our society, competition is inevitable and useful.
(c) Low grades discourage some students.	Those students would probably be discouraged anyway.
(d) There are adequate substitutes for final grades: (1) pass-fail system of grading; and (2) teachers' written comments on students' performance.	These are poor substitutes; they are not precise enough. Both might be a disadvantage to students competing for the sometimes limited openings in graduate schools.

An evaluation of points opposed to your own will also help you appraise your own.

8. *Be honest and fair to opposing views.* If your credibility is questioned by your readers, you will find it more difficult than you otherwise might to get them to believe anything you say. You will find it less difficult if you treat opposing views fairly. Your readers are more likely to find you honest and trustworthy if you consider dispassionately and in sufficient detail positions opposed to your own. This is where making a list of points in opposition to yours will come in handy.

9. *Restate your position.* Especially in argumentation, your essay will profit from a concluding paragraph that summarizes and emphasizes what you have said in the body of the essay in support of your thesis.

Regardless of how many of these suggestions the limitation of a short essay permits you to adopt, there is one bit of advice you would do well always to keep in mind: The burden of proof is on you. An *assertion*—a statement without support or reason—will fail to convince your audience that your position is valid. Presume that your readers will be both alert and skeptical. Don't overestimate their credulity. It is *your* job to convince *them* by giving support or reasons for every statement you make.

HOW TO KEEP AIR CLEAN

Sydney Harris

Sydney J. Harris wrote "It's How You Ask It," pages 258–260.

---

1 Some months ago, while doing research on the general subject of pollution, I learned how dumb I had been all my life about something as common and familiar—and essential—as air.

2 In my ignorance, I had always thought that "fresh air" was infinitely available to us. I had imagined that the dirty air around us somehow escaped into the stratosphere, and that new air kept coming in—much as it does when we open a window after a party.

3 This, of course, is not true, and you would imagine that a grown man with a decent education would know this as a matter of course. What *is* true is that we live in a kind of spaceship called the earth, and only a limited amount of air is *forever* available to us.

4 The "walls" of our spaceship enclose what is called the "troposphere," which extends about seven miles up. This is all the air that is available to us. We must use it over and over again for infinity, just as if we were in a sealed room for the lifetime of the earth.

5 No fresh air comes in, and no polluted air escapes. Moreover, no dirt or poisons are ever "destroyed"—they remain in the air, in different forms, or settle on the earth as "particulates." And the more we burn, the more we replace good air with bad.

6 Once contaminated, this thin layer of air surrounding the earth cannot be cleansed again. We can clean materials, we can even clean water, but we cannot clean the air. There is nowhere else for the dirt and poisons to go—we cannot open a window in the troposphere and clear out the stale and noxious atmosphere we are creating.

7 Perhaps every child in sixth grade and above knows this; but I doubt that one adult in a hundred is aware of this basic physical fact. Most of us imagine, as I did, that winds sweep away the gases and debris in the air, taking them far out into the solar system and replacing them with new air.

8 The United States alone is discharging *130 million tons of pollutants a year* into the atmosphere, from factories, heating systems, incinerators, automobiles and airplanes, power plants and public buildings. What is frightening is not so much the death and illness, corrosion and decay they are responsible for—as the fact that this is an *irreversible process.* The air will never be cleaner than it is now.

9 And this is why *prevention*—immediate, drastic and far-reaching—is our only hope for the future. We cannot undo what we have done. We cannot restore the atmosphere to the purity it had before the Industrial Revolution. But we can, and must, halt the contamination before our spaceship suffocates from its own foul discharges.

Questions About "Argumentation"

1. What is Harris' proposal?
2. What is his main argument? Does he have any other(s)? Explain.
3. Does Harris' argument convince you to accept his proposition as valid? Explain.

Questions on Diction and Writing Techniques

1. Does Harris make clear to you what he had in mind about the infinite availability of fresh air? If so, how? Where, elsewhere in this essay, does he explain an idea in a similar manner?
2. What does "moreover" (par. 5) signal to you?
3. What is Harris' purpose in writing "but" in paragraph 7? Find another instance of his choice of this word for a similar reason.
4. How much of this essay is exposition?

For Discussion, Reading, and Writing

1. What, according to Harris, is frightening about the discharge of impurities into the air?
2. What, according to Harris, is our only hope for the future?
3. "Spaceship" is an often-used metaphor for the planet Earth. Why, in view of the information in this essay, is it apt?
4. Write a paragraph or two in which you argue for the prevention or curtailment in your home town of any one kind of discharge that now pollutes the air there.
5. Write a letter (one that you perhaps would like to mail) to any newspaper (including that on your campus), in which you argue for or against a view expressed in one of its editorials.

EITHER/OR

C. P. Snow

C. P. Snow (1905–1980), English physicist and author, had a varied career that included holding several important positions in the British government and writing novels.

1 Scientists *know* certain things in a fashion more immediate and more certain than those who don't know what science is. Unless we are abnormally weak or abnormally wicked men, this knowledge is bound to shape our actions. Most of us are timid, but to an extent, knowledge gives us guts. Perhaps it can give us guts strong enough for the jobs in hand.

2 Let me take the most obvious example. All physical scientists *know* that it is astonishingly easy to make plutonium. We know this, not as a journalistic fact at second hand, but as a fact in our own experience. We can work out the number of scientific and engineering personnel it needs for a nation-state to equip itself with fission and fusion bombs. We *know* that for a dozen or more states, it would take perhaps only five years, perhaps less. Even the best informed of us always exaggerate these periods.

3 This we know with the certainty of—what shall I call it—engineering truth. We also, most of us, are familiar with statistics and the nature of odds. We know, with the certainty of established truth, that if enough of these weapons are made by enough different states, some of them are going to blow up—through accident or folly or madness. But the numbers do not matter; what does matter is the nature of statistical fact.

4 All this *we know*. We know it in a more direct sense than any politician can know it, because it comes from our direct experience. It is part of our minds. Are we going to let it happen?

5 All this we *know*. It throws upon scientists a direct and formal responsibility. It is not enough to say scientists have a responsibility as citizens. They have a much greater one than that, and one different in kind. For scientists have a moral imperative to say what they know. It is going to make them unpopular in their own nation-states. It may do worse than make them unpopular. That doesn't matter. Or at least, it does matter to you and me, but it must not count in the face of the risks.

6 For we genuinely know the risks. We are faced with an either/or and we haven't much time. The *either* is acceptance of a restriction of nuclear armaments. This is going to begin, just as a token, with an agreement on the stopping of nuclear tests. The United States is not going to get the 99.9 percent "security" that [it] has been asking for. This is unobtainable, though there are other bargains that the United States could probably obtain. I am not

going to conceal from you that this course involves certain risks. They are quite obvious, and no honest man is going to blink at them. That is the *either.* The *or* is not a risk but a certainty. It is this: There is no agreement on tests. The nuclear arms race between the United States and the Soviet Union not only continues but accelerates. Other countries join in. Within, at the most, six years, China and six other states have a stock of nuclear bombs. Within, at the most, 10 years, some of those bombs are going off. I am saying this as responsibly as I can. *That* is the certainty. On the one side, therefore, we have a finite risk. On the other side, we have a certainty of disaster. Between a wish and a certainty, a sane man does not hesitate.

7 It is the plain duty of scientists to explain the either/or. It is a duty which seems to me to live in the moral nature of the scientific activity itself.

Questions About "Argumentation"

1. What is the idea whose acceptance Snow proposes in this essay?
2. What argument(s) does he offer in support of the idea?
3. There is a kind of faulty argument called the either-or fallacy, so called because it assumes only two options although there may be more. Does Snow commit this error? Explain.
4. How many times does Snow write "*know*"? What is his argumentative purpose in repeating the word?
5. "Between a wish and a certainty, a *sane man* [italics added] does not hesitate" (par. 6). Is this an example of name calling? (See "Getting Personal: *Ad Hominem*," pages 302–303.) Explain.

Questions on Diction and Writing Techniques

1. Mark in your text those words that are new to you, but whose meaning you inferred from their context. Define them in your own words. Compare your definitions with those in your dictionary. Look up in your dictionary any other words that are new to you. Use the words in both groups in sentences.

2. What transitional words does Snow choose to help achieve coherence within his paragraph?

For Discussion, Reading, and Writing

1. Which of these statements, according to Snow, are true (T), which false (F)?
   - A. ______ Scientists are more truthful than journalists.
   - B. ______ A scientist's knowledge is more dependable than that of politicians.
   - C. ______ Scientists should concern themselves with facts and nothing else.
   - D. ______ There is no certainty that if the nuclear arms race continues some nuclear bombs will go off.
   - E. ______ Some scientists recommend bomb shelters as a solution to the nuclear bomb problem.
2. Write a paragraph or two in which you argue for or against any point Snow makes.
3. Increasingly, major U.S. corporations are placing advertisements in national and local newspapers (often on the Op-Ed page) and in magazines, taking stands on public issues. Find one such ad that interests you and write a short essay for or against the point of view it expresses.

"I WANTS TO GO TO THE PROSE"

Suzanne Britt Jordan

Suzanne Britt Jordan teaches English at North Carolina State University at Raleigh.

1 I'm tired—and have been for quite a while. In fact, I think I can pinpoint the exact minute at which I first felt the weariness begin. I had been teaching for three years at a community college. I had, for quite a while, overlooked ignorance, dismissed arrogance, championed fairness, emphasized motivation, boosted egos and tolerated laziness. I was, in short, the classic modern educator.

2 One day a student, Marylou Simmons, dropped by my office. She had not completed a single assignment and had missed perhaps 50 per cent of her classes. Her writing, what little I saw of it, was illogical, grammatically incorrect and sloppy. "Can I help you, Marylou?" I said cheerily, ever the understanding and forgiving teacher. Her lip began to tremble; her eyes grew teary. It seemed she had been having trouble with her boyfriend. "I'm sorry, but what can *I* do?" I asked. Suddenly all business, Marylou said, "Since I've been so unhappy, I thought you might want to just give me a D or an Incomplete on the course." She smiled encouragingly, even confidently. That's when the weariness set in, the moment at which I turned into a flaming conservative in matters educational. Whatever Marylou's troubles, I suddenly saw that I was not the cause, nor was I about to be the solution.

3 When I read about declining SAT scores, the "functional illiteracy" of our students, the namby-pamby courses, the army of child psychologists, reading aides, educational liaisons, starry-eyed administrators and bungling fools who people our school systems, my heart sinks. Public schools abide mediocre students; put 18-year-olds, who can't decide what to wear in the morning, into independent study programs; excuse every absence under the sun, and counsel, counsel, counsel. A youngster in my own school system got into a knife fight and was expelled—for one week. I noticed in the paper that bus drivers regularly see riders smoking marijuana and drinking wine on the bus at, for God's sake, 8 in the morning. I could go on, but the public knows well enough the effects of a system of education gone awry.

4 Consider for a moment what caused the mess. A few years ago people began demanding their rights. Fair enough. They wanted equal education under the law. I'm for it. Social consciousness was born. Right on. Now, enter the big wrong turn, the one that sent our schools into never-never land. We suddenly, naïvely, believed that by offering equal opportunities we could (1) make everybody

happy, (2) make everybody well-adjusted, (3) forgive everybody who failed, and (4) expect gratitude to boot. When students were surly, uncooperative, whiny and apathetic, educators decided they themselves didn't know how to teach. So they made it easier on the poor, disadvantaged victims of broken homes, the misfits, the unloved. Well and good. But the catch to such lofty theories is evident. Poverty, ignorance and just plain orneriness will always abound. We look for every reason in the world for the declining test scores of our children, except for stupidity and laziness.

5 I'm perfectly aware that I sound like an old curmudgeon and it frightens me more than it offends you. But I have accepted what educators can't seem to face. The function of schools, their first and primary obligation, is not to probe tender psyches, to feed and clothe the homeless, nor to be the papa and mama a kid never had. The job is to teach.

6 The teacher's job is to know his subject, inside out, backward, forward and every which way. Nothing unnerves a student more than to have a teacher who doesn't know his or her stuff. Incompetence they cannot abide. Neither can I.

7 Before educators lost their way and tried to diversify by getting into the business of molding human beings, a teacher was, ideally, someone who knew a certain body of information and conveyed it. Period. Remember crochety old Miss Dinwiddie, who could recite 40 lines of the "Aeneid" at a clip? Picture Mr. Wassleheimer, who could give a zero to a cheating student without pausing in his lecture on frog dissection. Every student knew that it wasn't wise to mess around with a teacher who had the subject down cold. They were the teachers we once despised and later admired.

8 I want them back, those fearsome, awe-inspiring experts. I want them back because they knew what a school was for and didn't waste any time getting on with the task at hand. They were hard, even at times unjust, but when they were through, we knew those multiplication tables blindfolded with both trembling hands tied behind our backs.

9 Before the schoolmasters and the administrators change, they will have to shake off the guilt, the simpering, apologetic smiles and the Freudian theories. Which is crueler? Flunking a kid who has flunked or passing a kid who has flunked? Which teaches more about the realities of life? Which, in fact, shows more respect for the child as a human being?

10 Just today I talked to a big blond bruiser of a football player who wants to learn the basics of grammar. I didn't tell him it was too late. You see, he was a very, very good football player, so good that he never failed a course in high school. He had written on a weekly theme, "I wants to go to the prose and come fames." He may become a pro, may even become famous, but he will probably never read a good book, write a coherent letter or read a story to his children. I will, however, flunk him if he does not learn the material in the course. My job means too much to me to sacrifice my standards and turn soft. Suppose that every time my student played football badly, the coach said it was "just a game." Suppose the coach allowed him to drink booze, stay up all night, eat poorly and play sloppily. My student would be summarily dismissed from the team or the team would lose the game. So it goes with academic courses.

11 The young people are interested, I think, in taking their knocks, just as adults must take theirs. Students deserve a fair chance, and, failing to take advantage of that chance, a straightforward dismissal. It has been said that government must guarantee equal opportunity, not equal results. I like that. Through the theoretical fog that has clouded our perceptions and blanketed our minds, we know what is equitable and right. Mother put it another way. She always said, "Life is real; life is earnest." Incidentally, she taught me Latin and never gave me air in a jug. I had to breathe on my own. So do we all.

Questions About "Argumentation"

1. What statement does Jordan affirm in this essay?
2. Is the anecdote of Marylou Simmons valid as an argument in favor of Jordan's position? Explain. Is paragraph 10?
3. To better understand what Jordan is saying in this essay, write a summary of it in a paragraph of a hundred words or less. Explain in a paragraph whether Jordan convinces you of the validity of her position.

Questions on Diction and Writing Techniques

1. Mark in your text those words that are new to you, but whose meaning you inferred from their context. Define them in your

own words. Compare your definitions with those in your dictionary. Look up in your dictionary any other words that are new to you. Use the words in both groups in sentences.

2. Does Jordan make clear to you what she means by "the classic modern educator"? Explain.
3. Underline the sentence in paragraph 1 that exemplifies Jordan's use of coordination. What is the advantage of combining similar grammatical elements in a series as Jordan does in that sentence?
4. Underline the three three-word sentences in this essay. What is their effect?
5. Find four sentence fragments in this essay. Rewrite each to make it a complete sentence. Which versions do you prefer? Why?

For Discussion, Reading, and Writing

1. When did the weariness Jordan talks about set in?
2. What was "the big wrong turn" (par. 4)?
3. What is it, according to Jordan, that educators nowadays can't seem to face?
4. The main idea of this essay is (circle one):
   A. When giving a student a grade, teachers should take into account his or her personal problems.
   B. Public schools abide mediocre students.
   C. The job of teachers is to teach.
   D. Flunking a kid who has flunked is not cruel.
   E. Government must guarantee equal opportunity, not equal results.
5. Write a paragraph arguing for or against any idea Jordan expresses in this essay.
6. State in a declarative sentence what you consider to be the characteristic(s) of an ideal teacher. Write a paragraph or two to convince someone to agree with your opinion.

WHO KILLED BENNY PARET?

Norman Cousins

Norman Cousins was for many years the editor of *Saturday Review.* This essay appeared there on May 5, 1962, soon after the notorious Emile Griffith–Benny Paret welterweight championship prize fight.

---

1 Sometime about 1935 or 1936 I had an interview with Mike Jacobs, the prize-fight promoter. I was a fledgling newspaper reporter at that time; my beat was education, but during the vacation season I found myself on varied assignments, all the way from ship news to sports reporting. In this way I found myself sitting opposite the most powerful figure in the boxing world.

2 There was nothing spectacular in Mr. Jacobs's manner or appearance; but when he spoke about prize fights, he was no longer a bland little man but a colossus who sounded the way Napoleon must have sounded when he reviewed a battle. You knew you were listening to Number One. His saying something made it true.

3 We discussed what to him was the only important element in successful promoting–how to please the crowd. So far as he was concerned, there was no mystery in it. You put killers in the ring and the people filled your arena. You hire boxing artists–men who are adroit at feinting, parrying, weaving, jabbing, and dancing, but who don't pack dynamite in their fists–and you wind up counting your empty seats. So you searched for the killers and sluggers and maulers–fellows who could hit with the force of a baseball bat.

4 I asked Mr. Jacobs if he was speaking literally when he said people came out to see the killer.

5 "They don't come out to see a tea party," he said evenly. "They come out to see the knockout. They come out to see a man hurt. If they think anything else, they're kidding themselves."

6 Recently a young man by the name of Benny Paret was killed

From *Saturday Review,* May 5, 1962, p. 14.

in the ring. The killing was seen by millions; it was on television. In the twelfth round he was hit hard in the head several times, went down, was counted out, and never came out of the coma.

7 The Paret fight produced a flurry of investigations. Governor Rockefeller was shocked by what happened and appointed a committee to assess the responsibility. The New York State Boxing Commission decided to find out what was wrong. The District Attorney's office expressed its concern. One question that was solemnly studied in all three probes concerned the action of the referee. Did he act in time to stop the fight? Another question had to do with the role of the examining doctors who certified the physical fitness of the fighters before the bout. Still another question involved Mr. Paret's manager; did he rush his boy into the fight without adequate time to recuperate from the previous one?

8 In short, the investigators looked into every possible cause except the real one. Benny Paret was killed because the human fist delivers enough impact, when directed against the head, to produce a massive hemorrhage in the brain. The human brain is the most delicate and complex mechanism in all creation. It has a lacework of millions of highly fragile nerve connections. Nature attempts to protect this exquisitely intricate machinery by encasing it in a hard shell. Fortunately, the shell is thick enough to withstand a great deal of pounding. Nature, however, can protect man against everything except man himself. Not every blow to the head will kill a man—but there is always the risk of concussion and damage to the brain. A prize fighter may be able to survive even repeated brain concussions and go on fighting, but the damage to his brain may be permanent.

9 In any event, it is futile to investigate the referee's role and seek to determine whether he should have intervened to stop the fight earlier. This is not where the primary responsibility lies. The primary responsibility lies with the people who pay to see a man hurt. The referee who stops a fight too soon from the crowd's viewpoint can expect to be booed. The crowd wants the knockout; it wants to see a man stretched out on the canvas. This is the supreme moment in boxing. It is nonsense to talk about prize fighting as a test of boxing skills. No crowd was ever brought to its feet screaming and cheering at the sight of two men beautifully dodging and weaving out of each other's jabs. The time the crowd comes alive is

when a man is hit hard over the heart or the head, when his mouthpiece flies out, when blood squirts out of his nose or eyes, when he wobbles under the attack and his pursuer continues to smash at him with poleax impact.

10 Don't blame it on the referee. Don't even blame it on the fight managers. Put the blame where it belongs—on the prevailing mores that regard prize fighting as a perfectly proper enterprise and vehicle of entertainment. No one doubts that many people enjoy prize fighting and will miss it if it should be thrown out. And that is precisely the point.

Questions About "Argumentation"

1. What is Cousins' purpose in this essay?
2. What conclusion does he reach about the death of Benny Paret?
3. Does he sufficiently explain his view of the cause of Paret's death to convince you to accept it as valid? Explain.

Questions on Diction and Writing Techniques

1. What is the derivation of "colossus" (par. 2)? How is the word related to "colossal," "Colosseum," and "coliseum"?
2. What is Cousins' purpose in writing: "pack dynamite in their fists" (par. 3), "hit with the force of a baseball bat" (par. 3), "smash at him with poleax impact" (par. 9)?
3. In paragraph 9 Cousins, using different verbs, might have written "when his mouthpiece *falls* out, when blood *comes* out of his nose or eyes, when he *falters* under the attack." Which version do you prefer? Why?
4. What is the topic sentence of paragraph 9? Is the paragraph unified (see pages 26–29)?
5. Define "mores" (par. 10) and write a sentence using it appropriately.

6. Comment on whether paragraph 10 performs well the function of a concluding paragraph (see page 33).
7. Explain the purpose and the effect of the writer's use of the interview as a source of material.
8. Explain how Cousins' organization contributes to the convincingness of his essay.

For Discussion, Reading, and Writing

1. What questions were raised by investigations of the Paret fight? What, according to Cousins, did the investigations overlook?
2. Would Cousins have explained his subject more convincingly if, in paragraph 6, he had used vivid language as, for example, Mailer did in "The Death of Benny Paret" (pages 95–97)? Why or why not? If your answer is Yes, rewrite the paragraph. Be prepared to discuss, in class, description as a means of affecting the reader's attitude toward a subject.
3. Write an argumentative essay on any subject that interests you, incorporating information gathered in one or more interviews with fellow students, teachers, or any other persons (you may be able to borrow a tape recorder from the audiovisual department of your college).
4. Find in any newspaper under "Help Wanted" an ad that seeks to fill a position that you might qualify for, and might indeed like to have. Write a letter giving convincing reasons why you should be given the job.

Glossary

Active Voice and Passive Voice: A verb may be active—Betsy *blew* the whistle—or passive—The whistle *was blown* by Betsy—depending on whether the subject in a sentence is the actor or the recipient of the act mentioned in the verb.

Allusion: A passing reference to a literary or historical figure or event: "Language must be protected not only by poets but by the saving remnant of people who care—even though, as the flood rises, their role may be nearer *Canute*'s than *Noah*'s." (Douglas Bush, "Polluting Our Language")

Anecdote: A short narrative about an interesting incident.

Argumentation: See pp. 371–375.

Causal Analysis: See pp. 347–352.

Cause and Effect: See pp. 347–352.

Chronological Order: In a paragraph or essay, the placement of material in temporal sequence.

Circumlocution: A roundabout expression: *due to the fact that* (instead of *because*); *at that point in time* (instead of *then*); *for the simple reason that* (instead of *because*); *in the event that* (instead of *if*).

Cliché: An expression that is stale and ineffective because of overuse: *cool as a cucumber*; *strong as an ox*.

Coherence: The cohesiveness of the sentences in a paragraph and of the paragraphs in an essay. Also, the mechanical means of holding together sentences or paragraphs. It is not to be confused with *unity*, a term that refers to content.

Comparison and Contrast: See pp. 271–276.

Concluding Paragraph: A paragraph that sums up, evaluates, or draws a conclusion from the rest of the essay.

Connotation and Denotation: The *connotation* of a word is its associated or implied meaning, as opposed to its *denotation,* its definition. Beer may be *defined* as an alcoholic beverage brewed by fermentation from cereals. It may *connote* relaxation, good fellowship, well-being, and other feelings and thoughts, depending on one's associations.

Coordination: A technique for connecting similar grammatical elements in a sentence by combining them either into pairs—*Mary* and *Jane* played *ping pong* and *tennis*—or in a series—After graduation, Bill *took a vacation, got a job,* and *went to work.*

Deduction: See *Induction and Deduction.*

Denotation: See *Connotation and Denotation.*

Density, of a sentence: The amount of information or meaning a sentence contains.

Derivation: The origin or history of a word.

Description: See pp. 205–209.

Dialogue: Conversation between two or more persons.

Diary and Journal: Each is a daily or frequently made record of personal experiences. See pp. 143–146.

Diction: Choice of words.

Distance: A term used figuratively to indicate how personal or impersonal writing is, i.e., how close the writer appears to be to the reader.

Effect: See *Cause and Effect.*

Essay: A short prose composition on a restricted subject.

Exposition: See pp. 229–232.

Extended Definition: See p. 294.

Fable: A brief story told to teach a moral.

Figure of Speech: Expressive use of language, such as *simile* or *metaphor.*

General and Specific Words: General words include all of a group or class—*fruit, firearms, teacher.* Specific words refer to individual things—*apple, pistol, Professor Anne Smith.* See p. 86.

Illustration: See pp. 252–256.

Imagery: The nonliteral, expressive use of language. The term is synonymous with *Figure of Speech.*

Implied Thesis: See *Thesis and Implied Thesis.*

Induction and Deduction: Induction is a method of reasoning that proceeds from facts to a generalization. Deduction is a method of reasoning that moves from the general to the particular.

Inference: The process of deriving a conclusion from known fact. Also, the conclusion so derived.

Informal Essay: An essay whose purpose is not obviously serious.

Introductory Paragraph: The first paragraph of an essay, designed to announce its dominant idea, to attract the reader's attention, or to do both.

Inversion: The transposition from its normal place of an element in a sentence; for example, *He arrived home at two in the morning* (normal order); *At two in the morning he arrived home* (inverted order).

Irony: The use of words to express a meaning opposite to their apparent meaning, as in the statement, "He's a fine guy," made about a scoundrel. This is called *verbal irony* and is distinguished from *irony of situation,* which exists when the result of an effort is the opposite of what was intended or expected: A student of average accomplishment attends an all-night party, takes a final exam, and gets an A+.

Jargon: Obscure and pretentious language, often marked by long and highly abstract words.

Journal: See *Diary and Journal.*

Loose and Periodic Sentences: See p. 63.

Metaphor: A *figure of speech* in which an implied comparison represents that one thing *is* an unlike thing: "It is the East, and Juliet is the sun!" [*Romeo and Juliet*].

Mixed Metaphor: The combination in a sentence of two or more *metaphors* that evoke inconsistent images. Example: When the chips were down, Governor Jones called for a quarterback sneak.

Modification: A technique for increasing the *density* of a sentence by describing or by limiting or particularizing meaning. See pp. 57–59.

Narration: See pp. 176–180.

Paradox: An attention-getting device consisting of a statement that, although seemingly contradictory or absurd, may be true: "It is possible to get an education at a university" [Lincoln Steffens, *Autobiography*].

Paragraph: A unit of composition, generally consisting of two or more sentences, that develops a single idea.

Parallel Construction: The repetition of sentence elements that have the same grammatical function and form: *I came, I saw, I conquered.*

Passive Voice: See *Active and Passive Voice.*

Periodic Sentence: See p. 63.

Persona: The personality one reveals in one's writing.

Personification: The attribution of human qualities to abstractions or things.

Point of View: See p. 180.

Process: See pp. 331–334.

Pronoun Reference: The use of a pronoun or pronouns in a sentence to refer to a noun in a previous sentence or paragraph.

Rhetorical Question: A question not expected to be replied to, but asked for its rhetorical effect which is to make a greater impression than a direct statement would.

Sensory Diction: Words that refer to the experiences of the sense of hearing (*crunch, hiss, plop, rustle, scream, squeak*), of taste (*acidic, chocolaty, salty, sour, sugary, tart*), of touch (*fiery, freezing, hard, hot, smooth, soft*), of sight (*cloudy, glossy, polished, shiny, smoky, sweaty*), and of smell (*aromatic, moldy, odorous, perfumed, putrid, reeking*).

Sentence: A unit of composition that expresses a complete thought and that generally consists of at least one main clause.

Sentence Fragment: A word or group of words that is not a complete sentence, but nonetheless is punctuated as a sentence: He stayed home from school. *Even though he felt fine.*

Sentence Variety: The combination of successive sentences of different structures, lengths, and word orders, often with the purpose of avoiding monotony in a paragraph.

Simile: A *figure of speech* in which an expressed comparison is made between two unlike things, generally introduced by *as* or *like:* "What a piece of work is man . . . in action how like an angel, in apprehension how like a god" [Shakespeare, *Hamlet*]; "I wandered lonely as a cloud" [Wordsworth].

Slang: Very informal language—*cool cat, no sweat, far out, rip-off, zonked, quack.*

Specific Language: See *General and Specific Language.*

Standard Sentence: See *Loose and Periodic Sentence.*

Subject: What an essay is about. A subject may be broad or restricted. A broad subject, unlike a restricted subject, is one that is too general for a writer to handle in an essay of a given length. See p. 2.

Subordination: A technique for increasing the amount of information that a sentence contains. See p. 59.

Summary: A comprehensive but brief recapitulation of a piece of writing. See p. 39.

Symbol: Something that is itself and also stands for something else: The Stars and Stripes is a *symbol* of the United States.

Thesis and Implied Thesis: A *thesis* is a statement (sometimes called a thesis statement), often in one sentence, that summarizes the main idea of an essay. An *implied thesis* is one that is not expressed in so many words, but is suggested by the contents of an essay.

Tone: The attitude of the writer toward the reader and toward the subject. In a way, it is like tone of voice; we say of a speaker, "Her tone of voice was angry" or "He spoke in a subdued tone." Compare the tone in these sentences: "Would you please move your car out of the way?"; "Get that goddam jalopy the hell out of there!"

Topic: A *subject* sufficiently restricted for a writer to be able to explain it to his or her readers in an *essay* of a given length.

Topic Sentence: The sentence in a paragraph that expresses the main idea of the paragraph.

Transitional Words and Phrases: Words and phrases used to indicate a relationship between consecutive sentences in order to add a thought (*in addition, also, again, furthermore*), to introduce an illustration (*for example, for instance, to illustrate, thus*), to indicate a conclusion or result (*in conclusion, to sum up, as a result, consequently, accordingly*), or to qualify or contrast (*however, but, still, nevertheless, on the other hand*).

Unity: Consistency of material in an essay or paragraph.

Voice: Aside from meaning the form of a verb, as in *active* and *passive voice,* the term means the unique personality that a writer reveals in his or her writing.

Index of Terms, Authors, and Titles

ABOUT THE AUTHOR

Morton A. Miller, since graduating from Columbia College in 1935, has had a varied career as a World War II combat photographer, a producer of educational films, a playwright, a general contractor, a land developer, and, since 1969, a teacher. Out of his experience with teaching composition in colleges and with writing occasional essays for journals this text has evolved.